THE Power OF Inquiry

KATH MURDOCH

Dedication

This book is dedicated, with love, to my precious daughters Gretta and Holly.

May the power of inquiry drive you to be ever curious, ever courageous and ever compassionate citizens of the world.

THE Power OF Inquiry

ISBN: 978-0-9758412-1-1
Published by Seastar Education
PO Box 683
Northcote Vic 3070
Australia
Email: seastar@netspace.net.au
Website: www.kathmurdoch.com.au
© Kath Murdoch 2015

The Power of Inquiry

In her classroom our speculations ranged the world.
She aroused us to book waving discussions.
Every morning we came to her
carrying new truths, new facts, new ideas,
Cupped and sheltered in our hands like captured fireflies.

John Steinbeck

Foreword
by Guy Claxton

Learning in classrooms – in fact learning anywhere – proceeds on a number of different levels. Learning is like a river that is choppy and fast moving on the surface, but moves more slowly in its depths. Activity on the surface is easy to see; activity lower down is harder to see, but just as influential. The movements in the depths can gradually alter the course of the river. And these deep currents also influence the more visible changes on the surface. On the surface of a classroom we have the acquisition of *knowledge and information*. "Hydrated copper sulfate crystals are blue" is easy to say, and it is easy to check if someone "knows" it. It is harder to tell if they "understand" it, because understanding depends on the integration of that "fact" with a whole lot of other concepts like *molecule*, *chemical bonding* and *the periodic table*.

Lower down comes the development of *skills, techniques and strategies* which expand our capacity to do useful and interesting things. Can you actually make a paper boat that will carry a load of coins without sinking or tipping over? Can you use a dictionary to look up words by yourself? And below skills there are a collection of things we call *habits, dispositions, values, attitudes and interests*. They are broader than skills and harder to "test". Are you generally cheerful? Or timid? Or honest? To answer that, I have to follow you around, see how you behave in a variety of contexts, and make judgements about you. That's more subtle and time-consuming than counting the crosses in boxes on a multiple-choice questionnaire.

Learning at these levels is always going on simultaneously. At the same time as you are learning about some period of history, you may also be learning the skills of listening carefully, imagining vividly and writing coherently, and you are also gradually cultivating attitudes of, for example, dependency on your teacher to direct and correct you, or credulity in the face of authoritative text. You can't avoid it: being a teacher means influencing learning on all levels – for good or ill.

Recent research forcibly reminds us that the slow development of these habits of mind is just as important as acquiring knowledge and getting good grades. Grades get some students through certain useful gateways – though we should always remember that the grading game is rigged so that a sizeable proportion of students *don't* get the key to the door. But even for the successful youngsters, grades do not guarantee they will do well on the other side of the portal. For that they need attitudes like determination, collaboration, and the willingness to be independent and accept responsibility. And curiosity. And a love of reading and learning. An 11-year-old's success in adult life is better predicted by their *pleasure in reading* than by their level of *reading ability*, for example.

And this line of argument brings me to Kath Murdoch's marvellous and much-needed book – for the earlier the seeds of these dispositions are sown, the stronger they grow. Primary education is the third leg – after home life and pre-school – of a long formative journey that leads on through secondary school to college, university and working life. Primary education only makes sense in terms of the long game of which it is just one phase. Instead of being passively blown this way and that by the shifting political and bureaucratic winds, every school principal has to instil in their staff, and in all the stakeholders of the school, a vivid sense of "the kinds of young people we are trying to produce". And this means, above all, the attitudes and values with which we are trying to imbue them, in the firm belief that those qualities are the ones that the next generation – every one of them – will need most.

My own view is that these core 21st century virtues come in three clusters: self-control, sociality and learning. Self-control enables you to modulate your feelings and actions in the light of long-term priorities and differing contexts. Sociality enables you to be a good friend, a good comrade, a good neighbour and a good citizen (though of course each of these "goods" needs arguing about and customising in different societies.) And learning means being a skilled researcher, a courageous explorer, a curious thinker, a meticulous detective, and a critical consumer of information and opinion. For each of these, primary school is a crucial incubator – or a missed opportunity. If children are allowed to learn that reading is drudgery, unrelated to their worlds and concerns; that mistakes are inevitable signs of stupidity and carelessness; that morality is

what passes for thinking); and that this method of teaching is entirely compatible with a concern with literacy, numeracy, and the rigours of scientific or historical research. When people disparage inquiry and project-based learning, they have met it – if they have met it at all – being done badly or superficially. Kath Murdoch shows us, step by step, how to do it well. When it is done well, it is a demanding and sophisticated form of teaching. But teachers who have put in the effort to master this subtle art are rewarded handsomely. They see their children becoming powerful, confident, capable, articulate, convivial managers of their own learning. They see the river of learning turning in the right direction. They feel part of an education worthy of the name.

'... teachers who have put in the effort to master this subtle art are rewarded handsomely. They see their children becoming powerful, confident, capable, articulate, convivial managers of their own learning.'

In every country I know, there are schools doing this kind of teaching – but not enough. This kind of education is not scaling up fast enough, and too many children are still suffering a

what you can get away with; that self-respect depends on being able to make other people afraid of you; that trying to grapple with difficult ideas is a waste of time; that thinking with your hands is inferior to thinking with words; that winning quiz shows is the apotheosis of human intelligence – if these currents are allowed to form deep in the river of learning in any primary school – then it is not educating but mis-educating.

What Kath's book shows so brilliantly is that cultivating curiosity, perseverance and thoughtfulness through well-designed inquiries and projects is completely possible; that it is profoundly different from the lazy laisser-faire caricature of inquiry that still, sadly, informs some people's thinking (or

kind of teaching more suited to the 19th than the 21st century. Partly it is because we are all creatures of habit, and Kath's way requires us to question and change existing habits – an effortful process. Partly because some school leaders are timid and unimaginative. Partly because too many politicians are doctrinaire and ill-informed. And partly because there has been a lack of clear guidance – not enough guide books that are both deeply grounded in good science and packed with practical seeds of possibility and tried-and-tested illustrations. This book removes this latter hindrance to progress. I hope you enjoy it as much as I did. And please, don't just agree with Kath – actually do something different with your students tomorrow.

Acknowledgements

To say that this book has been a long time in the making would be an understatement. It has existed in various forms for several years… sticky notes written hastily after teaching a class, lengthy musings typed at altitude on long flights, drafted and redrafted chapters saved to my desktop and notes and ideas on my phone. Its gestation has been wide and long. This is due in part to a busy schedule, a growing fondness for the immediacy of blogging and a preference for being out there *doing* it over writing about it – but it is more than that. Looking back, I see how much my thinking has evolved over this time. This is not the same book I set out to write some three years ago.

It has taken time. And – like most creative enterprises – it has taken collaboration. Several people have helped bring this book to life and I am eternally grateful for their time and their skills:

Guy Claxton – Emeritus Professor of Learning Sciences at the University of Winchester – who not only contributed a stunning foreword to the book but whose work has been so profoundly influential on my learning over many years. Conversations with Guy about the book (including the vexed issue of the title!) have been very helpful in refining and clarifying my thinking. I am indebted to Guy for his contribution.

Meredith Flanner and Annie Quail who gave me detailed feedback on early drafts of the book. They are two exceptional teachers and I benefitted enormously from their advice and suggestions.

Graeme Murdoch, who designed the book. I have long admired the skill my brother has applied to his work and was so thrilled when he agreed to take on this challenge with me. The first thing I said to him was 'I want it to look beautiful'. He has more than met my request and has done so with extraordinary patience and good humour – not to mention his tolerance for my tendency to break into hits of the eighties at any given moment.

Stephen Ray, my husband, for incidental and very valuable feedback as the book has evolved. His work in the field of facilitation with adults has helped fine-tune my thinking about the role of the inquiry teacher. I am grateful beyond measure – especially for the cups of tea.

Chris Reed and the wonderful staff of **Mother Teresa Primary School** in Melbourne who allowed us to photograph the students and surrounds in their beautiful school.

Ed Sloane who is responsible for most of the photographs in the book. His ability to capture the essence of what I wanted to support the text was masterful.

Justine Hutchinson who beautifully captured a sense of wonder in the front cover photo.

Sam Trafford and **Kerryn Burgess**, for their efficient and thoughtful editing and for seeing what I had stopped seeing.

And…

While these people had a direct role in the production of this book, there are so many others who have contributed to my thinking and learning over the years. Indeed it is true to say that each school, each teacher and each child with whom I have worked has helped grow my thinking in some way. With over 30 years of teaching now behind me, it would be impossible to do justice to all those I should acknowledge. But there are several who stand out as having been particularly important in this journey and whose voices can be heard in these pages.

I was so very blessed to have Keith Pigdon and Marilyn Woolley as my lecturers and then later my colleagues at the University of Melbourne. Their work was quite definitely ahead of its time and set me on a path of inquiry from the very early days of my teaching career. Jo Parry was the first teacher I saw in action to truly inspire me as a teacher and to instill in me a hunger to do this job the best possible way I could. She showed me what it meant to really *honour* the child and to remain authentic and grounded in all I do. She remains a true mentor and friend. Dr Julie Hamston – with whom I have had the pleasure of writing in the past – brings her stunning intellect to our conversations and always succeeds in stretching and invigorating my thinking. David Hornsby and Debbie Sukarna instilled a passion for literacy in me as a young teacher that has never subsided. Jeni Wilson and

I worked together as teacher educators for many years and I am grateful for what our collaboration has taught me.

While my early teaching and collaborations were based in Australia, the last decade has presented me with the extraordinary opportunity to work with teachers and children all over the world. They say travel grows the mind and there is no doubt that my experiences of working in schools in very different contexts and countries has done just that. It has been an enormous privilege to work in schools throughout New Zealand, Asia, America, Africa and Europe. It would be impossible to name each individual school and indeed each teacher who has welcomed me into their classrooms, their planning meetings and their professional learning workshops – not to mention their willingness to guide my own inquiries into their part of the world. I am so very grateful to those amazing teachers who commit to educating children around the world. Not only have I connected with some extraordinary educators – I have made friends for life. Thank you – you know who you are!

There are several schools around the world with which I have had an ongoing partnership for the past few years – schools that have made a long-term commitment to developing real and rigorous inquiry. My partnership with these schools has included significant time in classrooms, working with children. I wish to acknowledge the contribution each school has made to this book in some way:

Canadian International School, Hong Kong
Castlemaine North Primary School, Australia
Elsternwick Primary School, Australia
English Schools Foundation, Hong Kong
Footscray Primary School, Australia
Hartwell Primary School, Australia
International School of Manila, The Philippines
International School of Prague, Prague
Island Bay Primary School, New Zealand
Jakarta Intercultural School, Indonesia
Macquarie Primary School, Australia

Merri Creek Primary School, Australia
Mother Teresa Primary School, Australia
Ringwood Heights Primary School, Australia
Roberts McCubbin Primary School, Australia
St Fidelis Primary School, Australia
St Clares Primary School, Australia
St Bernadettes Primary School, Australia
United World College of South East Asia, Singapore
Yokohama International School, Japan
Zurich International School, Switzerland.

In addition to the educators I have met and worked with throughout my career, there are many who have influenced my thinking without us ever having met. The digital revolution has made it possible for me to connect with educators all over the world through my virtual professional learning network. This has made it possible for me to inquire and (I hope) to inspire inquiry any time, anywhere.

I am also indebted to the scholars – some of who are no longer with us – whose research has informed my thinking. They are quoted and referenced throughout but in particular, I wish to acknowledge, in particular, the profound influence of: Garth Boomer, James Beane, Jerome Bruner, Donald Graves, David Perkins, Howard Gardner, Linda Darling Hammond, Art Costa, Ron Ritchhart, Carol Dweck, Guy Claxton, Lilian Katz, Sir Ken Robinson, Martin Seligman, Dylan Williams, Anne Davies, Carol Kuhlthau, Lynne Erikson, Grant Wiggins, Gerard McTighe, Peter Johnston, Stephanie Harvey and Debbie Miller.

I am convinced that becoming an inquiry teacher has its foundations not only in our professional learning and experience but in our personal lives. As my siblings and I grew up, we were acutely aware of the value our parents placed on learning – ours *and* their own. They provided us with rich experiences in nature, nurtured and challenged our thinking and remained ardently curious about us, others and their world. For this I am eternally grateful. It helped make me the teacher I am.

The Power of Inquiry

Contents

CHAPTER **1**
PAGE **12**

A fresh look:
WHY AND HOW DO WE USE INQUIRY
IN TODAY'S CLASSROOMS?

CHAPTER **2**
PAGE **26**

Creating the space:
HOW CAN WE DESIGN LEARNING
ENVIRONMENTS FOR INQUIRY?

CHAPTER **3**
PAGE **38**

Beyond topics:
WHAT'S WORTH
INQUIRING INTO?

CHAPTER **4**
PAGE **54**

Inviting uncertainty:
HOW CAN WE GROW A CULTURE
OF QUESTIONING AND CURIOSITY?

CHAPTER **5**
PAGE **74**

Finding our way:
WHAT ROLE CAN FRAMEWORKS AND MODELS PLAY
IN SCAFFOLDING INQUIRY LEARNING?

CHAPTER **6**
PAGE **94**

Assets for life:
HOW CAN INQUIRY NURTURE SKILLS AND DISPOSITIONS
FOR LIFELONG LEARNING?

CHAPTER **7**
PAGE **110**

To each their own:
WHY MAKE IT
PERSONAL?

CHAPTER **8**
PAGE **132**

Staying accountable:
WHAT DOES ASSESSMENT LOOK LIKE
IN THE INQUIRY CLASSROOM?

CHAPTER **9**
PAGE **160**

Together is better:
HOW CAN WE GROW AN
INQUIRY SCHOOL?

CHAPTER **10**
PAGE **178**

Building the repertoire:
WHAT STRATEGIES HELP POWER UP
INQUIRY TEACHING?

PAGE **192**

Additional resources

The Power of Inquiry

Introduction

To suggest that learning is *not* about inquiry is, in many ways, nonsense. The act of inquiry is critical to our learning and growth. From the moment we are born, we make sense of our world through exploring, testing and evaluating. We learn through experience and our desire to make meaning from that experience. We question others and we question ourselves. One only has to spend time with a four year old to witness the power of inquiry – be it their intense engagement in exploratory play or the barrage of questions from the back seat of the car! As we grow, most of us continue feel much more engaged and more committed to learning something when we are interested, curious or have a real need to find out.

The power of harnessing our inclination to inquire has not been lost on those involved in formal education. Scholars have long advocated the importance of nurturing active and independent investigation. Indeed, John Dewey claimed that the future of our civilization depended on 'the widening spread and deepening hold' of the inquiring mind. More recently, Noam Chomsky asserted that to be 'truly educated' is to know how to be a skilled inquirer:

'That means knowing, understanding many things but also – much more important than what you have stored in your mind – to know where to look, how to look, how to question, how to challenge, how to proceed independently, to deal with the challenges that the world presents to you … in cooperation and solidarity with others.'

For more than thirty years, I have pursued an inquiry into inquiry. At the heart of this pursuit has been my passion for working *in schools* with teachers and children. This privileged work regularly re-affirms my heartfelt belief that we are indeed at our 'learning best' when engaged in the powerful act of inquiry – be it challenging, playful, individual, collaborative, closely guided or independent. It also affirms that teaching *itself* is an act of inquiry. The very best teachers bring an open minded, inquiring disposition to all they do.

Understanding how inquiry helps 'power up' learning impacts profoundly on the way we think about and interact with students, the nature of the tasks we design, how we choose to use our time, the design of the physical environment, how we assess learning and the way we work with our colleagues. This view of inquiry – as a way of being rather than something we 'do' a couple of afternoons a week – has led to the writing of this book. My intention is to share important shifts in thinking and offer fresh insights into quality practice while acknowledging the value of what has gone before.

While its contents are well informed by academic and classroom-based research, this book is first and foremost a *practical* guide. The material will be of most relevance to primary teachers but it is my hope that those working with secondary students will also find much that is relevant and timely for their settings. Following chapter 1, each subsequent chapter is driven by a big question central to inquiry. They may be read in isolation but, collectively, they seek to represent a picture of inquiry in the contemporary classroom as necessarily demanding and complex – yet ultimately manageable and intensely rewarding.

Kath Murdoch

• Dewey, J. (1916/1980). *Democracy and Education*. In J. A. Boydston (Ed.) *John Dewey: The Middle Works*, 1899-1924 (Vol. 9). Carbondale, IL: Southern Illinois University Press.
• Chomsky, N. (May 26, 2015) *On Being Truly Educated*, The Brainwaves Video Anthology, retrieved from https://www.youtube.com/watch?v=eYHQcXVp4F4

'The spirit of inquiry
is fundamental
to living mindfully.'

(Kabat-Zinn, J., 2005)

~ C H A P T E R ~

one

A fresh look:

WHY AND HOW DO WE USE INQUIRY IN TODAY'S CLASSROOMS?

INTRODUCTION

Historically, inquiry learning has suffered from a bit of an image problem. In some circles (particularly those with a conservative agenda) the term conjures up pictures of wishy-washy teachers encouraging students to 'find out for themselves' and of students free to explore anything in which they are interested. Over time, inquiry learning has been accused of being an approach lacking in structure, depth and clarity and has been criticized for relegating the teacher to the non-interventionist role of 'guide on the side'. Interestingly, inquiry has also come under fire from the view that it focuses on process *at the expense* of content.

As I write this book, toward the end of 2014, I can say with great conviction that the inquiry classrooms I see around the world are a far cry from the rather worn cliché of the chaotic and content-free classroom in which the teacher hovers tentatively on the sidelines. Quality inquiry classrooms are places where *highly intentional* teachers work hard to grow the capacity of all students to learn. These teachers work diligently to help students *know what to do when they don't know*, to develop deeper understandings of how the world works and to build and refine a set of skills and dispositions that will enable learning to continue life-long and life-wide. Like other serious proponents in the field, I have long argued that quality inquiry must challenge students to engage with *significant conceptual understanding* of their world. The 'content' is vital. One has to inquire into *something*, and that 'something' should be conceptually important ideas within and across disciplines.

Perhaps, in our desire to help students become more independent learners, we have misconstrued the teachers' role (and the role of 'content') as less significant. John Hattie hits the nail on the head when he suggests that we can 'confuse the outcome…[that of fostering inquiry learners]…with methods of teaching that abrogate responsibility by the teachers to actually make a difference' [Hattie, accessed 2014 www.visiblelearningplus.com].

'AND' – NOT 'OR'

Of course so *many* significant and enduring approaches to teaching can be misinterpreted or perhaps deliberately hijacked. Education is full of what are often described as 'false dichotomies' – for example, you either 'teach phonics' or you don't, you support system level testing or you are dead against it, you value process or content and, when it comes to inquiry, you *either* let students find out *or* you tell them. When inquiry is similarly over-simplified or pitted against terms such as 'direct instruction,' it is easy to critique and dismiss as ineffective.

I would suggest we would be much better served to think of the 'and' rather than the 'or'. Growing inquiry learners requires strong teacher knowledge of a wide range of techniques and practices. Providing information directly to the student is *one of the techniques* we use as required and so too is the practice of challenging the student to find something out for themselves. While there is a strong emphasis on techniques that encourage the learner to actively and more independently seek, sort and synthesize, this does not preclude some carefully placed direct instruction within our daily repertoire.

SO – WHAT IS IT?

Simplistic, monochromatic views of inquiry are frustrating at best and divisive at worse, and can lead to problematic misconceptions. So let's take a moment to explore what an inquiry approach means in the context of today's classrooms. As an approach to teaching and learning, inquiry has a long and rich history. It is perhaps most famously grounded in the early work of Dewey (1938), Bruner (1966) and Vygotsky (1978). Researchers in the field have long argued for the use of *inductive* approaches to learning – wherein the learner is challenged to gather and analyze information, review it against existing knowledge, seek connections, notice patterns and gradually build an understanding of a concept.

In short, these theorists claim that it is the student who needs to do the 'heavy cognitive lifting'. Dominant teaching practices present information (rules, laws, principles) together with examples, then ask students to replicate what they have been told. Inquiry teachers challenge (scaffold) learners to come *to* understanding through tackling a problem, looking for connections between case studies or analyzing data they have gathered. As they engage with a learning episode through inquiry, students gradually construct and deepen those principles for themselves:

> *'A growing body of research suggests that students learn more deeply and perform better on complex tasks if they have the opportunity to engage in more authentic learning such as projects and activities that require them to employ subject knowledge to solve real-world problems. Studies have continued to show positive impact on learning when students participate in lessons that require them to construct and organize knowledge, consider alternatives, engage in detailed research, inquiry, writing and analysis and to communicate effectively with audiences.'* (Newman, Marks and Gamoran, 1995, cited in Barron and Darling-Hammond, 2008)

Inquiry refers not only to the nature of the learning but also to the disposition of the teacher. Teachers who work this way see the learner as an *active participant* in the learning process. While the term 'active' relates to being physically active and having opportunities to engage in direct, hands on experiences, it is vital that it is also understood in a cognitive sense. Inquiry learning is an approach that demands high-order thinking. The student is continually challenged by the teacher, and tasks are designed to prompt students to question, predict, gather, analyze, synthesize and reflect.

The way the classroom is organized, the way resources are used, the classroom discourse, and the method of planning, documenting and assessing are all designed to have students 'do the (cognitive) heavy lifting'. Inquiry is an approach that places the learner and learning central to what the teacher thinks, says and does. Learning happens through thorough *investigation* which in itself is driven by powerful questions often framed by authentic contexts and real-life problems and purposes. In an inquiry classroom, students move through processes that help them think beyond facts and come to understand deeper concepts. These processes also emphasize the explicit learning of interdisciplinary skills such as self-management, collaboration, communication and of course research itself. Importantly, inquiry is an approach that favors a more connected, integrative pedagogy (although it is *not* synonymous with an integrated curriculum). Teachers help learners see that the tasks in which they are engaged are part of a larger and transferable process.

AND SO TO THE WHY…

'People don't buy what you do – they buy why *you do it.'*
(Sinek, S., 2009)

Effective teachers know *why* they do what they do. The best strategy for dealing with ill-informed critique of inquiry is to be clear about the purpose and benefits of the approach and to be able to articulate how inquiry works within a contemporary setting – informed by current evidence of 'what works' in classrooms. Even teachers who have become very comfortable with inquiry-based approaches should return regularly to the question '*why* do I work this way?' When we have clarity of purpose, the 'whats' and the 'hows' are strengthened.

WHY INQUIRY?

- It is widely acknowledged that we are **more motivated** to learn when we are genuinely interested in or curious about the subject or when we have a problem we need to solve.

- Inquiry requires and strengthens 'whole of life' **transferable skills** including critical thinking, planning, self-management, organization and communication.

- Inquiry teachers focus **their attention on student learning** – and because planning is responsive and recursive, they *inquire into their students*, constantly asking 'what is this student revealing to me and what do I need to do next?' Because inquiry demands an approach to planning that is ongoing, there is a stronger connection between the plans teachers make and the needs and interests of students as they are assessed.

- In an increasingly **globalized and digital world**, we are inundated by huge quantities of information which is available to us almost any time and anywhere. This is vastly different from the context many teachers grew up in and demands different skills. Students need to learn how to effectively and safely locate, access, evaluate, use and contribute to this ever-evolving global information bank, and that's what inquiry is all about.

- At a time when system-level curricula around the world are still criticized for being over-crowded, an approach to learning that encourages **integrative, connected thinking** is vital.

- Inquiry involves students in locating, gathering and critiquing information using an increasing number of digital tools, therefore sharpening **digital literacy skills**.

- Contemporary inquiry practices seek to engage students in tackling real world questions and problems through **authentic** contexts at both local and global levels.

- Inquiry helps develop students' **agency**. Through quality questioning and involving students in actively gathering and analyzing information, the student gradually develops a sense of control over and responsibility for themselves as a learner. They learn to learn. Teachers nurture independence by gradually releasing responsibility and encouraging students to 'make meaning' using high-level thinking skills and strategies.

- Finally, the act of inquiry itself has become more and more mainstream. Kulthau *et al.* (2011) argue, 'In the past decade we have seen research transformed from a traditional academic exercise into an important part of every day living' (Kulthau *et al.*, 2007: 3). Think about it. We are now more inclined to research and manage our own travel arrangements, or to decide on the next car we will buy by reading all we can on various dedicated websites. We owe it to students to equip them with the skills they need for what has now become such a **central part of how we live and work**.

SO, IF INQUIRY IS SO WORTHWHILE, WHY ISN'T EVERYONE USING IT?

Even when teachers agree that inquiry as an approach has worth, it can be daunting to implement. There are several reasons for this, which I'll outline below.

Inquiry can be messy. Not in a literal sense (although that too sometimes!) but 'messy' in that, by being more responsive to what students say, do and reveal, there is less the teacher can tightly control from the outset. Many teachers remain uneasy with approaches that can't be rigidly planned, controlled and scripted. Inquiry requires us to respond to students' needs and interests, not just at the 'beginning of a unit' but throughout the day. Ironically, this requires an acute understanding of broad learning purposes and a strong intentional stance on the teacher's part. Inquiry moves the act of teaching out of the realm of control and authority to one of complexity, nuance and some shared responsibility.

As stated earlier, inquiry has also suffered from a reputation as a somewhat loose and *free-for-all approach* that lacks rigor, and perhaps because of this, there has been a lack of specific, quality advice on inquiry-based instructional strategies. Vague labels like 'guide on the side' or 'facilitator' don't help and can perpetuate ambiguous and ill-conceived learning experiences for students. If there is one message I want to get across in this book, it is the critical role of the teacher in enabling learning through inquiry. Our aim is to grow independent, learning-powered individuals, but our role in that process remains critical as it is demanding and complex. Inquiry teaching is not for the faint hearted!

When not rejected due to perceived lack of rigor, inquiry can also be *made unnecessarily complex* by being talked about only as a conceptual framework with limited examples of how it actually looks in the classroom. Like other elements of education, inquiry abounds with jargon that can render it inaccessible. The reality is that teachers can often access the approach best by reflecting on the intuitive ways in which they successfully help students learn.

When we move to the heart of inquiry, it is about engagement, about lighting a fire within students so they *want* to investigate and find out more. Inquiry is not a single 'method' or a program. Inquiry is really a 'way of being' as a teacher – it is about how you think about learning and the relationship between teaching and learning. It is about how you see yourself and is at the heart of what you do and why you do it.

TEACHING THROUGH INQUIRY

I am an inquiry teacher – someone who is committed to nurturing inquiry learners whether they are primary school students or experienced teachers. When I teach this way, I notice I am questioning, prompting, observing, naming, scaffolding, guiding and listening, and these acts are more present in my repertoire than telling, controlling, cajoling or even entertaining. When the beauty of that high-quality learning moment takes place, I am truly joyful. Every committed, passionate teacher knows that feeling. I am joyful because I can feel myself connecting to the learner in a way that simply makes sense. I feel myself teaching *the person* – not the subject. I feel myself truly supporting *learning* rather than simply espousing information, demonstrating something or setting a task and hoping it will 'stick'. I feel myself empowered by my role in empower*ing* the learner. When I teach with an inquiry mindset, I feel the thrill of not quite knowing what is going to happen next, *yet* knowing where we are headed… and that delicious frisson that happens when we all start making connections, both expected and unexpected.

Inquiry teaching has often been described using the metaphor of a journey – and that is so apt. When I am working this way, it's like travelling with my learners to a destination that I, as the (active) guide, can see at least *some* of: maybe the tips of the trees, the church spires – I have some markers on the horizon. Gradually, the view reveals itself to my fellow travellers. They don't all see it the way I do and they don't necessarily see it the same way or at the same time as their companions do, but we have some common understanding and are enriched by our diversity. And we learn a lot along the way.

I am often reminded of why I love inquiry teaching when I am lucky enough to find myself in nature with children. We all know that amazing moment when we are walking with children and we notice something extraordinary – perhaps we see it but they don't. So we wait…we don't want to spoil the thrill of discovery. We may subtly guide them, help them move in the right direction and then suddenly – they see it: 'Wow! Look at that!' And we delight in watching them discover something for themselves. In the same way, my inquiry mindset reminds me to remain open to new pathways. There are times when the route, or even the destination I have in mind, is changed. Intent on what I *thought* was the direction, I am persuaded to take another path. So as an inquiry teacher, I lead and guide but I must also be prepared to be lead and be guided in turn.

TEACHING AS INQUIRY

While I was writing this book, I came across a recent talk given by the wonderful Tim Costello. In this talk, he argued that many of us have a question, or questions, that guide our whole lives. For Costello, the question was how we can achieve justice in a painfully unjust world. Similarly, Amy Tan, when describing the creative process of writing, refers to the way she found herself 'walking the world' with questions in her head and how those questions helped her observe and gather ideas and thoughts for her books. I think that having an inquiry mindset means that you do, indeed, walk the world with questions in your head. It may be that the question drives a burning, life-long vocation as it does for Tim Costello, or perhaps we find ourselves moving in and out of various quests, driven by a kind of insatiable thirst for learning. Having an inquiry mindset means we are relentlessly and passionately curious.

Inquiry teachers provide a natural and infectious role model for their students and they remain curious about the students *themselves*, about their learning, about their teaching and most importantly about the relationship between the two. They regularly ask themselves: 'How is what I am doing impacting on this child's learning? How am I making a difference?' For the inquiry teacher, learning is delightfully problematic and layered and there will never be an end to it.

Bringing an inquiring disposition to our work as teachers also prompts us to think more rigorously about the relationship between what we do and say and what happens for our students. When we ask ourselves 'What are my students revealing to me?', we position ourselves to act in accordance with our discoveries. We plan, teach, inquire and plan some more. Inquiry teachers see the work they do with students as an opportunity to learn *about* their students and, in turn, an opportunity to meet their needs and interests more effectively.

FROM A 'SUBJECT' TO AN APPROACH ACROSS THE DAY

Thinking of inquiry as something we 'do' (eg, when we do a 'unit of inquiry' on Thursday afternoon) is problematic. Teachers are familiar with the concept of *a cycle or framework* for inquiry that helps us design an ongoing journey of learning for students – often over several weeks. Tasks are organized around a broad sequence of 'phases' that moves students from an exploration of their prior knowledge through to deeper understanding as a result of research, analysis and synthesis. This process is generally framed by questions generated by both teachers and students. This cycle can be applied to short and long-term investigations. The use of inquiry as a planning framework for such units is powerful and effective; however, when we see it *only* in this context we run the risk of treating it like a separate subject in the curriculum (see chapter 5 for more on inquiry frameworks).

Inquiry is *an approach to teaching and learning* regardless of whether this teaching is done within a unit of inquiry or a one-off lesson. An inquiry teacher has a view of their role as a teacher that impacts on what they say, do and think about *everything* that happens in the classroom. The teacher's mindset is absolutely critical to the successful implementation of inquiry in the classroom. It is far more significant than any planner, scope and sequence, framework, program or set of strategies. This mindset goes to how we think about the act of teaching itself.

Teachers with an inquiry mindset generally see learn___ a two-way process and view students as capable and curious. The expectation that accompanies this is that students can (and should) actively investigate questions, problems and challenges – coming to both expected and unexpected conclusions. Teachers tell me time and time again that when they remain open in this way, they meet their intentions by travelling down much more engaging and meaningful pathways. This means being open minded and managing a degree of uncertainty while keeping the big picture in mind. Primary teachers have long used the phrase 'gradual release of responsibility' in relation to teaching reading. An inquiry-oriented teacher applies this same principle across the day. In the wise words of Maria Montessori, our task is to help students 'learn to do it for themselves'. How fascinating to have that same idea echoed almost a century later by Sugata Mitra (2010), whose famous 'hole in the wall' experiments remind us how much students can learn and teach each other if they are motivated by curiosity and given the space and time to learn. Our teaching reflects our mindset, but using strategies and changing what we *do* can also change how we think and feel.

Being an inquiry teacher means more than being able to design tasks within a cycle of inquiry or inviting students to ask and pursue problems and questions. Inquiry comes from a deeper commitment to reflective, process-oriented learning. The inquirer (both teacher and learner) sees themselves and their learning as a 'work in progress.' They are driven by the desire not to simply accumulate or conquer a body of knowledge but to make meaning of the ever-changing knowledge landscape of which we are part. This includes acquiring knowledge, but it is *understanding* that is the ultimate quest.

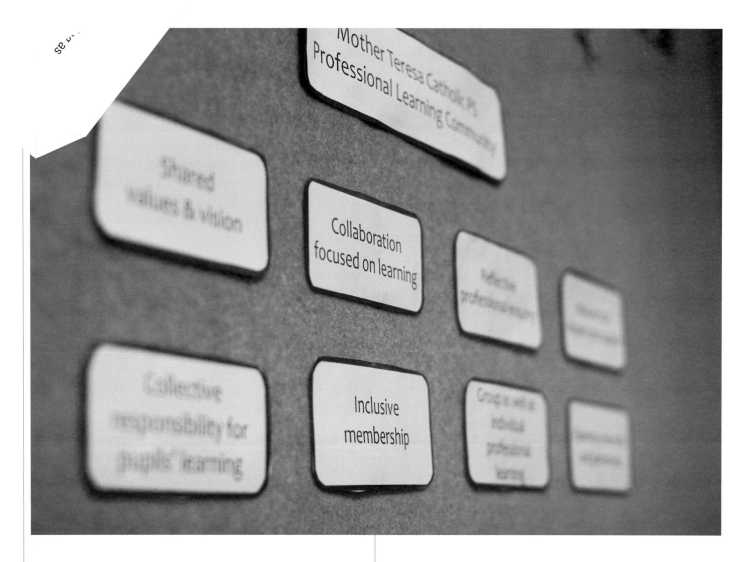

A PRINCIPLED APPROACH

'Great teachers…inside their hearts and their heads, as part of their deep inner core, have an enduring set of principles by which they teach and lead. Such principles offer guidelines against which to measure the worth of external resources. They promote a holistic or big picture for us all to work towards.'
(Dalton and Boyd, 1992)

For thirty years, I have worked with teachers and children in the field of inquiry. One of the questions that stays with me, day in, day out, is 'what makes an inquiry teacher?' Why are some teachers so willing to step back and allow the learner some control over their learning while others struggle to let go and to relinquish power? Why do some teachers so easily locate learning experiences within a bigger picture while others become fixated on specific, narrow outcomes in isolation, reducing their students' opportunity to make useful connections? Why do some teachers happily ask questions, admit uncertainty and relish the opportunity to grow and learn new ways of doing things while others cling to their 'known', fail to look beyond the familiar and see questions or uncertainty as a sign of weakness? My hunch is that this question of 'What makes an inquiry teacher?' will stay with me for the remainder of my career.

What I do know is that effective inquiry teachers are guided by a set of core principles. Clear, well-articulated principles are essential. Once established, principles become the filter through which we judge our actions. They are more than 'beliefs' or opinions – they are informed and highly defensible positions that keep the light on what we do. For principled inquiry teachers, tension can arise when external expectations or initiatives (such as mandatory testing) conflict with these positions. This is why principles are even more effective when they are shared and when they guide the practice of the whole school, not just the individual. Articulating the principles that underpin inquiry-based learning help define and grow a culture of inquiry.

It is important to develop a set of principles as a staff. The following principles provide an example and are also foundational to the content of this book. These principles guide my own practice and reflect my 'inquiry mindset'.

CORE PRINCIPLES GUIDING THE INQUIRY TEACHER'S PRACTICE

01: OWNERSHIP Learning is an active process of construction (not reproduction) and is enhanced when each learner has a voice in, and can make real choices about, their learning.

02: INTEREST Providing opportunities for learners to identify and explore their own interests, beliefs and questions promotes deeper engagement.

03: REFLECTION Learners benefit from continual reflection on and through the learning process. Self-knowledge and metacognition enhance learning and build self-efficacy.

04: PURPOSE Learning should be guided by real purposes and situated in authentic contexts.

05: PRIOR LEARNING Learning is more powerful when the learner can make connections between the new and the known – where there is recognition of their prior knowledge.

06: TRANSFER Learning is powerful and useful when we can transfer it to, and make connections with, other contexts. It is important to know how learning connects to a bigger picture.

07: COLLABORATION Cooperation, interaction and mutual respect enhance opportunities for learning. We learn from and with others.

08: RESILIENCE Emotional resilience, a positive self-image and a 'growth mindset' help the learner set and work towards challenging goals and learn from mistakes.

09: TIME Deeper learning requires adequate time for investigation, processing and creating, and communicating learning. In inquiry, *less is more.*

10: FEEDBACK The learner should be given continual and specific support, guidance and feedback to take their understanding and skills further.

11: ENVIRONMENT Learning environments (physical and emotional) should promote care, curiosity, flexibility and independence.

12: OPENNESS Learning should be approached with openess, flexibility and curiosity.

13: JOY Learning – even when challenging and difficult – should be invigorating and joyous and feed the desire to do and learn more.

FROM PRINCIPLES TO PRACTICE

When guided by these principles, there are certain teaching practices that become less acceptable – or unacceptable – in the learning space. For example, if we hold to the principle of 'purpose' – believing that learning happens best when situated in real contexts for authentic purposes – then we have to question the use of random worksheet exercises such as word mazes or fill-the-gap texts. 'Busy work' like this does not support any inquiry learning principles and is therefore off the menu for the inquiry teacher. When teaching with an inquiry mindset, we shift the way we teach.

A MINDSET DOES NOT MEAN A 'SET MIND'

I like to think that my inquiry mindset acts like a filter for all the decisions I make about what I do and say as a teacher, but I also acknowledge that learning happens when there is the best fit between what the teacher does and what the child needs as a learner. As the great Donald Graves once said, 'the enemy is orthodoxy'. If a methodology becomes blind ideology or our principles start to become rigid rules, we are in trouble.

There are moments each day where I choose to provide information rather than have my students seek it out or I provide no choice in a task. This does not mean I have stopped becoming an inquiry teacher. Far from it. David Perkins (2006) suggests that what we need is a rich constructivists' tool kit. We need to know how to help students inquire and to make connections but we also need to recognise those moments when, for want of a better word, a more 'traditional' approach might be best for that child in that moment with that particular learning intention. Perkins uses the term 'pragmatic constructivism' to describe this approach, and it is a term I have warmed to.

It can be useful, therefore, to see inquiry on a continuum as illustrated below. While the inquiry classroom will emphasize the elements that lie towards the left of this continuum, those more associated with the elements on the right may still be part of the instructional landscape at times.

MORE	LESS
active	passive
open	closed
integrated	separated
differentiated	homogenized
formative	summative
concept-driven	fact-driven
collaborative	competitive
transferable	fixed
student-centered	teacher-centered
negotiated	prescriptive
authentic	simulated
complex	simplistic
connected	fragmented
deep	surface
explicit	hidden
transparent	covert
continuous	intermittent

BECOMING AN INQUIRY TEACHER: AN INQUIRY IN ITSELF

Not long ago a friend with an interest in martial arts shared with me the concept '*shuhari*', which describes the stages one goes through while training. The meaning of this Japanese word goes something like this: *Shu* means to defend, protect or abide by the law of something. *Ha* is about less reliance on the rules and about innovating. *Ri* refers to a kind of freedom from the rules; the *intention* of the rules is so embodied that the practitioner no longer needs to be guided by them. He or she creates and innovates in a new, fluid, higher dimension.

This struck a chord with me, as I witness and share teachers' journeys towards becoming more inquiry based. At first, we seek to know what the 'rules' are. We want recipes and planners and steps and rules. For this reason, I still find myself giving teachers who are very new to the approach samples of fully planned units to follow for their first attempts at working this way. But gradually we are less and less reliant on rules and recipes. As a deeper understanding of inquiry takes root, so too does the teachers' confidence to innovate and create, until ultimately, he or she is in flow. From being a teacher who *does* inquiry, he or she becomes an inquiry teacher. What is said, done and valued in the classroom happens through the powerful, critical lens of inquiry.

The path towards becoming an inquiry teacher is not necessarily linear, nor is it linked to the number of years one has been teaching. One of the qualities associated with inquiry teaching is actually being able to see something anew, as if for the first time. Inquiry teachers have to be prepared to 'reinvent the wheel' with their students. Jardine and Kraemer argue that we should consider the term 'experienced teacher' somewhat differently when it comes to inquiry.

'It is possible to have taught for many years and not be 'experienced' in the sense inquiry requires. In fact it is quite possible to have taught for many years and to have become less and less experienced – less and less open to new experience.' (Jardine, D. and Kraemer, M., 2011: 2)

Regardless of our years of experience, teaching is a profession in which one is continually learning. The bulk of our work resides in the classroom and is intimately bound to what we say and do with students. The following table identifies some of the key techniques that can be used to more effectively nurture students as empowered inquirers.

'The path towards becoming an inquiry teacher is not necessarily linear, nor is it linked to the number of years one has been teaching. One of the qualities associated with inquiry teaching is actually being able to see something anew, as if for the first time.'

WHAT DO INQUIRY TEACHERS DO?

INQUIRY TEACHERS...	EXAMPLE FROM DAILY PRACTICE
01. Create a **flexible, equitable learning environment** where students exercise some **choice** and where independence is fostered.	• Provide students with a range of seating possibilities. • Create spaces for group learning, quiet individual learning, etc. • Help students learn to make wise choices about where to carry out a learning task.
02. Link investigations to **authentic contexts** and purposes. Show students how their discoveries are connected to the world beyond school. Real audiences and real purposes drive learning. Teachers with an inquiry mindset harvest what goes on in the classroom, school, and local and global community for learning contexts. By situating inquiry within such contexts, we show students how learning applies to 'real life' right now – not once schooling is finished.	• An investigation of persuasive texts in literacy may have more power if students are able to choose an issue/cause they wish to persuade a real audience about. • Students investigate what stick insects need to survive before they purchase some for their classroom. • Students learn to calculate percentages by studying household or school water use. What percentage of overall water consumption is used at the drinking fountain? How could we measure this?
03. Frame their teaching around **open-ended questions or problems.** This positions students as investigators/researchers and the question can be returned to during and at the end of the lesson. Inquiry teachers are great question posers. They use questions to prompt student thinking and they question in ways that allow for pondering, theorizing, revising and connecting. A 'stand alone' lesson can be driven by a rich question just as a sustained 'big picture inquiry' can be driven by a compelling question. When we use questions as a driver for our teaching, we position the learner as a researcher – the student is doing the learning rather than having the learning 'done' to them.	• What does 'long' mean? How can we measure what's long? • I wonder how many ways the long 'ee' sound can be made in words? How could we find out? • What makes a great Haiku poem? • How could we work out the most effective way of throwing the ball?
04. Provoke, model and celebrate curiosity. Inquiry teachers provoke, expect and relish questions. Inviting students to explore authentic problems or meet challenges will inevitably give rise to numerous questions along the way. Build in time for students to raise and explore questions meaningful to them. Help students see that questions are a sign of great thinking – not of ignorance.	• Share fascinating objects, images, film clips, stories and dilemmas, and ask 'What does this make you wonder?' and 'What questions are going around in your head?'. Make students' questions visible by recording, sorting and displaying them – and *return* to them to help students reflect on how their thinking is changing. • Begin an art lesson by exposing students to a slide show of inspiring art works without any commentary from the teacher (exposure to works without expectation), simply allowing students to absorb and respond – *then* use the questions to help build students' understanding.

WHAT DO INQUIRY TEACHERS DO? (CONT'D)

INQUIRY TEACHERS...	EXAMPLE FROM DAILY PRACTICE
05. Allow time for students to figure it out for themselves ('flip' the lesson). Inquiry teachers give students time and opportunities to discover and make meaning for themselves. That is not to suggest that the role of the teacher is obsolete or peripheral – this approach is strategic.	Rather than 'front load' at the beginning of a lesson or unit, present a challenge/question/problem and begin by assessing how much students know and how much they can do. Follow by providing, for example, a range of texts to investigate, equipment to work with, or a group challenge to pursue. Once students are involved in exploring the problem or question, the teacher is better able to teach at the point of need and by observing, listening and questioning as the students are engaged in learning. Specific, targeted instruction then happens during or later in the lesson.
06. Use probing questions and thinking prompts as much as possible as teaching tools – so that students do more thinking for themselves more of the time. Teachers with an inquiry mindset remain curious and open to what their students are revealing to them through their actions and words. This means stepping back, noticing, analyzing work samples and bringing these samples to collaborative planning meetings. It means using what students say and do to inform what we say and do. It also means saying less and listening more.	• What do you notice about this group of words? • I wonder what kinds of patterns you are seeing as I read these poems to you? • Tell me more about how you came to this answer. • Talk to each other about how you think that works. I am going to move around the room and listen in.
07. Invite students to **raise questions/wonderings** throughout a lesson and use their questions as a springboard for teaching. Inquiry teachers build a culture that lets students know that **questions are a sign of good thinking** – not a sign of ignorance.	• Using strategies like 'see/think/wonder' can build question-asking into the fabric of a lesson. • Record and celebrate questions that students raise, come back to these and have students attempt to answer as they gain more information.
08. Involve students in **making some decisions** about aspects of the learning experience, even within a lesson. A student voice in decision making is one of the key tenets of inquiry-based learning.	• If students are to work in groups they suggest the best way to organize the groupings. • Students can choose the way they will demonstrate their understanding of something. • Students should help design rubrics and other assessment frameworks.
09. Use a **'layered' or 'split screen' approach** to the lesson. Guy Claxton (2006) has coined the phrase 'split screen teaching' to describe the technique of focusing not just on what is being learned – but on how the learning is happening. An inquiry mindset brings with it a continual focus on the act of learning itself. As students are going about a learning task (whether it is composing a piece of writing, listening to a guest speaker, or reading through information as part of a research task) they are mindful of how that learning is happening and of what they are using/doing as thinkers, collaborators, self-managers or communicators. In an inquiry classroom we are always inquiring into learning itself.	As students work on a math problem in small group, you might ask them to notice the way they are strengthening their collaboration skills as they give feedback to each other.

WHAT DO INQUIRY TEACHERS DO? (CONT'D)

INQUIRY TEACHERS...	EXAMPLE FROM DAILY PRACTICE
10. Use **transferable routines and strategies** within the lesson. When students can use or apply a strategy in different contexts, the possibilities for inquiry are extended.	In a music lesson, students might practice using the 'connect, extend, challenge' routine to analyze a piece of music (this can also be used in a range of other subject areas). Make sure you are explicit about the transfer – how it works the same and differently across subject areas.
11. Help students **make connections between ideas,** between subjects, between inquiries. Making connections builds understanding.	As students are working in teams to choreograph a simple dance, ask them to stop and make a connection to another task they have done recently that has required this same kind of thinking.
12. Are **open** to **unexpected pathways** for inquiry. They remain attuned to the potential for spontaneous investigations to arise and are not hesitant to work with them. Teachers with an inquiry mindset are thorough and thoughtful planners. They are, however, also open and awake to an unexpected moment in which quality inquiry can take place. This can be a challenging balance to strike. On the one hand, we need to be intentional and clear about our learning goals; on the other hand, we need to give ourselves permission to work towards those goals in ways we had not anticipated.	A sudden weather event such as a hail storm could be used for some on-the-spot science inquiry: • What *is* hail? • What causes it to happen? • How do you know? • How could we find out more? • What questions come to mind as we watch this?
13. **Access students' prior learning** and make the process **of 'constructing understanding'** as explicit as possible. In an inquiring classroom, the students are *building* understanding for themselves with skillful questioning, prompting and scaffolding from the teacher.	Have students identify something they already know/expect/ anticipate/predict at the beginning of the lesson, then consciously stop to review and reflect to identify new thinking.
14. **Allow some open-ended exploration time.** Inquiry involves a certain amount of 'play', and through such play, students will often make discoveries for themselves which are more powerful than anything they might be 'told'.	Provide time: • to explore manipulatives during a math lesson. • to skim and scan through a text before using any specific strategy. • to play with equipment/space (safety considered) during PE and use this as an opportunity to observe skills and areas of need. • to play with instruments during a music lesson – what can we learn about how this instrument works through open exploration?
15. **Limit whole-class instruction.** Structure lessons so that the bulk of the teaching is done with small groups and individuals.	The 'whole–part–whole' formula works well for inquiry. The trick is to keep the 'whole' brief and focused.

WHAT DO INQUIRY TEACHERS DO? (CONT'D)

INQUIRY TEACHERS...	EXAMPLE FROM DAILY PRACTICE
16. Encourage students to do the **talking and thinking** rather than doing it for them!	Reduce 'hands-up conversations'. Instead, use strategies like 'think–pair–share' when conducting whole-class conversations.
17. Build **reflective thinking into** the daily routine. Teach students how to reflect and expect this as part of how we 'do things'. When we stop to think about what we have done, why we have done it, what we have learned, how we feel and what we might need to do next, we give ourselves an opportunity to clarify and make meaning from our experiences. Teaching with an inquiry mindset means that we, as teachers, become habitually reflective. It requires discipline to deliberately stop, look back and take stock, but it is critical to the success of inquiry and a valuable disposition for life.	Sentence starters, thumbs up/down and other quick reflective techniques can be a practical way to build reflection in without making it a time-consuming part of the lesson.
18. Consider the tasks students are doing as **learning strategies** rather than activities. Make sure students know why they are doing what they are doing.	• Display the **learning intentions** (as questions) for the lesson. • Ask students to tell you what they believe the learning purposes are. • Ask students: 'Why are we doing this?'.
19. Provide opportunities for **personal learning** pathways.	Create a routine in the week such as 'iTime' (see chapter 7) that allows students to investigate current passions or work on a skill they wish to develop.
20. Are **inquiry learners**.	The best inquiry teachers are *continually inquiring into their own practice*. They show students that *they* are learners too – and bring an inquiry mindset to their own teaching. One of the most powerful ways we can nurture an inquiring disposition in our students is to show them *our* fascination in the world, our hunger to learn, our delight in discovery, our willingness to find out more and our preparedness to change our thinking. An inquiry mindset can be contagious when we make it visible and audible to others.

REFERENCES AND FURTHER READING

• Aitken, G. (2009) 'The Inquiring teacher: Clarifying the concept of teacher effectiveness', http://www.educationalleaders.govt.nz/Leadership-development/Leadership-programmes/First-time-principals-modules/Module-2-Teaching-effectiveness.

• Bruner, J. (1966) *Towards a Theory of Instruction*, Harvard University Press, Cambridge, MA.

• Claxton, G. (2006) 'Expanding the Capacity to Learn: A New End for Education?', opening address to the Annual Conference of BERA, Warwick University.

• Dalton, J. and Boyd, J. (1992) *I Teach: An Inspiring Guide to Classroom Leadership*, Eleanor Curtain Publishing, Melbourne.

• Dewey, J. (1938) *Experience and education*, Simon & Schuster, New York.

• Dweck, C. (2006) *Mindset: The New Psychology of Success*, Random House, New York.

• Jardine, D. and Kraemer, M. (2011) 'On the Nature of Inquiry: The Experienced Teacher', http://galileo.org/teachers/designing-learning/articles/the-experienced-teacher/.

• Kabat-Zinn, J. (2005) *Wherever You, There You Are: Mindfulness Meditation in Everyday Life*, Hyperion, NY.

• Kuhlthau, C., Maniotes, L. and Caspari, A. (2007) *Guided Inquiry: Learning in the 21st Century*, Libraries Unlimited, Santa Barbara, CA.

• Mitra, S. (2010) 'The Child Driven Education', Ted Talk, Oxford, http://blog.ted.com/2010/09/07/the-child-driven-education-sugata-mitra-on-ted-com/.

• Montessori, M. (1949) *The Absorbent Mind*, Kessinger Publishing LLC.

• Perkins, D. (2006) 'Constructivism and Troublesome Knowledge' in Meyer, J. and Land, R. *Overcoming Barriers to Student Understanding: Threshold Concepts and Troublesome Knowledge*, Routledge, Abingdon, UK, pp. 33–47.

• Sinek, S. (2009) *Start with Why: How Great Leaders Inspire Everyone to Take Action*, Portfolio, Penguin, US.

• Vygotsky, L.S. (1978), *Mind in Society*, Harvard University Press, Cambridge, MA.

• West-Burnham, J. and Coates, M. (2005) *Personalizing Learning*, Network Educational Press, Stafford.

How well do I know my students as people? Do I know what interests them? Do I know what they are passionate about?

Am I an inquirer? Do my students see and hear my questions about the world? Do I wonder aloud? Do I show them what it means to be curious and passionate about learning? Do I explore and connect with the world?

Do my students know *why* they are doing what they are doing? *Do I?* Are my purposes clear and shared? Is this worth teaching?

Do my **walls teach** or simply 'display'? What does my classroom say about what I value? What does it say about me?

What do my students **reveal** to me? Do I use this evidence to inform my planning? Am I listening?

Am I teaching my students *how* to inquire? Do they know what they are learning about learning?

How do I give my students **voice?** Do they **participate** in decisions made about their learning? Do I hold all the power? Am I prepared to let go?

'Given a rich learning environment,
learning becomes like the air —
it's in and around us.'

(Sandra Dodd)

~ C H A P T E R ~

two

Creating the space:
HOW CAN WE DESIGN LEARNING
ENVIRONMENTS FOR INQUIRY?

INTRODUCTION

It almost feels a little retrograde to be writing about *classroom environments* for inquiry when we are on the cusp of an exciting movement that is changing the very concept of the 'classroom' itself. Students do not need to come to 'a classroom' to inquire. We can inquire anywhere, any time – particularly when we have a device in hand. I have no doubt that we will see an increasing trend towards flexible timetables, community-based learning and more creative use of learning spaces within and beyond schools. That said, the majority of teachers with whom I work still interact with a group of students in a dedicated, physical space for most of the time.

After years of working in a wide variety of learning spaces, I can say with confidence that quality inquiry learning *can* happen just about anywhere – from the smallest, most under-resourced schools through to the lush, privileged surrounds of wealthier settings. I have seen some beautiful inquiry facilitated in very traditionally designed classrooms, just as I have seen more

flexible, digitally connected, indoor–outdoor environments go to waste when there is little understanding of *how* to make the most of them. Choosing to forgo inquiry because the physical environment does not lend itself well enough is, in short, a bit of a cop-out. Having said that, there is also no doubt that inquiry teachers find their work can be significantly supported and made easier when the environment is sympathetic to, and indeed generative of, more student-centered and investigative approaches.

Teachers (and students) can create environments that work for or against learning. As so beautifully described by proponents of the Reggio Emilia philosophy, the environment can be seen as the child's third teacher, the first and second being the parent and teacher. The inquiry classroom is, above all, a space that nurtures an inquiring culture. This is achieved partly though the physical use of furniture, walls and objects and also through the relational and emotional space that is 'built' over time.

'Teachers (and students) can create environments
that work for or against learning.'

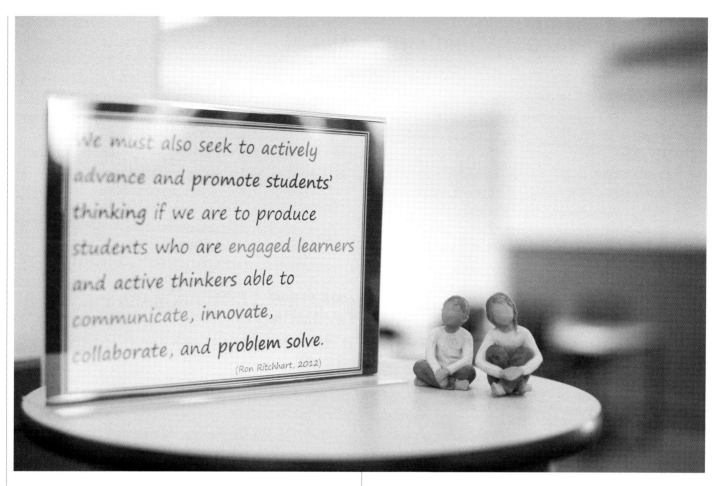

We must also seek to actively advance and promote students' thinking if we are to produce students who are engaged learners and active thinkers able to communicate, innovate, collaborate, and problem solve.

(Ron Ritchhart, 2012)

THE EMOTIONAL ENVIRONMENT
Building relationships

'The truth is that when we scrub joy and comfort from the classroom, we distance our students from effective information processing and long term memory storage. Instead of taking pleasure from learning, students become bored, anxious and anything but engaged.' (Willis, J. 2007:1)

While the physical environment needs to be as supportive as possible of inquiry, it is the 'emotional' environment that is the key to real success. Simply put, inquiry requires risk taking, and students are more likely to take risks in environments where they feel safe to express themselves and to be challenged. There is ample evidence to convince us that students' learning is hampered when they are stressed or feel they are under threat. Teachers exert enormous power without even realizing it. What we do and say has a profound influence on students' feeling and thinking. Any good teacher knows that it is, in the end, the quality of the relationships they hold with their students – and the relationships fostered *between* students – that determines much about the kind of learning that takes place. Ample evidence exists to link the child's sense of safety and security to the degree to which they will confidently explore the world around them (Engel, 2011).

For the inquiry teacher, relationships are paramount. Inquiry teachers depend on their deep knowledge of their students to guide them in questioning, prompting and helping determine individual learning paths. They need to establish a trusting and connected community of learners if they are going to successfully challenge them to wrestle with higher order thinking, authentic problems and complex ideas. Relating well to students and building connected and respectful relationships between students can be, in itself, the focus of an inquiry process. Many teachers begin their year by posing such questions as:

- *How can we get to know each other as people and as learners?*
- *How can we make this classroom a place where learning thrives?*
- *What kind of learning community do we want to be?*
- *How can we connect with each other and with ourselves?*

When we use such questions as the basis for an inquiry we develop inquiry strategies at the same time as building relationships. It's a win-win. There are countless resources on relationship building available to us. The techniques I list on page 30 only scratch the surface. Suffice to say, the emotional climate of the classroom has a huge influence on the degree to which an inquiry approach will work with your students. It is worth putting time into. Like all relationships, the connections we have with our students needs regular attention – it's not just something to attend to at the beginning of the year.

STRATEGIES FOR BUILDING COMMUNITY AND CONNECTING WITH STUDENTS

- Ask students to **share 'who they are'** by bringing in objects or photos that represent themselves and their lives. Have them share and compare, looking for similarities and differences.

- **Create a class blog** or use online tools that allow for regular dialogue between you and students and among students as an ideal way of communicating. This is often the preferred milieu of the students themselves. Blogs also allow connections to be made with students in other classes and other schools across the world. This strengthens the understanding of ways in which we are part of multiple communities.

- Invite students to **write you a letter (or a post)** about why you are lucky to have them in your class – and you can write one to say why they are lucky to have you!

- Use the informal 'before the bell goes' time in the morning to **chat to individuals about their lives**. It makes such a difference to a child when their teacher remembers the football match they were playing in, the cousins who were coming over, or the pet they had to take to the vet. The time before the school day officially starts can be the greatest opportunity to build rapport.

- **Greet each student** in the morning as they come into the room. Use their names. Expect them to use yours in return.

- **Play games** that foster teamwork, connection and fun.

- **Co-construct agreements** about behavior and expectations. This is critical to the beginning of the year but should be revisited regularly. If students have participated in developing these agreements they are more likely to adhere to them. Inquiry classrooms are places in which students must have a voice – and must be held to the decisions they help make.

- **Establish** a routine of **regular class/group meetings**. This might be a weekly event that is eventually run by the students themselves. The class meetings give students an opportunity to air concerns, make suggestions, solve problems, reflect and plan.

- **Set some class goals** – some things you want to achieve as a group. It might be to raise enough money to sponsor an endangered animal or to beat your best time at a circle game. Set the class a challenge to collaboratively organize an event such as a welcome to new families. There is nothing quite so galvanizing as a shared goal – and the sense of camaraderie that comes from this can form powerful bonds between students.

- Send a simple **note** (slipped into a student's bag/locker), or an **email**, **message or text** letting them know you are glad to have them in your class, that you noticed a kind thing they did that day or simply that you believe in them. This can be more powerful than 'praise' in front of the group.

- **Allow students to get to know _you_.** You as a person as well as a teacher. Relax your guard, tell stories, share, show them some photos of the important people and places in your life. Quality relationships are a two-way street. Smile.

- Above all, **be the inquirer you want to see!** _Show_ students how curious about and connected with the world you are. Wonder aloud. Share the things that make you curious, the puzzles and problems you encounter as a learner. Think aloud. Show them what it means to be a courageous, capable, curious and committed inquirer.

CREATING A COLLABORATIVE COMMUNITY

In their work on Literature Circles, Short and Pierce (1998) point out the interesting paradox that is the co-existence of individuality _and_ 'groupness' in an effective learning community. They argue that the community becomes effective not because it strives for homogeneity amongst its members but because it recognizes and values diversity. The diversity 'increases and expands' the resources available to the group and makes for a richer, more dynamic learning context. Similarly, George Otero's wonderful work in the field of relational learning reminds us of the power of interdependence between learners in a learning community and the importance of respecting and learning from difference:

'The more we respect others, in all of their diversity and multiplicity, the more we as learning selves can benefit and grow. It is only by seeing people as they are that we can learn from their experiences and absorb the valuable things they are prepared to teach us. Learning selves are respecting selves.' (Otero, G., 2001:8)

Inquiry classrooms demand complex collaborative skills. As we'll see in chapter 6, skills can be 'inquired into' and taught explicitly. Clear and focused time spent on learning how to learn with others is never time wasted. There is now a significant body of research that suggests there are learning benefits for students when they work together on a collective task. When students are challenged to work on a collective task and given the right kind of support and explicit instruction and reflection time, they learn how to negotiate, articulate and justify their thinking, respect and resolve differences, give and accept feedback, play a range of roles, compromise and build communication skills. In the digitally connected inquiry classroom, collaboration is not simply about students working in class-based groups. It may involve tasks carried out in collaboration with community members or students in other schools – even other countries.

WHAT DO WE OBSERVE IN THE INQUIRY CLASSROOM?

Before we continue, let's take a moment to consider what we might expect to see happening in the inquiry classroom. Determining ways to create and nurture the visible, physical and emotional space should be informed by our understanding of how inquiry teachers and students *use* the space. The following table outlines some of the key activities happening in a typical inquiry classroom.

STUDENTS ARE...	TEACHERS ARE...
• working in different areas and not necessarily on the same task • talking to each other • moving around the space • accessing technologies and other resources as needed • working in small focus groups with the teacher for short, intensive instructional sessions • using materials • using anchor charts (and/or digital equivalents) and other reference items to check criteria, intentions or requirements for a task • recording and documenting their thinking in a range of ways • working on sustained projects rather than one-off activities • negotiating with teachers and others about learning tasks and how they will approach them • setting and reflecting on personal goals • generating, recording and exploring questions • self and peer assessing • returning to tasks to re-work them based on teacher feedback • offering their expertise to other students • inviting peer assistance as well as teacher assistance • talking about their learning • expressing ideas and opinions • taking time to laugh and enjoy learning • sitting, standing, moving to different parts of the space	• working in different parts of the space – most often with small groups and individuals • listening • interacting with students – moving around the space • talking with individuals and small groups of students – engaging in deeper dialogue to elicit thinking • questioning students to encourage deeper, challenging thinking • modelling skills and processes • making intentions clear and explicit throughout the day • helping create visible records of learning (digital or hard copy) • collaborating with other teachers and adults in the learning space • using sophisticated language of learning and cognitive terminology, e.g. ' classify', 'reflect', 'analyze', 'predict' • observing and documenting student learning – capturing learning with photos, video, notes etc. to be used for planning • listening to students • using a wide range of resources: visual, print, hands-on etc. • conducting quick 'check-ins' for understanding • giving specific feedback • thinking out loud – modeling what it means to be an inquirer • posing questions, providing interesting provocations • inviting students to help plan tasks, excursions and other learning experiences • maintaining clear, shared expectations – helping students observe protocol for a safe and active environment • encouraging full participation • referring to the anchor charts, menus and criteria lists around the room to help build independent learning • reflecting • taking time to laugh and enjoy learning

MAKING LEARNING PRINCIPLES VISIBLE

Sample from St Clares Primary School, Melbourne.

ST CLARE'S PRIMARY SCHOOL IS A LEARNING COMMUNITY.
All members of the community are learners – staff, parents and children.
AS A LEARNING COMMUNITY WE RECOGNISE THAT:

We can learn anywhere, any time.

Learning is social, cultural and dependent on relationships.

Our emotional and physical wellbeing are keys to learning.

Learning is multi-sensory.

Each one of us learns differently but we can all strengthen our learning capabilities.

Feedback from others has a powerful impact on our learning.

Motivation is enhanced when we understand and own our learning.

Time and reflection are integral to learning.

WHAT DOES YOUR CLASSROOM SAY ABOUT YOU AS A TEACHER?

Whether we like it or not, we send clear messages to students, parents and the wider community about what we value through how we choose to use our learning spaces: what goes on the walls, the use of technologies and shared spaces, how we arrange furniture, the objects we keep in the learning space and the condition and type of gardens and outdoor spaces. The agreements we make about the use of physical environments also impact on student learning. If, for example, each student is allocated their own table and is expected to stay at that table for all tasks, we immediately limit opportunities for flexible groupings, collaboration and choice. If we lock most materials away in storerooms and keep control over what can and can't be used, we limit opportunities for the development of resource management and organizational skills *and* we send clear messages about our power. We also make more work for ourselves by not including students in the shared responsibility for their environment.

INVOLVING STUDENTS IN THE DESIGN OF THE LEARNING SPACE

The way we create the classroom space can, in itself, be an excellent *context for inquiry*. Many teachers now understand that setting the room up before the students arrive actually deprives them of an important opportunity to develop a sense of shared ownership of, and commitment to, their environment. Some questions that can help students contribute to classroom design include:

- What do we need to have in this space to help us as learners?
- What could we do without?
- What furniture arrangement would best suit *you* as a learner or *us* as a learning community? How does this fit with others? How could we compromise?
- How can we make this space a place we *want* to learn in? How do we want to feel in here?
- How will we make sure this space is cared for? What systems and agreements do we need?
- What parts of this space should be shared? What parts should be personal?
- How can we create pockets for quiet, small-group and whole-group learning?
- How can we make our learning space look and feel special and inviting?
- What do we need to do to ensure we care for the space?
- What responsibilities come with being here? Who should do what?
- How will we manage our devices and other equipment?

A SPACE THAT HONORS THE AESTHETIC

The words 'classroom' and 'beauty' are rarely used in the same sentence – and for good reason. For so long, classrooms have been anything but beautiful. Functional, industrial, disciplined, sterile interiors have perhaps been used as ways to ensure students ar enore compliant. Alternatively, classrooms can be somewhat chaotic, busy environments full of 'dingle-dangles' hanging from the rafters, walls strewn with colorful posters and student work, resources piled high in and on shelves.

Of all the learning spaces I visit, the ones that regularly leave me most inspired and that lean most toward inquiry are those more mindfully designed and 'curated' by teachers who see the connection between the physical space and learning. These teachers seem compelled to ensure the learning environment holds some beauty, and this, in turn, sends out a deep message of respect to the learner. It says: 'I care about you. I want you to be in a space that is nurturing and pleasant to be in. I want you to feel at home, inspired and valued'.

Most of us know the impact that being in a beautiful environment can have on us. Creating beauty in classroom spaces can be a relatively straightforward accomplishment and does not require a degree in interior design! Beauty does not necessarily mean 'pretty' but it does, in this case, mean compelling – a classroom environment that honors the aesthetic appeals to the senses, invites the learner to wonder and is a place in which one wants to be and learn.

Some simple suggestions:
- Use **natural materials** where possible. Wood, cane, raw fabrics and natural materials have an aesthetic and environmental quality that makes a significant difference to the 'feel' of the classroom environment.
- Include indoor **plants** and/or window boxes, perhaps grown from seedlings by the students.
- Try **baskets** rather than plastic containers for resources.
- Place **lamps** in some areas to soften the lighting.
- Install soft, sheer **curtains** (e.g. shower curtains) to divide areas and provide some interest and softening of the space.
- Offer cushions, bean bags and **couches.** These make a difference to the feel of the space and can also provide more open areas in which to move and learn.
- Try a **variety of tables** and seating of different sizes. Like adults, children like to work in different places at different times. Include some tables to stand at rather than sit at. Include some low tables.
- Use cloths to cover tables, particularly where **objects of interest** are placed; scented oil burners/infusers (these can be the non-open-flame variety) and additional rugs/mats that help define small-group spaces.
- Introduce **Fish tanks**, terrariums – well-designed enclosures for suitable animals.
- Pay attention to **natural light sources**. Covering the windows with posters can restrict the flow of natural light into the room, which is both energy wasting and potentially less inviting to the learner.
- Above all, **avoid clutter**. If you are not a tidy person by nature this may be a challenge, but it is one you need to rise to in the professional context of school. Inquiry learning requires self-management and independence. Children learn so much by example – so if we want students to be independent, organized and careful with and respectful of their belongings, then we need to show what that looks like.

ATTENDING TO THE NEEDS OF INDIVIDUAL STUDENTS

Of course, each class is composed of students with a range of needs and dispositions. The way we set the classroom up must take into account the particular needs of some students who may be challenged by an over-stimulating environment or may require more space in which to move around.

A SPACE THAT NURTURES CURIOSITY AND WONDER

There is a lot we can do in and with the physical environment to nurture that all-important disposition of curiosity in our students. Contemporary museums and galleries do this well by positioning intriguing objects, signs and artworks in ways that capture our attention and invite us to look more closely. Regardless of what students might be currently inquiring into, the classroom should be a place that invites investigation and routinely intrigues students.

TRY THESE STRATEGIES

A '**wonderwall**' – this can be a permanent fixture in the room that is used and re-used for different inquiries. Display students' names and/or photos on the wall under which they can post their questions.

'**Wonderboxes**' – these serve a similar purpose to a wonderwall. Noodle boxes can be personalized. Provide a set of ready cut cards to write wonderings on.

Cozy book corner
– a café-style area where students can comfortably curl up with a book.

Living things – plants and animals (with attention to the relevant guidelines regarding animals in classrooms) are a fantastic source of wonder for children. Animals are a natural stimulus for ongoing inquiry.

Video booth/ movie-making, viewing and editing area.

Tinkering station
– fill it with tools and materials, old toys and gadgets.

Mini art studio – containing art materials and supplies, and work in progress.

Photos, images and art – the internet is full of *amazing* images that inspire wonder. Try having one displayed on your interactive whiteboard at the start of each day. Display intriguing images from books on a bookstand.

The lab – devoted to science exploration.

Global communications center – a fancy name for a device dedicated to Skype/FaceTime conversations.

Collections – these may change from week to week and be curated by the students themselves. They could include rocks, bones, shells, stamps, cards – the possibilities are endless.

The 'cave' – a place to retreat to, to work alone or when something requires intense concentration.

Intriguing objects – reserve a small table in the room for a weekly object of intrigue and invite students to try to figure out what it might be, where it is from, etc. Have students write their thoughts on Post-it notes.

A 'cabinet of curiosity' – this may be a small second-hand cupboard with the doors taken off or a simple boxed shelving unit into which interesting items are placed.

Question of the day – reserve a space in the room to write an intriguing question of the day. These questions are generally open-ended and may be philosophical, mathematical, ethical or fantastical. Here are some examples:

- Is it better to be a kid or a grown up?
- Is it ever OK to lie?
- If you could re-name yourself, what would you choose? Why?

- If you could go back in time, where would you go and in what time period?
- Do animals have feelings?
- What makes you who you are?

- How do you know if you are healthy?
- What jobs might not be around when you are an adult?

- Why do leaves fall off trees in autumn/fall?
- What is snow? How is it made?
- If you were an animal, what would you be?

A FLEXIBLE SPACE

Inquiry learning means learning in different ways and often with different people. Not all students will be doing the same thing at the same time, and teachers need to be able to work with individuals and small groups throughout the day. All this requires furniture arrangements and agreements that allow movement and choice. There is no need for a table and chair for every student. Flexible learning spaces allow students to position themselves in different places in the room for different purposes: sometimes sitting at a table, sometimes in a beanbag, sometimes standing at a bench, sometimes on the floor, or perhaps outside in an area just off the classroom if you are lucky! Inquiry classrooms take re-imagining. The idea of who 'owns' what, changes.

Consider:

- tables in groups – or tables that lend themselves easily to team work
- semi-supervised spaces or 'nests' where students can cluster together while still in view
- tables that can be easily moved and rearranged
- an area that lends itself to chairs or cushions being placed in a circle for whole-group discussions
- a space that is clear or can be quickly cleared for a whole-group gathering
- an area or pod of tables ideal for small-group instruction
- a variety of chairs/bean bags and places students can sit
- stable tables or clip boards
- standing tables
- an interactive whiteboard that can be easily managed and accessed by students
- an outdoor area in which some students can choose to do their learning
- resources (laptops, iPads, pens and pencils, etc.) on shelving units that are accessible to students
- bags outside rather than inside the room
- mini whiteboards
- room dividers (on wheels so they can be easily moved around)
- an area of the classroom set aside for complete silence: quiet spaces created by corrals, tents or sheer screens
- teaching in and from different areas – moving an easel and whiteboards around so there is no obvious front to the room
- removing large teachers' desks

A SPACE THAT HELPS TEACH

Traditionally, primary classroom walls have, at best, been used to 'show off' student products. While celebrating some student learning is important, there are other ways this can be done and more productive ways to use the walls. The concept of working walls has been around a long time and is very relevant to inquiry approaches. Rather than the walls being seen as a place to display finished work, the walls become a visual record of work in progress. Even more importantly they become, a visual reference to support students' thinking and decision making as they inquire. So rather than displaying 25 copies of a worksheet students have completed, the walls will hold:

- menus of strategies students have learned; these can be referred to and built on throughout the year
- agreements and routines that remind students of 'how we do things around here'
- current essential questions for inquiry
- samples, photos and annotations about the inquiry journey
- work in progress (this may look less 'polished' than the finished product but is much more authentic)
- learning intentions/goals for individuals and groups
- signs and descriptors of the processes and procedures being used by the students (these can be written by the students as a way of 'curating' the classroom and sharing their learning processes with others)
- criteria for tasks that have been developed with students (these can be referred to when self-assessing and when working through the task itself)

AN INTELLECTUALLY CHALLENGING ENVIRONMENT

'[The teacher's] words change the life of the classroom. They change the worlds the children inhabit, and consequently who they can be, what they will feel, what they can know, and what will be 'normal' behavior' (Johnston, 2012)

Inquiry learning is, by its nature, intellectually challenging. Students are working with open-ended questions, issues or problems and are expected to participate not just in what they are learning but in the design of the learning experience itself. In the hands of an expert practitioner, this approach leads to greater intellectual engagement. As has already been said, a climate of trust and connectedness is vital to risk taking. But 'feeling safe' is not sufficient. As inquirers, our students also need to feel challenged, and indeed, to relish feeling challenged!

In short: we need to be careful we don't confuse the need to be supportive and caring with an absence of challenge.

In an inquiry classroom, our aim is to create an atmosphere that is, as Kohn describes, one of 'exuberant discovery' (Kohn, 2004) or, in a similar vein, one that induces a state described by Caine and Caine (1994) as 'relaxed alertness'. Establishing a safe, trusting emotional climate opens the gate to rigorous intellectual activity, and this is where the great joy of inquiry learning can be most keenly felt. We want our students to be courageous thinkers – to posit theories, to question texts and each other, to critique the purpose of tasks, to find and solve problems and to be able to receive critical feedback without feeling they are being judged or bullied.

In his wonderful book *Opening Minds*, Peter Johnston offers a powerful metaphor for the language of the inquiry teacher. He remarks that talk in a student-centered classroom is like 'conversational jazz'. A great inquiry teacher is a highly skilled improviser, carefully using his/her talk to scaffold thinking, honor the child, model curiosity, respect difference and most of all to ensure the student owns their learning. And when we use our talk in ways that achieve all of these things, we engage students at an intellectual level. So, what can we do to create a joyful, intellectually challenging environment?

- **Keep the bar high!** *Expect* your students to think and to participate. Use the language of learning with them. Don't dumb it down. If a five year old can learn to say 'Tyrannosaurus Rex' then they can learn the words 'investigate' and 'reflective'.

- **Make your own thinking 'audible' to students.** For example, 'Oh – that idea is really challenging me! I need to think more deeply about that.'

- **Help students to feel how deeply satisfying an intellectually rigorous task can be.** We can do a lot by modelling our own sense of satisfaction when we have persisted through a challenging task. 'Oh, this is challenging, but I really want to figure it out! I need to stick with it…there must be a way to make it clearer to myself….' 'Oh, that feels very satisfying. I had no idea how to do that, but now, I do!'

- **Acknowledge the role of confusion in learning.** Give some *value* to confusion. When we are bewildered and puzzled, we are on the brink of learning. We don't want children to adopt 'confusion avoidance' strategies by aiming low and shying away from challenge. They need to see confusion as a valid and often important part of the learning process. The famous 'zone of proximal development' we have learned from Vygotsky reminds us that students are in the best position to learn when

they are neither too comfortable nor too confused, when they still need some help to figure it out but are getting there. Some confusion is often a sign that learning is about to take place. Notice it and name it:

- *'I can see you are really persisting with your thinking here. Well done – it's so satisfying to have to dig deeper, isn't it?'*
- *'I wonder if any of you are starting to change your minds about that? I am not so sure about my initial ideas now – it can be a great feeling to let go and find a new way of thinking about something.'*
- *'Does this prompt some questions for you? I love it when there are more questions about something than there are answers? It makes it so fascinating.'*
- *'Are you making connections? What does this remind you of? It's a buzz when you can recognize a pattern or a link, isn't it?'*
- *'What are you noticing about your thinking? Share what's happening in your head with someone else. Isn't it interesting that we all have different ways of working it out?'*
- *'Oh – I'm noticing a change in the atmosphere. Some of you look really puzzled. Who is in the zone of confusion right now? That's OK – let's figure out what we need and what we need to ask to make our way through. I feel some learning coming on. Don't you?'*

- **Expect participation by all** – not just the chosen or willing few. Get rid of 'hands up' during discussions. When you ask a question, give students time to think and rehearse with others before asking a few to share their thoughts. 'Hands up' reduces participation and engagement. It is an instrument of control rather than of quality discourse.

- **Limit 'whole-group' conversations.** Too much time 'on the floor' inevitably means too much teacher talk.

- **Introduce students to powerful thinking routines** and strategies they can use across the day (see chapter 10 for a range of strategies).

- **Consider the quality of your questions** and the manner in which you question students (see chapter 4 for questioning ideas).

- **Ensure that what students are inquiring into is rich and relevant.** We disengage from something intellectually when we lack any connection with it and when we fail to be fascinated by or see worth in what we are learning about.

- **Vary the dynamics across the day.** High energy, interactive group time needs to be balanced by opportunities for individuals to experience 'periods of autonomy and quiet' (Cain, 2013). This is particularly important in newer, open-learning environments. Without spaces that allow students to retreat and work quietly and individually, these environments can become overwhelming and stressful for some. Similarly, making all tasks collaborative is frustrating for learners who thrive when they have opportunities to work alone. Choice and attention to balance are important ingredients in intellectual engagement.

- **Allow some down time.** Schools can be exhausting places. With teachers' workloads and community expectations increasing, many teachers bemoan the sense that they 'just don't have time to have fun any more'. What an indictment on our system! Our brains need some time off. Programs that are overly structured and fast-paced can rob the learner of important time to rest the mind and allow learning to bed down. In short, give students a break. Many argue that, contrary to popular opinion, it is vital for students to be able to spend some time 'daydreaming'. When the mind is at rest and is permitted to travel, we can be our most creative. '*Good daydreaming is when the mind is working on information and for that information to lead students on journeys of imagination and discovery.*' (Hawkes, 2010:2)

- **Stop talking (as much).** Just as important as our talk in the classroom is our silence. In the inquiry classroom, this is not the compliant 'heads down and work' silence of the past – but the mindful, respectful silence following a question, within a conversation, at various points in the day. Teachers talk too much and students often spend their day drowning in a sea of unnecessary talk.

We can nurture curiosity and thinking through what we say, but also through choosing *not* to say anything at all. To listen, we need to stop talking. To wait. To breathe. To slow down.

Over the past few years, we have learned a great deal about the importance of students' personal 'mindsets' in determining the degree to which they will persist with thinking. The work of Carol Dweck (2007) has been pivotal in this regard. Again, it is the language we use as teachers that can be instrumental in fostering a preferred 'growth mindset' over a 'fixed' one. Students with a fixed mindset tend not to find inquiry easy.

Where inquiry invites the learner to wrestle with knowledge as problematic and messy, those with a fixed mindset often yearn for the 'right' answer and do not cope well when their efforts to 'find out' meet with failure. Giving students feedback on the processes they are using rather than simply what they are 'producing' is one way to help ensure a growth oriented mindset and a true culture of inquiry.

THE INQUIRY CLASSROOM: A SPACE OF POSSIBILITY

I once heard the ideal classroom described as the 'space of possibility.' In this space, students have agency and are active participants in the complex, dynamic process that is learning. The environment we create impacts on the learning our students experience. There is a lot we can do to enhance inquiry by attending to the physical space and the emotional and intellectual climate within it. When we fail to examine the environment in which learning is taking place, we often fail to remove the most fundamental roadblocks to quality inquiry. So take a look around. Walk into your classroom as if you were visiting it for the first time. What does it say about you? Your beliefs? Your approach to teaching and learning? Would you want to be a student in your classroom? Is this a place that invites curiosity, wonder, thinking and joy? Is this a 'space of possibility'? Is this an inquiring classroom?

REFERENCES AND FURTHER READING
- Barron, B. and Darling-Hammond, L. (2008) 'Teaching for Meaningful Learning: A Review of Research on Inquiry Based and Cooperative Learning', Edutopia.org. Can be retrieved at http://www.edutopia.org/pdfs/edutopia-teaching-for-meaningful-learning.pdf.
- Cain, S. (2013) *Quiet: The Power of Introverts in a World That Can't Stop Talking*, Random House, New York.
- Caine, R. and Caine, G. (1994) *Making Connections: Teaching and the Human Brain*, Dale Seymour Publishing, Lebanon, IN.
- Dodd, S., www.sandradodd.com.
- Dweck, C, (2007) *Mindset: The New Psychology of Success*, Ballantyne, New York.
- Hawkes, T. (2010), quoted in MacGibbon, A., 'New Thinking Backs Daydream Believers' *The Age*, 16 August 2010.
- Johnston, P. (2012) *Opening Minds: Using Language to Change Minds*, Stenhouse, Portland, ME.
- Kohn, A. (2004) 'Feel-bad Education', *Education Week,* 24(3) pp. 44–45, http://www.ascd.org/publications/educational-leadership/summer07/vol64/num09/The-Neuroscience-of-Joyful-Education.aspx.
- Otero, G. (2001) 'Deepening Dialogue: The Learning Self', accessed at http://www.learningtolearn.sa.edu.au/tfel/files/links/DeepeningDialogue_1.pdf.
- Short, K. and Pierce, K. (1998) *Talking About Books*: Literature Discussion Groups in K-8 Classrooms, Heinneman, Portsmouth, NH.

For great question of the day ideas, see:
- http://wonderopolis.org – subscribe and you will have a wonder of the day emailed to you every day)
- http://www.101qs.com – a great website that inspires interesting math questions.
- Gilbert, I. (2007) *The Little Book of Thunks*, Crown House Publishing, UK.
- White, T. (2007) *Could You? Would You?*, Kane/Miller Books, Australia.

'We need a curriculum of big questions...
We need a pedagogy free from fear
and focused on the magic of children's innate
quest for information and understanding.'

(Sugata Mitra, 2013)

~ CHAPTER ~

three

Beyond topics:
WHAT'S WORTH
INQUIRING INTO?

CONTEXTS AND CATALYSTS FOR INQUIRY

Inquiry learning is all about giving students the skills, the dispositions *and* the opportunities to investigate – to find out information, make meaning and take action based on what is discovered. It follows, then, that just about anything can, in theory, be 'inquired into'. As already discussed in chapter 1, criticisms of inquiry are often leveled at those who suggest that content is irrelevant and that it is all about process. To some extent the idea that inquiry is 'content free', as is sometimes suggested, is a nonsense. Students have to be inquiring into *something* – there is always content. When I think of the term 'content' I think of it quite simply: content is what the students are *learning about* and *learning to do* as they inquire. It is the *worth* of that content and the ways in which teachers conceptualize and scaffold learning about the content that makes the difference. Quality inquiry teaching is all about helping move students to deeper understanding and a stronger grasp of targeted skills. To do this well, teachers need to select and design contexts that lend themselves best to inquiry *and* they need to be clear about what they hope students will learn.

The term 'context' is preferable to 'topic' or 'unit'. A context suggests a situation, be it a problem, project, event or place in which the learning can take place. There is no doubt that some contexts lend themselves much better to inquiry than others. Skilled teachers can quickly spot an opportunity for quality inquiry and also know how to design one. They recognize that inquiry journeys are triggered in different ways and from different starting points.

Much has been written about the characteristics of contexts that lend themselves well to inquiry. I would agree students inquire more readily and powerfully when:

- students can see the **relevance** of the inquiry in some way (to their lives/the community around them/their interests)
- the context lends itself to the use of **primary sources** of information as well as secondary ones
- the inquiry would be regarded as one of **worth** to people beyond the classroom
- it is easy to **make connections** between this and other investigations or other learning
- students bring some **prior knowledge** or experience to the question. They may have already done some thinking about this in their lives, and therefore they have some connection with this. The inquiry builds on what has gone before
- there are **multiple perspectives** on, and ways of thinking about, this problem or project
- the context lends itself well to the **curriculum** (state-/school-based)
- the context lends itself to building understanding of **concepts** as well as skills and dispositions.

BALANCE AND VARIETY

Over the course of a year, a healthy classroom engages learners in a wide variety of inquiries. A journey of inquiry may occur within the time frame of a single lesson or a year-long project. Some inquiries will involve the whole class in a highly structured, guided, shared process while others will be more individualized and independent. Some inquiries arrive unexpectedly while others are more planned events. As the examples below illustrate, inquiries come in all shapes and sizes. Whether spontaneous or carefully planned, whether shared or more individual, whether driven by action or philosophical pondering, there are some basic features that characterize most – if not all – journeys of inquiry:

- They are generally driven by **questions** – both teacher and student generated.
- They require active **research**/investigation/experimentation by the student.
- They most often seek to connect learning with students' **real-life experiences**.
- They are as much about **process** as they are about content – and content is **conceptual**.
- Students experience **connected learning episodes** – one task is clearly linked to the next rather than being simply an 'activity'.
- The learning is **responsively** planned (rather than fully mapped ahead in detail).
- Aspects of the learning tasks/assessments are **co-constructed** with students.
- The planning is **emergent** – the detail of the process unfolds rather than being pre-determined.

TYPES OF INQUIRY
PROJECT-ORIENTED INQUIRY

Typically, a project-oriented inquiry is **driven by some kind of task/action/product** that is worked toward over several weeks. The inquiry process is essentially that which helps learners find out more about what they need to do and know about in order to **achieve this practical goal**.

Project-based inquiries really start with the end in mind – the action is a given. In these inquiries, students know what it is they will do with the knowledge they have gained. Many of us engage in this kind of inquiry in our day-to-day life, which makes these contexts very authentic. There is a strong sense of purpose driving the investigation and the final project is often practical and tangible. Through the duration of the project, essential skills and broader understandings can still be gained. Even a small project like creating a school worm-farm can lead to bigger understandings about sustainability.

Many school activities lend themselves beautifully to project-based inquiries. Special events, camps, performances, exhibitions, gardens – all these things can be the 'action' that occurs through an inquiry process. Knowing what the inquiry sets out to achieve can be a powerful motivator for learning. Students have a goal and a real purpose for their learning. Here, we are not waiting to decide what action to take – the action *is* the inquiry. What is most important about this kind of project-based inquiry is that teachers are careful to identify the understandings, skills and dispositions that lie within it. The project itself is the context for *learning*. While the task of designing, creating and managing an effective worm-farm is wonderfully motivating for students, it is the teacher's role to help students demonstrate what they have learned about, for example, the role of decomposers in an ecosystem, the reason why waste needs to be managed and the life cycle of living things (depending on the learning goals established from the outset). Teachers are also responsible for considering the skills that need to be made explicit in this context. For example, students may be learning how to better manage themselves in a team, how to evaluate something they have designed, how to set up a system for monitoring progress or how to use language to persuade others.

Some examples of project-oriented inquiries:
- Students design and make a vegetable garden in the school grounds.
- Students design models to take to the school board – sharing their ideas for the new playground.
- Students take on the responsibility of designing, making and evaluating the props for a school production.
- Students work in teams to investigate, write, film, produce and edit their own short films for a class or school film festival.
- Students design a website to promote the school.
- Students create a classroom museum to show others about changes in the local area
- Students redesign the canteen menu

Sample questions to drive project-oriented inquiries:
- How can we attract more native **birds** and **animals** to our garden?
- What kind of **canteen menu** should we have at our school?
- How can we **communicate** our learning at school to others in the wider and global community?
- What do we need to do to make a successful **puppet theatre?**
- How can I create an **artwork** to promote wellbeing?
- How can we **redesign assemblies** to better involve the parent community?

- How can we plan a **successful camping trip**?
- How can we create an **enclosure** to keep our classroom pet healthy and happy?
- How can we **create and sell something** at a profit so we can contribute to our favorite charity?
- How can we redesign the **playground** for greater fitness and fun?
- How can we build an **energy efficient vehicle**?

PHILOSOPHICAL/ETHICAL INQUIRY

The 'philosophy for children' approach has had a huge impact on the broader field of inquiry learning – and indeed on the ways in which teachers can support and extend students' thinking through structured conversations. For the purposes of this chapter I am presenting the notion of a 'philosophical inquiry' in a less formalized way than may be found in the literature devoted to the method. Philosophical inquiry encourages students to explore questions that go to the heart of what it means to be human. This kind of inquiry can work within and beside other inquiries or simply be the focus of an inquiry in its own right. Characterized by an emphasis on dialogue, philosophical inquiry encourages students to explore their values and beliefs as well as exercising their creativity and metacognition.

Many questions lend themselves to philosophical inquiry. These questions typically have many answers, or perhaps may never really be answered at all:

- What makes me who I am?
- Does the past make us who we are?
- What is art?
- What is imagination?
- Do we need heroes?
- Is it ever OK to steal?
- What matters more – the fly or the elephant?
- How well do your family know you?
- Who knows you best?
- Can we be happy and sad at the same time?
- Is dreaming thinking?
- How do we know what is real?
- How do we know if something is true?
- What is a miracle? Do miracles happen?
- Is it better to give or receive?
- What's worth saving?

ISSUES/PROBLEM-ORIENTED INQUIRY

In issues-based inquiries, the emphasis is on the location and exploration of a problem in order to, hopefully, reach some kind of recommendation for actions and solutions. Unlike project-based inquiries, problem-based inquiries do not have a specific end in mind; rather, they seek to come to some kind of solution or action through the investigation of the issue or problem. The action presents itself as a result of the investigation. Problems for inquiry can be large or small. They may have global or local significance. They offer a powerful and authentic purpose for investigation as, by their nature, the inquiry is happening because of a need to sort something out or alleviate a situation. Many issues that offer loads of potential for inquiry are right under our noses!

Environmental, social and health-related issues are all part and parcel of being in a community, and inviting students to participate in the process of exploring these issues through the inquiry process is a highly authentic and personal context for learning. Problems that lend themselves to student inquiries may be on a global or local scale. Local problems mean more potential for direct experience and active learning, but technologies now allow us to become much more involved in addressing problems and issues in other places and in collaboration with communities around the world. Some teachers use a problem or issue in their own environment (e.g. caring for the local waterway) and set up a partner class elsewhere that is doing the same thing in their local environment. Sharing experiences and ideas in this way is a highly motivating form of collaborative inquiry.

Some examples of issues-/problem-oriented inquiry:
- How can we make our school a safer place?
- How can we reduce our energy use in the school?
- What can we do about the school's waste?
- How can we attract more native birds to our yard?
- Can we help clean up the local waterway?
- Can we re-design our classroom space so it is better for learning?
- What can be done about traffic at pick-up time?
- How can we deal with bullying in our school?
- What kind of canteen should we have? What food should be sold?
- What can we do to support refugees and homeless or disadvantaged people in our country?
- How can we make a difference to children in developing countries?
- What can we do about our endangered animals?
- How can we help our local community meet the needs of young people?

EVERYDAY PROBLEMS AS A CONTEXT FOR INQUIRY

Problems arise as a natural part of being in a community and these can be, in themselves, a powerful context for inquiry. When we ask students to consider how they might solve a problem, the process of inquiry finds a very natural home. Some examples of problems that can be 'inquired into' include:

- **Managing time**: what can we do about the fact we are late getting to specialist classes or we never seem to be ready to start after the bell goes?
- **Managing resources**: what can we do about the fact that the bag area is always messy and there is constant 'nagging' to keep it tidy? How can we find a solution?
- **Managing behavior**: what can we do about the fact that we still have people talking over others when we are in discussion, despite our agreement?

To inquire into these issues often means having students take on the role of data gatherers ('What is happening?') followed by trialing and testing suggested interventions and working out ways to monitor progress.

PLAY AS A CONTEXT FOR INQUIRY

Generally associated with – but by no means exclusive to – the early years, some powerful inquiries can emerge in the context of open exploration of materials and ideas. Skilled teachers know about the power of play to stimulate curiosity and wonderment and to lead to short or long-term investigations. Essentially, inquiry that emerges from play is often less predictable than other forms. The teacher must be on the look out for moments where a child wonders, questions, puzzles, notices or seeks more information. At times, the inquiry that emerges is completely 'organic' – it happens as naturally as walking and the child leads the way. At other times, the child may show some signs of interest into which the teacher adds a provocation. A provocation may be in the form of a question, a challenge, materials or a comment that stimulates further wondering. Play-based inquiries arise out of tinkering, experimenting, talking and interacting with natural and human-made objects. Essentially, it becomes an inquiry when questions are asked or problems are posed and when there is some form of investigation that then happens in response.

Examples of inquiry that arise from play are numerous. Within a play context, problems, projects and even philosophical questions arise that can be investigated. Skilled teachers become adept at setting up the physical environment within and outside the classroom to stimulate questions and investigations. Natural objects are often a great way to get this kind of learning going. For example, a teacher sets up some

- A wide variety of seeds can be classified, used to create patterns and eventually planted. Avoid directed activities like making seed pictures – keep this open-ended.
- Freezing objects in ice and timing how long it takes the ice to melt can be the basis for students to predict and to draw the change in shape over time.
- Water with a variety of objects can be used to test out floating and sinking theories.
- Water with a variety of substances to mix with it – some soluble, some not – can encourage children to naturally predict, test and describe. Include various sized containers, eye droppers, spoons, funnels and tea strainers.
- Paint charts and sample colour cards can be used to stimulate inquiry into colour in natural and other objects.
- Collections of different rocks, pebbles, shells, feathers and other natural materials can be sorted, classified, examined, drawn and wondered about.
- An overhead projector on a table can be used with various objects to project shadows.
- X-rays and other medical paraphernalia can be used to stimulate inquiry.

(see chapter 7 for more information on play-based inquiry)

CONTEXTS FOR INQUIRY WITHIN THE DISCIPLINES

There remains some confusion between the concept of an 'integrated curriculum' and that of 'inquiry'. While an integrated curriculum is more about the organization of learning experiences to ensure valid connections between disciplines, inquiry is an approach to teaching and learning itself. Although the terms 'integration' and 'inquiry' mean quite different things, inquiry, at its best, does foster deeply integrative thinking. This kind of thinking can transcend the sometimes-unhelpful subject compartmentalization that remains in many schools. Inquiry is a process that can find a home within a specific discipline but can also help students think across disciplines. While each discipline has a particular approach to inquiry within it (e.g. historical inquirers use particular approaches and tools that are distinct from, say, scientific inquirers) there are also some generic ways of inquiring that are shared across disciplines. The table on the following page identifies inquiry questions that work within disciplines. They are by no means mutually exclusive – in fact many of these questions can be developed as highly interdisciplinary investigations. I have written extensively elsewhere about the dangers of forced or inauthentic integration (Murdoch and Hornsby, 1997), but when the integration of these areas is authentic and deep, powerful learning takes place.

beautiful big shells on a table and maybe a sand tray and some water too. The children naturally hold the shells to their ears, prompting questions and theories about the sound they make. The inquiry begins from there.

Teachers who design play-based experiences for their students become attuned to the kinds of provocations that best stimulate investigation. Following are some examples of such provocations:

- Cooking opportunities and equipment gives many possibilities for inquiry through both role play and actual cooking experiences.
- Glass marbles of various sizes and colours are presented near a light box and various ramps and tunnels. The physics-based questions arising out of these materials stimulate wonderful questions and explorations about light, colour and shape.
- A deftly placed baby bath, dolls, towels, soap, etc. will often lead to a conversation about the best way to bath a baby.

INQUIRY WITHIN DISCIPLINES

HUMANITIES	SCIENCES	HEALTH & WELLBEING
• How and why do people seek homes in new places?	• What makes things move?	• How can I care for my body?
• What is work and why do people do it?	• What makes the earth work and how can we care for it?	• What makes my body work?
• How does popular culture change over time?	• What lies beneath us and why does it matter?	• What makes a good friend?
• Where is the past in the present?	• Where is the science in cooking?	• Why do humans play games and what makes a great game?
• Poverty: whose responsibility?	• What makes a great construction?	• How do humans change over time?
• How does where we live affect how we live?	• What's it made of and why?	• What makes us happy?
• What makes a great leader?	• How do we know it is true?	• What does it mean to be fit?
• Who has power?	• What's out there and how do we know?	• How safe are we?
• Does the past make us who we are?	• How do living things change as they grow?	• How safe is our school/community?
• Can we belong to more than one culture?	• How do living things survive in changing environments?	• How can we make a difference to the lives of others?
• What makes a good home?	• How does climate affect ecosystems?	• What is a healthy/unhealthy relationship?
• How can we improve our school/community?	• How does science influence sport?	• What makes a good pet and why do people have them?
• Are we the same as other people, or different? In what ways?	• How could we design the most efficient bicycle?	• Why do people eat what they eat?
• How and why do people explore?	• How do humans and animals relate?	• How do our choices affect our health?
• What makes a great community?	• How do animals communicate?	• Is practice enough for success?
• Why do people belong to groups?	• How have different inventions changed the world?	• What does being successful mean?
• Why is history worth knowing?	• How does electricity work and how does it impact on our lives?	• What makes a great team?
• What legacy will we leave behind?	• How and why does organic matter decompose?	• How do our body systems work to keep us alive?
• Whose history is it?	• How do scientists think and work?	• Why do we believe that?
• How do we know if we weren't there?	• How does the land change?	• Can one person make a difference?
• What makes this place unique?	• Where does it come from and where does it go?	• What do people believe and why?
• How and why do we move from place to place?	• How are living things connected?	• How are religions the same and different?
• How do places change over time?	• What natural cycles and systems help keep our planet working?	• Can conflict be good for relationships?
• What can a map tell us?	• What is matter and how does it behave?	• How am I connected to my past?
• How do we govern ourselves?	• How do our senses help us find out about the world?	• What's my story?
• Do we need rules?	• What happens when we mix things?	• How can goal setting improve my health?
• What stands the test of time?	• How do living things protect themselves?	• How and where can I sek help?
• How and why do we remember/commemorate events of the past?	• How are the earth, sun and moon connected?	• How can my talents contribute to the community?
• How can I have my say?	• How are landforms shaped?	• How can I keep others and myself safe?
• Who should rule and why?	• What is a fair test?	• How do people face challenges in their lives?
• Why do we have money?	• What is energy – where does it come from and how is it used?	• How do peoples' lifestyles affect their health?
• What does it really cost?	• What is the reason for the seasons?	
• Does technology change our lives for the better?	• What makes sound?	
• What happens when cultures collide?	• What makes light?	
• Who was here first? How do we know?		
• What makes a fair trade?		
• Were they the 'good' old days?		
• What makes the news and why?		

INQUIRY WITHIN DISCIPLINES (CONT'D)

ARTS	MATHEMATICS	LANGUAGES
• How do people express their identity?	• How do we measure time?	• How do people tell their stories?
• Can art persuade?	• What is long?	• What makes a great poem, song, story
• Do we need art?	• What makes a pattern?	or film?
• Why and how do people make music?	• What math do we need to build a cubby	• How do we get our message across?
• Can art build bridges?	house, gymnasium, or racing track?	• What do authors do and what choices do
• What makes music?	• How can we measure…?	authors make?
• Can art change our beliefs?	• What are the shapes in our environment	• How has communication changed over
• What can dance teach us about	and are shapes important?	time?
culture?	• Can numbers lie?	• Is Shakespeare relevant?
• What choices do painters, sculptors	• What do graphs tell us?	• How are symbols used to communicate
and composers make?	• How can we measure change?	meaning?
• What makes good design?	• Why do we need mathematical	• Why read fiction?
• What does a designer need to think	operations?	• Where do words come from?
about?	• What's the value in numbers?	• How do words make us feel?
• How and why do we design?	• How do we make a reasonable	• How can words paint a picture?
• Does art have power?	estimation?	• How can we use non-fiction to be better
• Can art divide?	• How does data influence others?	researchers?
• Is there bad art?	• What is 'equal'?	• How can we create a great non-fiction
• How does art change over time?	• What are some different ways to count?	text?
• What inspires us?	• Why do we need fractions?	• Can fiction be true?
• What is the role of the arts in this	• How are the four operations connected?	• What can fairytales, legends, myths and
community?	• What strategies help us solve problems?	fables teach us?
• What does it mean to be an artist?	• How can we change the shape of	• What makes a great speech?
• Where is the science in art?	a shape?	• How can props enhance communication?
• How are feelings and art connected?	• What's the world's most useful shape?	• How has social media changed the way
• How does music heal?	• How do we know where we are?	we communicate?
• How is art valued?	• How can we find patterns?	• How can the media influence our
• How can art teach us about others?	• How can we tell what time it is?	thinking and decision making?
• What influences an artwork?	• When should we multiply, add, subtract	• How do advertisements persuade us?
• Do artists have a responsibility to their	or divide?	• How is French like/not like English?
audience?	• Where is the math in our school	• How can we have a successful
• How do we make/use art in our	grounds?	restaurant experience in Japan?
everyday lives?	• What, why and how do we buy?	• How can we have a successful public
• How can we combine artforms?	• Where is the math in our music?	transport experience in Italy?
• Where is art in nature?	• How can you describe a million?	• How might we get to know others in
		Indonesia?
		• How could we tell people in China about
		our home country/family/school?
		• What gives words power?

CONTEXTS AS CASE STUDIES – WINDOWS ONTO A BIGGER CONCEPTUAL PICTURE

While inquiry journeys will lead to important learning in themselves, I always like to think each one as a case study – a part of a whole or an example of something that exists in a much broader context elsewhere.

I recently worked with a group of 6–7 year olds who had become fascinated by bees. Triggered by a dramatic incident where a bee was spotted in the classroom, many of the children had theories and plenty of wonderings. The teacher quickly sensed an opportunity for quality inquiry. She gathered the children's questions together and the class worked to organize the questions around their main interests. Some of the questions were quite specific and closed ('What kind of bees do we have in Australia?'), while others were more complex ('How do bees make honey?) Once the questions had been established, the teacher asked the students to draw, write and talk about what they thought they already understood about bees and what they might do to find out more.

The students looked at websites, watched clips and browsed simple non-fiction texts and posters. They returned to their questions and considered which ones they could now answer and which ones remained uncertain. They also added new questions – they had become interested in people who kept bees.

Later that week, the children Skyped a bee keeper in the local area who showed them how he housed and cared for the bees and how he collected honey. The children remained intensely interested in this investigation. They learned a lot, and by the end of the inquiry, they were well able to provide informed responses to their own questions. They also appeared to have a new respect for a creature they once feared, as they had found out more about its vulnerability in our rapidly changing environment.

A study of bees was a great context for inquiry for these children, but the important thing was not so much what they had learned about bees but the *concepts*, *skills* and *dispositions* this investigation helped to develop. It could have been an inquiry into spiders, into seahorses or whales. The case study was simply a vehicle for developing the concepts of interdependence, lifecycles, roles and community.

The best contexts for inquiry lend themselves to learning that goes beyond the content of the inquiry itself. Great contexts for inquiry have some 'conceptual congruence' and give students insights into big ideas that they will, ideally, visit time and time again across their schooling.

In his book 'Future Wise', David Perkins (2014: 52) suggests four characteristics of big understandings that can drive worthwhile learning:

- **Insight:** the understanding helps to reveal how our physical, social, artistic or other worlds work.
- **Action:** the understanding leads us to taking action, personally, professionally or in other ways.
- **Ethics**: the understanding sets us up to a more caring or humane mindset.
- **Opportunity:** the understanding is likely to come up in various contexts and circumstances

A skilled inquiry teacher helps students make connections. Even when an inquiry is very specific, the teacher considers how this vehicle could be used to contribute to an enduring bigger-picture understanding. Inquiring into the way bees adopt particular roles within a colony can help young students understand more about the need for defined roles in other communities and about the concepts of 'roles' and 'community' themselves. *When teachers help students see the connections between the specific understandings they are gaining and similar ideas in* other *contexts, deeper learning occurs.*

HOW DO WE JUDGE THE CONCEPTUAL 'WORTH' OF AN INQUIRY CONTEXT?

A good context for deeper inquiry entices the learner *beyond* the facts and towards concepts. If we simply say, for example, that we are 'learning about bees' then the inquiry is simply that – finding out interesting facts about bees. These facts will, for the most part, be forgotten soon after the inquiry is over. As soon as we ask a question like 'Why are bees so important?', then we have to make meaning of those facts – we have to think more broadly and deeply.

If an inquiry is anchored in a specific discipline, it is important to identify the concepts that are central to that discipline. When an inquiry easily connects with a few key concepts, we can help lift students' thinking beyond the facts they find in order to explore and develop bigger ideas that stand the test of time.

The following table identifies some key concepts within broad discipline fields. Some appear in more than one field and several are very transferable. Some are macro concepts stretching across all disciplines. These really big ideas include change, diversity, interdependence, systems, patterns and cycles. Macro concepts can be a useful way to connect several disciplines in a highly integrated inquiry.

When selecting or considering a context for inquiry, ask yourself; 'Does this investigation help students learn more about key concepts? Can we use it to work towards an enduring understanding?

KEY CONCEPTS WITHIN DISCIPLINES

HUMANITIES

- change over time
- interdependence
- power
- community
- diversity
- culture
- equity
- leadership
- rights and responsibilities
- peace and conflict
- identity
- supply and demand
- resources
- location
- democracy
- collaboration
- economy
- colonization
- work
- diversity
- freedom
- oppression
- migration
- citizenship
- consumption
- ritual
- celebration
- continuity
- tradition
- justice
- revolution

SCIENCES

- systems
- change
- life and living
- variables
- cycles
- energy
- diversity
- habitat
- structure and function
- matter
- survival
- force
- design
- technology
- adaptation
- natural/manufactured
- ethics
- sustainability
- diversity
- organism
- evidence
- design
- variable
- measurement
- properties
- interdependence
- causation

HEALTH & WELLBEING

- growth
- change
- relationships
- choice
- responsibility
- resilience
- conflict
- identity
- wellbeing
- nutrition
- fitness
- emotion
- influence
- fairness
- morals
- values
- beliefs
- achievement
- lifestyle
- trends
- safety
- spirituality
- leisure
- balance

ARTS

- symmetry
- form
- imagination
- structure
- creativity
- abstraction
- expression
- performance
- perspective
- process
- product
- balance
- line
- dynamics
- composition
- pattern
- audience
- movement
- design

MATHEMATICS

- addition
- change
- subtraction
- multiplication
- division
- value
- measurement
- equal
- whole
- fraction
- shape
- time
- unit
- pattern
- shape
- order
- value
- variation
- proof

LANGUAGES

- structure
- composition
- expression
- meaning
- perspective
- plot
- genre
- voice
- style
- origin
- form
- inference
- symbolism
- metaphor
- schema
- audience
- authorship
- imagery
- patterns

NAMING CONTEXTS AS QUESTIONS

Big questions are a powerful way to frame an inquiry journey This will be explored in more depth in chapter 4, but the sample inquiry questions shared in this chapter offer a multitude of potential contexts for investigation. When one moves a unit of study from a topic to a question, there is an immediate and significant difference in how that topic is being positioned. For example, a study of 'materials' can be a good context for scientific inquiry, but when we frame this study as a question – 'What's it made of and why?' – the emphasis is immediately on inquiry. The deliberately ambiguous use of the word 'it' opens up huge possibilities. Students are not passively 'doing' a study of materials, they are actively investigating the relationship between the properties of a material and its use. Similarly, we can have our kids study safety, but if they *inquire* into the question 'How can we make our school a safer place?', we move the context from a passive to an active and authentic one.

FROM THE PLANNED TO THE SPONTANEOUS

Some of the most successful inquiry journeys I have witnessed – and those that students often evaluate the most favorably – have been those that emerged unexpectedly. These precious moments are seized upon by savvy teachers who learn to recognize a context for inquiry worth exploring even though they had not planned to do it. So many opportunities for spontaneous inquiry arrive on our doorstep each week. For example the curious object a child brings in for 'news' time, the unexpected thunder storm, the fascinating photo on the front of the newspaper, the natural disaster on the other side of the world, the equipment that broke down unexpectedly, the death of the beloved classroom goldfish, a moment in a picture book that leaves us spellbound, the construction work that has just started in the street, the leaves falling from the trees in the yard or the spider appearing on the classroom wall. There is much that we can bring to the classroom in the form of questions and provocations we create to trigger inquiry and open up the world to our kids. Similarly, there is much that the world brings to us that, though unexpected, is just as valid. Staying awake to the possibilities of a spontaneous inquiry can be exhilarating for teachers and students alike, but students will benefit most when the teacher sees the conceptual worth of the moment. We ask, 'What might this engaging moment help my students understand more deeply about the way the world works?'

CLARIFYING INTENTIONS

Regardless of the context or starting point for an inquiry, clarity of intention is vital. Over the many years in which I have worked with teachers on designing quality learning experiences for students, the questions that remain critical around the planning table remain the same:

- *What is it we hope students will come to understand more deeply through this inquiry? (understanding goals)*
- *What knowledge might they need to help them to move towards this understanding?*
- *What is it we hope students will be able to do more competently? (skills)*
- *What learning dispositions will this inquiry help students practice and develop further?*

Of all these questions, the challenge to clarify *understanding* goals is often the one that is most difficult and the one on which we may need to spend the most time. Despite the fact that we know so much more about the power of being clear and intentional, we can still become easily seduced by the pull of 'activities' students might do rather than thinking about the learning we want to see.

SOME EXAMPLES OF UNDERSTANDING GOALS
FOR LOWER PRIMARY STUDENTS

- *The way things move depends on a variety of factors including their size and shape.*
  Concepts: cause and effect, movement

- *Stories can help us learn about our families, our culture and our past. There are many ways to share these stories.*
  Concepts: past and present, story, communication

- *Our lives are both the same as and different from the lives of our parents and grandparents when they were children.*
  Concepts: change over time, same and different

- *Materials have different properties that influence how they are used and what they are used for.*
  Concepts: materials, function, connection

- *There are strategies we can use to help ourselves manage conflict and get along productively with others.*
  Concepts: conflict, strategies

FOR MIDDLE–UPPER PRIMARY STUDENTS

- *Different art forms can be used individually and in combination to communicate ideas and feelings to others.*
  Concepts: art, communication

- *Our community has changed over time and continues to change. Certain events in our community's history have particular significance for people, for a range of reasons.*
  Concepts: significance, change, perspective

- *There are many ways in which individuals and groups can contribute to or bring about change in their communities. Participation can benefit both the community and the individual.*
  Concepts: participation, action, cause and effect

- *Products and systems are often designed or made for particular purposes or users. Designers take many factors into account when developing products and systems.*
  Concepts: design, evaluation

- *Living things (including humans) have features and characteristics that can help them adapt to changing environments.*
  Concepts: change, characteristics, adaptation

THE BIGGER PICTURE:
USING A WHOLE-SCHOOL FRAMEWORK TO ENSURE CONCEPTUALLY ROBUST CONTEXTS FOR INQUIRY

When I first started working in the field of inquiry-based learning, it was standard practice for schools to develop a 'scope and sequence' chart of topics that would be covered (albeit using some form of inquiry) over the seven years of a child's schooling. While the intention of such programming was sound (ensuring adherence to system-level curricula; avoiding repetition; allowing for streamlined resourcing; providing coherence and predictability), the 'topics' were not always thoughtfully selected – nor were they seen as pathways towards a bigger conceptual picture. In short, many scope and sequence documents were (and still are) all about the 'topics'.

When schools design or adopt more conceptually based frameworks, contexts for inquiry become more flexible, responsive, adaptable and spontaneous. With a conceptual map or framework, the big ideas are the main game while the inquiries that might sit under them are seen more as pathways rather than ends in themselves. This big picture also helps teachers clarify the understanding goals for their inquiries.

The PYP program (the Primary Years Program of the International Baccalaureate) is well known for its six organizing themes. These themes provide an important reference point for teachers as they plan units of inquiry. Each unit is seen as widening and deepening the students' grasp of that big theme, be it how we organize ourselves, how the world works or how we express ourselves. I was first introduced to this notion of a 'spiral curriculum' when studying the remarkable work of Jerome Bruner (1961), who suggested that children can gain an increasingly complex understanding of big ideas by revisiting them through a range of contexts over time.

Using big ideas to frame the selection and design of learning journeys for students does not in itself make them inquiry-based; however, when teachers and students learn to see their inquiry through a conceptual lens the learning is more powerful, generative and sustained. Organizers of this kind vary from school to school but common themes to which they refer include:

- sustainability
- health and wellbeing
- creative expression
- social organization
- scientific laws and principles
- design and technologies
- citizenship and social responsibility
- continuity and change
- place and space
- culture and identity.

Creating a conceptual framework to guide and support the life of inquiry in your school is no easy task and there are many different ways of doing this. I like to think of the framework as being a little like a map. The major destinations (throughlines, organizers or conceptual lenses) need to be articulated but the route required to get there is dependent on the needs of the traveler. For some schools, all that is needed are the destinations, while others choose to identify at least some planned contexts of inquiry for all students. Regardless of the approach taken, conceptual organizers help provide guidance and accountability.

Whether an inquiry emerges from play, an unexpected event, a system level curriculum imperative, a problem to be solved or a project to be completed, we should *always* be asking the question: 'How does this fit into the big picture?'

SAMPLE WHOLE-SCHOOL CONCEPTUAL LENSES FOR INQUIRY PLANNING

These four broad, conceptual lenses help provide a framework against which to review and plan for some student inquiry – particularly those inquiries that connect with the disciplines of science and technologies, humanities, health and personal development, and the arts. The descriptions under each are designed to help teachers think about the conceptual underpinnings that link with students' investigations. They help us think beyond lower-level facts and towards understandings.

SOCIAL RESPONSIBILITY

Students will investigate local and global communities and consider the challenges and opportunities associated with living in a diverse society. This lens is about social organization and the ways in which people are connected to and have responsibility for each other. Students will explore the concept of change, discovering ways in which the past has made us who we are and how and why society changes over time. Students' will develop citizenship by building skills for active involvement in their community.

KEY CONCEPTS: diversity, social systems, change, citizenship, relationships, culture, history, citizenship

ENVIRONMENTAL SUSTAINABILITY

Students will investigate our dependence on a healthy natural environment. Investigations focus on the diversity and richness of the natural environment and the ways in which humans use and interact with the environment. Importantly, this lens emphasizes the need to care for and live responsibly with the environment – at a local, national and global level.

KEY CONCEPTS: interdependence, place, responsibility, environment, conservation, cycles, location

IDENTITY, CREATIVITY, WELLBEING

Students will investigate their uniqueness, talents and passions, and inquire into how to best nurture themselves – physically, emotionally, mentally and spiritually. This lens focuses on how we can work towards our potential, develop resilience, build healthy relationships and make wise choices. It fosters self-expression, resilience and creativity and explores how we change and grow. This lens is also about expression through the arts and how this in turn helps us communicate with others.

KEY CONCEPTS: expression, wellbeing, change, identity, choices, personal responsibility

THE PHYSICAL WORLD

Students will investigate the systems that govern physical phenomena in both the natural and built environment. They will become more aware of how science can help us explain the way the world works and the impact of science and technology on our lives. As students work through scientific problem solving, experimenting and gathering data, they become aware of the powerful role that design, technology and scientific thinking have in the world. This lens also promotes the processes used to innovate, create, make and evaluate.

KEY CONCEPTS: systems, innovation, ethics, design, classification, cycles

SKILLS AND DISPOSITIONS AS CONTEXTS FOR INQUIRY

Inquiry processes are most commonly associated with investigating questions that help us understand more about the way the world works and exploring the kind of concepts already outlined in this chapter. But these questions do not provide the only effective context for inquiry. Some of the most intriguing inquiry work I have seen in recent years has involved students inquiring into skills and dispositions – how they can achieve or improve them, what they mean, how they can be used in various aspects of their lives and what helps and what hinders their development.

Opportunities to inquire into *how* we go about the process of learning present themselves every day. If it is our intention to help students become better thinkers, collaborators, self-managers, communicators and researchers, then these learning assets (explored in depth in chapter 6) provide a compelling context for inquiry in themselves.

Students can inquire into many questions about skills and processes; for example:

- What makes an effective survey?
- How can we record our observations accurately?
- What roles can help a team function smoothly?
- How can we show someone we are really listening?
- What strategies help us manage our time more effectively?

Opportunities for inquiry can be connected to the learning goals students develop for themselves; for example:

- What helps me stay more focused on a task?
- How can I edit my own writing more effectively?
- What might be the best way for me to create a web page?
- What happens if I reduce my screen time?

The dispositions that support inquiry are fascinating to inquire into in themselves. Questions like the below can work in conjunction with other inquiries or as short, stand-alone investigations.

- What does it mean to be creative?
- How can reflection help us set goals?
- When is it a good time to be a risk taker?
- Can we become more courageous?

Exploring questions about skills, dispositions and processes is perhaps the most significant inquiry work our students can do. Most often, these contexts or avenues of inquiry are located within the scope of a larger focus. They work best if they are relevant to what is needed or being worked on at the time. For example, a team of students inquiring into how to design and make an enclosure for chickens may find themselves needing

to think more carefully about the roles they are playing within a group. Students investigating ways to make the canteen more healthy may find they need to investigate ways to design better surveys in order to get the information they need.

In this way, the context for inquiry becomes a home to the development of skills AND concepts. The richer and more meaningful the focus of investigation, the more opportunities it presents for inquiring into the learning itself.

Once you carry an inquiry mindset into your teaching – opportunities for *authentic* inquiry are bountiful. Great inquiry teachers quickly recognize something as 'inquiry-worthy' and they know how to make the most of the generative potential these contexts can bring. The question must continue to be 'Is this something *worthy* of investigation for these students/this student at this time?'

KEY ELEMENTS OF A QUALITY INQUIRY CONTEXT

Does this inquiry…

- link with significant concepts?
- promote the development of learning assets and dispositions?
- connect with students' interests/lives/needs?
- have the scope to link to system-level standards/curricula?
- generate opportunities for cross-curricula connections?
- invite students to participate in designing their learning journey?
- easily involve the community/experts and allow participation beyond school?

REFERENCES AND FURTHER READING

- Bruner, J. (1961, 1977) *The Process of Education*, Harvard University Press, Cambridge, MA.
- Erickson, L. (2006) *Concept Based Curriculum and Instruction: Teaching Beyond the Facts*, Corwin Press, Thousand Oaks, CA.
- Mitra, S. (2013) 'We Need Schools not Factories', accessed at http://www.huffingtonpost.com/sugata-mitra/2013-ted-prize_b_2767598.html.
- Murdoch, K. and Hornsby, D. (1997) *Planning Curriculum Connections*, Eleanor Curtain Publishing, Melbourne.

I wonder...

I wonder what Jake's teacher's name is.	I wonder why we do Japanese. (serena)	I wonder where the big kids door is to go home. cocc-Joy a ccec-Joy
I want to know all the teachers' names (Dominic)	I wonder why there is bark at the playground Trayground cece (Dominic)	I wonder where Zac is. (Niklesh) I wonder what is Kiara's studio. (sienna)
I wonder why there is a sandpit out there. (serena)	I wonder why we do cooking (Kara)	I wonder when the footy ground will be finished. (Kara) (Rhys)

A story of learning...through multiple lenses.

How does it change?

Understandings

Everyday materials can be physically changed in a variety of ways.

People use science and scientific thinking in their everyday lives.

Objects are made of materials that have observable properties.

I discovered...

I discovered that the sprinklers were was watering the grass seeds so that they will grow (Dom Noah Rhys)	I discovered that they are making the footy field because there is not enough space on the grassed area - the balls sometimes go over the fence. (Kara)	I discovered that builders are going to pour concrete on the path on Monday at about 1.00 (Noah Alexandra
I discovered that the worms have holed places spaces. Why were they moved? Some of the scraps were making a mess on the ground. (Rhys) (dominic)	I discovered that the Stephanie Alexander kitchen garden eat with in the prayer space. (Dominic)	

I'm still wondering...

where the big kids Door is to go out to lunch and recess and go home (cee-Jay)	why we do the stephanie Alexander kitchen garden (Dominic)	why is bark un the adventure playgro (Alexander Dominic Noah)
why we do are japanese and cooking. (Dominic) (Kara, serena	Why is there bark under the adventure Playground Alexander (Dominic) and (Noah	When garden be finish (Kara)

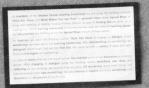

'If I had influence with the good fairy
who is supposed to preside over the
christening of all children, I would ask
that her gift to each child in the world
be a sense of wonder so indestructible
that it would last throughout life.'

(Rachel Carson, 1965)

~ CHAPTER ~

four

Inviting uncertainty:
HOW CAN WE GROW A CULTURE
OF QUESTIONING AND CURIOSITY?

INTRODUCTION

Questions are at the heart of inquiry. Questions give voice to our passions, our uncertainties and our curiosity. When we bravely release a question into the air, we are vulnerable, open and ready to learn. Where once, question asking was the teacher's territory, in an inquiry classroom, students' questions are as important as the teacher's.

Effective learners ask questions. They tend to be people who remain curious and who approach life with 'wonderment and awe' (Costa and Kallick, 2008). Questions help us discover and uncover new meaning. They are the bridge that takes us from the known to the new. One only has to spend time with very young children to know that, when they are left to explore the world, questions naturally arise out of life experience; indeed, some of the most profound questions we hear come from the mouths of babes. The research of Harvard University's Paul Harris (2012) shows the ways in which young children's questioning and subsequent interaction with adults helps them develop highly abstract concepts.

This same research also confirms that children's questions rapidly decrease as they enter and continue schooling. Susan Engel, an educational researcher who has specialized in investigating curiosity in children, agrees:

'Somehow the incessant curiosity that leads to so much knowledge in the first five years of life dwindles as children go to school.' (Engel, 2013:36)

In an inquiry classroom, curiosity is the grease that helps turn the wheel of learning. The inquiry teacher is passionate about not only sustaining the child's curious, questioning disposition but also strengthening it. This is not without its challenges. Indeed, the use of questions is one of the most commonly raised issues in my work with teachers: 'How do you get them to ask good questions?' 'My students don't want to ask anything!' 'My students don't know what a good question is!' 'I can't work with the questions my students ask!' 'How do I manage all those questions about so many different things?'

Inquiry teachers want their students to be questioners – to be curious, risk taking, wondering learners who are thirsty to find out, critique and explore the world. What can we do to encourage this? How do we keep curiosity and wonderment, and value and indeed build the students' ability to ask a range of questions to assist them to come to understand more about the world and themselves as learners? And how can we manage questions effectively when they are raised?

There are several strategies that help us make the most of the 'learning leverage' that questions potentially provide:

- provoking and modeling a curious disposition across the day
- valuing and working with children's questions and building their questioning skills and knowledge
- using sophisticated, thoughtful questioning/dialogue techniques in the classroom
- planning learning experiences around questions.

PROVOKING AND MODELING A CURIOUS DISPOSITION ACROSS THE DAY

Expecting children to ask good questions without being curious is like expecting a plant to grow without sunlight and water. We don't tend to ask questions about things that don't interest and intrigue us. We ask at a point of need or fascination. When we provoke, stimulate and sustain curiosity, students are more naturally inclined to wonder and articulate questions for further investigation.

In chapter 2, I identified some of the ways in which we can stimulate curiosity by attending to the physical and visual environment. There are several additional techniques that can be very effective in promoting wonder and stimulating questions.

SHARE A GLIMPSE OF WHAT'S TO COME
We are less curious about things we know *nothing* about. As soon as we know even a small bit of information about something or as soon as we have seen a part of something, we often become eager to find out more. Share with students some intriguing yet incomplete information. Show a small part of a picture and have the rest hidden. Cover a mystery object so that only the shape can be seen. Show the first 10 seconds of a film clip. Read the opening paragraph of a novel or the caption of an article.

When we 'tease' the brain like this, we are activating the mind's craving for connection. We want to make the part *whole* and we want to link this prior knowledge to new information.

USE POWERFUL PROVOCATIONS
For example, we can use stunning images, mysterious objects, an item of great beauty, a puzzle, an art work and found objects to provoke interest. Sometimes the best way to do this is to say very little and to simply place the provocation somewhere in the room and wait for students to notice and begin talking about it.

GETTING OUT THERE
Going beyond the classroom might be the very best technique for stimulating questions. Encourage your students to be explorers of the world and visit places connected to your

big question. Do this early in an inquiry in order to stimulate questions. Alternatively, take a walk for its own sake with the only instruction being 'What can you discover?' Issue your students with a 'wonder journal' at the beginning of the year and encourage them to record in it things that intrigue them, questions that come to mind, interesting photos, articles, a line from a book they are reading or a conversation they overheard. The prompts on page 71 can be used to stimulate documentation or you may leave the wonder journal more open-ended to use in any way that supports students' curiosity.

- **INVITE STUDENTS TO BRING AN INTRIGUING OBJECT, PROBLEM, IMAGE OR QUESTION.**
  Each student can be given a day when they are responsible for bringing in something that they believe might spark curiosity in others.

- **CREATE AN AREA OF THE ROOM DEVOTED TO WONDERINGS.**
  This could include wonder boxes, envelopes, wonder walls, or a 'cabinet of curiosities'.

- **POSE A 'QUESTION OF THE DAY'.**
  Gradually hand the responsibility of creating those questions to the students themselves (see the suggestions in chapter 2).

- **ALLOW STUDENTS TO SPEND TIME EXPLORING THEIR INTERESTS.**
  Paradoxically, something familiar and known can harness our curiosity as much as the novel or unexpected (see chapter 7).

- **ACTIVATE THE SENSES.**
  Our curiosity is not simply sparked by what we see and hear. The way things feel, smell and taste are powerful provocations. Multi-sensory experiences are an important element in an inquiry classroom.

- **DELIBERATELY CREATE TENSION AND 'DISEQUILIBRIUM'**
  Dewey (1991/1938) described the act of inquiry as a process that transforms an 'indeterminate' situation into one that is clearer and better understood. When a situation is indeterminate there is some conflict between current needs and realities. We might be puzzled, confused or uncomfortable – so we take action towards resolve. We are driven by a desire to move beyond that uncomfortable state.

One of the best ways to engage students and encourage them to want to explore further is to use a carefully constructed scenario that activates the emotions and creates an 'indeterminate' situation. Many teachers I work with choose to begin a journey of inquiry by involving students in a scenario that deliberately leaves them momentarily outraged or confused. Here are some examples:

- To activate an inquiry into **fairness**, teachers randomly gave some students more time, materials and attention in a lesson until the other students started pointing out how 'unfair' they were being.
- To activate an inquiry into making **healthy choices**, a teacher had a large Macdonalds' meal delivered to the classroom at snack time and began devouring it, to the children's horror!
- To activate an inquiry into **colonization**, a teacher organized for another class to come in and gradually take up residence in her classroom.
- To activate an inquiry into caring for the **environment**, a teacher tipped the contents of a rubbish bin all over the floor of the classroom before the students entered.

Capturing rather than deflecting resistance and tension can be a powerful way to begin a journey of inquiry. These provocations are often fun to plan but they also serve as powerful activators for inquiry. When our emotions are engaged, we are more likely to remember and involve ourselves in the learning. We want resolve and we seek to understand more. Of course, these provocations need to be de-briefed carefully but will often be the kind of events long-remembered by students.

TEACHER POWER

As discussed in the previous chapter, teacher behavior (our questioning, body language, tone of voice and feedback) has an enormous impact on the climate of the classroom. That climate will determine the degree to which students feel safe to ask questions. If we show students what being curious 'sounds like' by regularly and genuinely voicing our own wonderings, we also help teach the art of questioning in a more informal, natural way. The key to fostering an environment where students will feel safe to ask questions is to be comfortable with uncertainty ourselves. The founding principal of the Science Leadership Academy in the US, Chris Lehmann, describes inquiry as being prepared to 'live in the soup'. 'Inquiry means living in that uncomfortable space where we don't know the answer.' (Lehmann, 2013, quoted in Quillan, I. 2013: 1) Students need to see and hear us in that space, to see and hear our fascinations and uncertainties and finally, to see and hear our willingness to find out when we don't know**.**

MAKE IT WORTH WONDERING ABOUT

As discussed in chapter 3, meaningful contexts for inquiry need to be generated in order to engage students and to invite genuine questions. We ask about things we care about. Inquiries become meaningful when they: link to the immediate life of the student; connect to students' interests; target a specific project/action; explore an authentic issue; and provide ease of transference to other learning. Once students are invested in the inquiry and see it as purposeful, they have more reason to ask questions as a natural part of the process. For example, students engaged in the challenge of creating a school vegetable garden may need to ask many questions along the way: 'What grows best at this time of year?' 'How much will it cost to get the right materials?' 'Where will we make the garden?' 'Who will maintain it?' 'How will we protect it?'

Developing the capacity to ask questions remains a significant part of the inquiry teacher's role, but to make this work we need to attend to two things. Firstly (and somewhat ironically) we need to acknowledge that inquiry does *not always* begin with a question – questions can pop up along the way or even at the end of a process of investigation.

> 'The best way to find out things, if you come to think of it, is not to ask questions at all. If you fire off a question, it is like firing off a gun; bang it goes, and everything takes flight and runs for shelter. But if you sit quite still and pretend not to be looking, all the little facts will come and peck round your feet, situations will venture forth from thickets and intentions will creep out and sun themselves on a stone; and if you are very patient, you will see and understand a great deal more than a man with a gun.'
> (Elsbeth Huxley 1959: 272)

Curiosity and interest in something can take time to emerge. Some models of inquiry suggest teachers begin by asking students 'What would you like to find out about?' This strategy works beautifully some of the time. But, as the adage goes, we don't know what we don't know. A more natural approach to eliciting questions is to gather questions early in the process but assume there may be many students *not yet ready* to ask. *Invite* questions throughout the inquiry journey. Pause regularly to ask students 'What is this making you wonder?' 'Are there things you are interested in? Confused about?' As students gather new information and are exposed to new ideas and new perspectives, they are more likely to ask questions. Some of the best questions happen well down the inquiry pathway. Asking questions is not a 'stage' in a linear process.

VALUING & WORKING WITH CHILDREN'S QUESTIONS AND BUILDING THEIR QUESTIONING SKILLS AND KNOWLEDGE

The questions that arise as we inquire can, in themselves, be the subject of our inquiry. We need to help students to think more *about* the questions they ask by focusing on the many different kinds of questions that it is possible to pose. Commonly examined are 'open' and 'closed' questions, but there are many other ways of classifying questions. Once students have raised a range of questions, try exploring the following:

- *Which questions do you think will be the easiest for us to answer?*
- *Which questions are 'Google-able'? Which are not?*
- *Which seem to be the most commonly asked? Why?*
- *Which will be the hardest? Why?*
- *Which questions are you most/least excited about?*
- *Which ones are open/closed?*
- *Which do you think might be the most important?*
- *Shall we group them according to best ways to find out about them?*

Spending time exploring the nature and structure of the questions students have asked helps refine their ability to ask the right question for the right kind of investigation.

USING STRATEGIES AND ROUTINES TO GENERATE DIFFERENT KINDS OF QUESTIONS

At its most natural and organic, inquiry learning has students asking questions without too much prompting! However, while questioning *is* a natural part of inquiry, every researcher knows that careful thought needs to be given to the way we frame questions when particular avenues of investigation are being explored. The way in which a question is framed determines much about how we approach our 'finding out' and, therefore, the information we attend to.

Providing students with practice in various ways to develop and structure questions is an important role of the inquiry teacher. Grouping and classifying questions is certainly one very effective strategy but much can also be gained by giving students opportunities to generate questions within specific guidelines or scaffolds. Once you have exposed students to these structures, they act as something to 'lean on' when students might be struggling with articulating their wonderings or determining a path of investigation. The following strategies can be a useful way of generating and learning about questions.

THE FIVE WHYS

The 'five whys' entails asking a series of questions, each one beginning with a 'why' and linking to the previous answer.

- *Why should we wear a hat in summer?*
  (Because it shades our face.)

- *Why do we need to shade our face?*
  (To protect our skin.)

- *Why do we need to protect our skin?*
  (Because the sun can damage it.)

- *Why does it matter if our skin is damaged?*
  (Because this can lead to skin cancer.)

- *Why is skin cancer a problem?*
  (Because it can be life threatening.)

THE QUESTION MATRIX

Use the Question-Matrix to explore different question combinations (see page 67).

QUESTION THE ANSWER

Students are given the answer but must first come up with the question. **For example:**

- The answer is immigration – what is the question?
- The answer is justice – what is the question?
- The answer is contrast – what is the question?
- The answer is sunlight – what is the question?
- The answer is 32 – what is the question?

SPLURGE THEN REFINE

Give students a few minutes 'splurge' time to write down as many questions related to the inquiry focus as they can. It's 'no holds barred' time. Students just write without worrying about the quality. Once this is done, students get together to share and compare their brainstorms and to sift and sort. They might select the top 10 questions then prioritize them; sort them into open and closed; or group them into 'like' questions.

SEE, THINK, WONDER

This visible thinking routine (Ritchhart *et al*., 2011) is a simple yet effective method to help students generate questions. Beginning with a visual prompt (object, photo, painting, short video clip), children record what they *see*, what this makes them *think* about (or what they think is happening) and then what the prompt makes them *wonder*. The wonderings become questions for further exploration.

USING QUESTION STARTERS

Using question starters teaches children to ask questions in different ways. The Q matrix is a useful tool for this; or you can use an even more simple list of words or phrases that commonly begin questions:

- *Who*
- *What*
- *Why*
- *Where*
- *How*
- *When*
- *Did*
- *Could*
- *Might*
- *If*
- *Should*
- *Can*

QUESTION TOKENS

Give students a few tokens to 'spend' during a class discussion. Each token represents a question. When they ask a question, they spend a token. The aim is to spend all the tokens! This can be made more sophisticated by assigning the tokens to question types. For example, red tokens are closed questions and green tokens are open questions.

ASK THE PICTURE

Provide children with images in which people appear. Ask them to consider what questions they might ask one or more people in the image if they had the opportunity.

ASK THE AUTHOR

Provide students with a text and have them write questions directly to the author in the margin, as they read.

DE BONO'S SIX THINKING HATS

The well-known colored Thinking Hats of de Bono have been with us for many years. The framework, which acts like a kind of mental metaphor for the different ways we can think about a proposition, was developed to help people consider a problem or proposal from multiple standpoints. It is also a useful way to break down and streamline complex decision making. I have found the 'hats' to be a useful tool for helping students devise different kinds of questions to explore different elements of an issue or idea. See over the page for an example:

USING SIX THINKING HATS TO DESIGN QUESTIONS

WHITE HAT QUESTIONS	EXAMPLE
These questions should be about **facts** – they are likely to be closed questions and are designed to elicit information.	*What are the main causes of animal endangerment?*

YELLOW HAT QUESTIONS	EXAMPLE
These questions focus on the **positives** and **benefits** of a proposition/idea.	*How do zoos benefit animals?*

BLACK HAT QUESTIONS	EXAMPLE
These questions are designed to **critique** and **challenge** and elicit the possible problems within the idea/proposal.	*What's wrong with zoos?*

GREEN HAT QUESTIONS	EXAMPLE
These are questions to prompt **creative solutions** and **problem solving** or new ways of thinking about something.	*What might be some alternative ways humans could protect endangered animals?*

RED HAT QUESTIONS	EXAMPLE
These questions focus on **feelings** and are designed to elicit **emotional responses**.	*How do you feel about the potential extinction of some of our endangered species?*

BLUE HAT QUESTIONS	EXAMPLE
These questions focus on **thinking processes**.	• *Has your thinking on this issue changed over time? How and why?* • *What kind of thinking have you been doing?* • *What have you noticed about your thinking?* • *What is the most helpful hat for you to wear when thinking about this issue?*

USING SOPHISTICATED, THOUGHTFUL QUESTIONING/DIALOGUE TECHNIQUES IN THE CLASSROOM

Inquiry is a mindset. The inquiry learner brings a disposition of curiosity and intrigue to their learning. Inquiry teaches us how to look beyond the surface, how to maintain a sense of 'wonderment and awe', how to find important problems and address them and how to explore ideas from multiple perspectives. The questions teachers ask, and the manner in which they ask them, have an enormous impact on the quality of students' thinking. Our questions can promote or prohibit inquiry. Denis Palmer (1987) argues that focusing on quality questioning may result in one of the most important skills for 21st century learning: that of 'question finding'.

'Question finding is the ability to go to a poem, a painting, a piece of music or a document, a mathematical description, a science experiment – and locate a novel direction for investigation. The ability is difficult to teach directly, yet it may be one of the most important by-products of learning in an educational climate in which questions are varied, worth pursuit, authentic and humanely posed.' (Wolf, 1987: 7)

A great deal has been written about the art of teacher questioning. The following serves to summarise just some of the issues salient to inquiry learning in particular.

THE MINDFUL QUESTIONER – PAYING ATTENTION TO OUR QUESTIONS

Perhaps the most powerful thing we can do to is to be more *aware* of our questioning as we teach. By paying more attention to what we are saying, slowing ourselves down and pausing before and after questions, the quality and effectiveness of our questioning improves. Developing quality questioning techniques means considering not just the questions themselves but the ways in which we choose to ask questions – our questioning style and 'behaviour'. Discussions are an important part of the inquiry teacher's repertoire and can be a wonderful forum in which students clarify their thinking and benefit from hearing others' points of view. When we engage in quality conversations with students, we also get important windows into their thinking. Much of our formative assessment can take place in the context of conversations, providing we know what to ask and how to ask it.

COMMON QUESTIONING TRAPS

Questions designed to embarrass or humiliate the learner: asking a question to 'test' whether someone is listening is unnecessary and demeaning.

Questions that answer themselves: 'So, can you see the way adding these three numbers makes it easier to solve the problem?'

Over-use of closed questions or those with yes/no answers: 'So, who can tell me the name of this part of the world?'

Rhetorical questions: 'Are we ready to begin?'

Disjointed questions that fail to follow through a line of thought, and therefore keep the conversation at the shallow end.

Playing the 'guess what's in the teachers' head' game: asking a question and only expecting/accepting one answer.

Lack of 'wait time' before and after a question is asked.

Asking a limited range of questions that mainly focus on recall rather than deeper analysis and reflection.

Opting for whole-class discussions rather than the more effective small-group or one-to-one discussions where questioning can be more personalized.

Asking all the questions rather than encouraging students to question each other.

Poor listening to students' responses and not making eye contact with the student who is talking. Inauthentic listening.

Marginalizing students (often unconsciously) by directing questions only to students we suspect will know the answer.

Praising 'correct' responses in a way that decreases student risk taking or the sharing of alternative viewpoints.

Waiting until the end of an instructional period to ask questions rather than asking before and during.

Negative or judgmental feedback to what are deemed poor or incorrect responses rather than seeking more information or constructively challenging and probing to scaffold thinking.

THE TYRANNY OF RAISING HANDS

Having students raise their hands to speak is a widely used means of control when working with a large group. In some situations, this technique is useful: for example, a quick show of hands to find out who has brought back a form or who is going to the library. If, however, your intention is to help students participate actively in quality conversation, raising hands can be problematic. When students can only speak if their hand is raised:

- it's often the same students every time
- those who don't get 'chosen' switch off and stop listening
- the conversation is often stilted and superficial as those with hands up are selected in turn
- the teacher controls the conversation
- in an effort to be heard, students will fling their hands up before they have given adequate thought to the question
- students who take time to think are not chosen because their hand is not raised in time
- those with their hands up are often focused more on getting your attention than really listening to the other contributions.

WHAT ARE THE ALTERNATIVES?

It is very easy to have a manageable conversation, even with a large group, without needing to have students raise hands. Try the following techniques.

REHEARSAL TIME

Tell students you will be having a conversation with them but you will not be using the 'hands up' technique.

Instead you will:
- *Ask a question*
- *Give them time to think/talk to partners/jot down their ideas*
- *Invite a few students to share their thinking (it could be anyone – but all students have had time to think and prepare to share).*

Examples:
- **Turn to the person next to you** and ask them: 'What is your favorite picture story book and why?' Be ready to share your partner's thoughts with the rest of us.
- **No hands up please.** I will pick two people to share. What are two ways you already know that we can keep ourselves healthy? (The teacher waits 10 seconds and then asks two students.)
- **OK. Thumbs up if you agree** and thumbs down if

you disagree with this statement…and be prepared to defend your answer. 'Uniforms should be compulsory.'
- **Close your eyes everyone.** Think about some of the things that make a group work well, as we've been discussing. I am going to give you 5 seconds to think. Be ready to share your answers with your group.
- **Think to yourself and then I will ask you to share with a partner.** 'What are some of the differences between reptiles and mammals?'
- **Jot down some of your ideas** about how we could design a better book corner. When you are ready, bring your jotters to the floor and I will ask you to share your best idea with others.

CIRCLE FORMATION

Have students sit in a circle rather than a group all facing you. Introduce them to the idea that they will be having a non-hands-up conversation. The rule is that only one person speaks at a time and that they need to wait until there is a pause before they speak. In the early stages of this technique, you may use rules such as each child only having two speaking opportunities so the quieter students can participate.

TALK TOKENS

This technique works best with small groups but can be used with a whole class discussion. It also works best in a circle. Give students two 'talk tokens' and when they wish to say something, they 'spend' their token by placing it in a basket in the middle of the circle. They must try to use both tokens in the conversation, but once they have spent their tokens they can no longer contribute. This is a good strategy to raise awareness about how to share talk time in a conversation.

CONVERSATION PROTOCOLS

Eliminating hands up from a class discussion usually means that the students need to be more mindful of and responsible for the way they speak to each other. The conversation flows more naturally and deeply if they know how to build on what has been said, how to respectfully disagree, how to justify their opinion, etc. Learning how to hold a respectful and equitable conversation can be an inquiry in itself. Pose the question to students 'How can we help ourselves have an effective conversation when talking as a class?'

Support students by introducing them to some useful conversation connectors:

- *I agree with what…said about…and I want to add…*
- *I would like to ask…a question about…*
- *I have a different point of view about…*
- *The reason I think that is…*

- *Can I suggest another way of looking at that…?*
- *I disagree because…*
- *I can see your point of view but I am also thinking that…*
- *What you said about…made me wonder about…*
- *I want to add something to what…said about…*
- *Am I right in thinking that you are saying…?*
- *I am not sure I understand what you mean by…*
- *Could you explain that a little more?*
- *I am confused about…*
- *I would like to hear more from…about his/her ideas.*
- *[Students' name], do you have a point of view about this?*
- *Maybe we could agree to disagree about…*

CONFERRING – INQUIRING INTO STUDENTS' LEARNING

An effective way to modify our questioning behavior is to limit the amount of time we work with large groups. While the strategies listed above will certainly make those conversations more worthwhile, the larger the group, the harder it is to ensure participation by all. Setting up the classroom so that the dominant mode of dialogue is with small groups and individuals means we are more likely to connect with each student and to question them more thoughtfully. Scheduling regular 'conferring' time with groups and individuals is part of the routine for many inquiry teachers. 'Conferring' is the term commonly used to describe a deliberate conversation with students about their learning. It may be about a piece of writing they are working on, a text they are reading, a project they are investigating or an extended math problem they are working on. Conferring with students is more than the informal 'How are you going?' conversation we might have as we roam around the classroom. Good conferring is more deliberate and structured. It often relies on a routine set of questions and prompts to glean as much about the child's progress as possible. Conferring with students is formative assessment at its best. As we gain a sense of where the child is at, we can also provide on-the-spot, specific feedback and guidance about where to go next. Teachers who regularly confer with their students tend to have more personalized and differentiated programs and a deeper understanding of the needs of the students in their care.

USEFUL QUESTIONS FOR CONFERRING WITH STUDENTS

- *What would you like to share/show/tell?*
- *That's interesting – tell me more about that.*
- *That's interesting, keep going…*
- *How did you figure that out?*
- *What makes you say that?*
- *What went on in your head when I asked you that/when you did that/when you saw that?*
- *What can you tell me about this?*
- *What have you been trying to show/do/explain?*

- *How is what you're thinking connected to …'s thinking?*
- *Can you make a connection?*
- *I wonder if you can make a connection to something else you know?*
- *What puzzles you about this?*
- *Is there another way of thinking about this?*
- *What have you found most interesting? What has been the best thing about this for you?*
- *What did you notice about yourself when you said/did that?*
- *Could you share what you are thinking about this with the others?*
- *So what has helped you decide that? What evidence do you have for that idea?*
- *Which part is making sense?*
- *Which part is still confusing?*
- *What are you wondering?*
- *Which part of this do you think is the most important? Why?*
- *What are you planning to do next?*
- *What might you need to think about before you get started?*
- *Am I right in saying that you …?*
- *This is what I think you are saying … Is that right?*
- *Is there something else you would like to tell me about this?*
- *Is your thinking changing? How?*
- *How could you use this again?*
- *Where/when have you done this kind of thinking before?*
- *What do you need more help with?*
- *What might make this better?*
- *What are you most proud of?*
- *What would you like feedback on?*
- *What's the most important part of this?*

LISTENING TO WHAT IS SAID AND WHAT IS *NOT* SAID

When in conversation with students, the inquiry teacher is not only mindful of what students say but also mindful (and respectful) of the silences. We often mistake silence for confusion, disengagement or even resistance when it may well be indicative of reflection and deeper thinking. If students are not participating, we should (as appropriate) respectfully ask them why. When this is asked without judgment, the student may reveal learning we had not anticipated. For example: *'Jack, I notice you have not yet shared your thinking or taken part in the conversation. You may have good reasons for choosing to be silent right now but is there anything you would like to add?'* Students' silences can tell us as much as their words (Shultz,

2010). Paying attention to silence and avoiding quick judgments helps us become better inquirers into the needs and interests of our students.

ASKING BETTER QUESTIONS

Inquiry teachers know that the kind of questions they ask work in two ways. The question itself will prompt a certain kind of thinking and it will also model the art of questioning to the student. Inquiry teachers know how important it is for students to learn about different kinds of questions, so it is critical that we practice what we teach. The kind of questions we ask is determined by purpose. In an inquiry classroom, questions have a range of purposes, including:

- to engage students' interest/intrigue/curiosity
- to ascertain students' understanding of something (and, therefore, inform our teaching)
- to help students 'dig deeper' and take an idea further
- to help students critique and analyze something
- to promote divergent, creative thinking and to help students think beyond the obvious
- to help students make connections between ideas and establish patterns/relationships
- to scaffold students' planning or problem solving – to help them figure something out for themselves
- to promote reflection and encourage students to evaluate, self-assess and set goals
- to challenge or redirect thinking.

The research on quality questioning reveals a complex and often uncertain field. It is easy to assume that the best questions are open ended and at the 'higher' end of the cognitive spectrum, but simply asking higher-order questions does not guarantee higher-order thinking. Question-asking does not happen in a vacuum. The effectiveness of a question is linked to, among other things, student comfort levels and willingness to share their thinking, their facility with the language and their familiarity with the content. Lower-order questions may be needed to scaffold thinking to higher levels. Some closed questions may be needed to check facts before moving on to more complex generalisations. Most researchers agree that a combination of lower- and higher-order questions is superior to the exclusive use of one or the other.

There are a number of taxonomies and guides to teacher questioning that can help us take a more considered approach.

SOCRATIC QUESTIONING

Socrates was famous for his use of questions as an instructional tool, preferring to draw his pupils towards deeper thinking through questions rather than direct statements. Socratic questioning can be successfully taught to students as well as being used by teachers to encourage depth and breadth of thinking. The questions below encourage the student to inquire into their own thinking and to explore more deeply what, how and why they think. After a while, students can start using the Socratic questioning techniques when working with each other. Make an anchor chart with sample questions available for students to use when in discussion sessions.

Try using the following categories to strengthen your questioning and promote greater inquiry thinking.

'We so often mistake silence for confusion, disengagement or even resistance when it may well be indicative of reflection and deeper thinking.'

TO CLARIFY	• What do you mean by…? • Are you saying….? • Could you restate that in another way? • How does that connect with (the idea/concept/text being discussed)?
TO PROBE ASSUMPTIONS	• What makes you say that? • Where did you get that idea from? • Might there be another way of looking at that?
TO JUSTIFY AND SEEK EVIDENCE	• Can you give me an example of…? • How do you know that…? • How might someone argue against that? • How can you be sure? • Why is this so? • What is your evidence? • What would you need to change your thinking?
TO ELICIT OTHER PERSPECTIVES AND VIEWPOINTS	• Might there be another way of looking at this? • If you were…what do you think you would say? • How does this compare with …'s view? • Who would agree with you? Who would disagree? • Have you always thought this way?
TO EXPLORE/REVEAL IMPLICATIONS AND CONSEQUENCES	• So if that is true, what would it mean for…? • What might that lead to? • What if this is not the case?
TO THINK ABOUT THE QUESTION ITSELF	• Why do you think I asked that question? • Is there a better way of asking about this? • If we asked the question this way, how would our thinking change? • Was that a useful question?

SOLO TAXONOMY

The SOLO *(Structure of Observed Learning Outcomes)* taxonomy (Biggs, 1982) is a structured framework that helps students and teachers think more about the depth and sophistication of their learning. It is particularly useful in informing our assessment of and feedback to students. It is also useful as a guide to designing tasks and questions that increase the quality and quantity of thought. More discussion of the use of the SOLO taxonomy is in chapter 8.

An example of how the taxonomy might inform the kinds of questions we ask is as follows. SOLO is a hierarchical framework, presenting increasing levels of conceptual understanding as a student moves through a learning process. From a questioning point of view, this understanding can help us 'pitch' our question at the right level for where a student is at in their learning and it can also help us ask more challenging questions to help scaffold student progress to extended, abstract thought.

For example, within the context of inquiring into the important role of trees in the health of the atmosphere, we might ask the following questions:

- **Questions that may elicit a pre-structural response**: What do we call trees that lose their leaves? (The question may have little relevance to the role of trees in a healthy environment).
- **Questions that may elicit a uni-structural response**: What is respiration?
- **Questions that may elicit a multi-structural response**: What are some ways that trees can help give us cleaner air? How do trees work to keep the air clean?
- **Questions that may elicit an extended abstract response**: How do trees help keep the air clean and what other elements in the environment connect to this process?

PLANNING LEARNING EXPERIENCES AROUND COMPELLING QUESTIONS

'People are more likely to take a deep approach to their learning when they are trying to answer questions or solve problems that they have come to regard as important, intriguing or just beautiful. One of the great secrets to fostering deep learning is the ability to help students raise new kinds of questions that they will find fascinating'. (Bain, 2012:4)

It is increasingly common practice to drive a journey of inquiry through a 'big question' (see chapter 3 for examples). Variously described as an essential question, rich question, fertile question or compelling question, this helps to signal a

focus for learning and positions the experience as an inquiry-based one. Exploring the question 'What does it mean to make a wise choice?' feels quite different to announcing that we will be 'doing a unit on decision making'. I will use the term 'compelling question' here because it reminds us that the question we devise should, as much as possible, compel the learner to want to find out more. The question should ask something that is worth investigating.

Compelling questions can be devised by teachers or in conjunction with students. They may focus on skills or on 'content' but should allow for transferability. Compelling questions will often travel the arc of an inquiry and are returned to over and over again – each time with a deeper and more informed response. Numerous educators in this field have devised criteria for what makes a powerful inquiry question. Over the years, I have often found myself returning to the criteria outlined by Traver (1998):

- **open-ended** – yet focused enough to guide an inquiry
- **non-judgmental** – although answering them will require high-level cognitive work, including making judgments
- can be addressed in multiple ways from multiple **perspectives**
- have **emotive force** and **intellectual bite**
- are **succinct** – yet demand a lot.

I advocate sharing these questions with students from the outset of an inquiry. Display the question/s in a position that allows for easy reference. Have students record an initial response to them and then track the way that response changes over time.

Using a compelling question works well at lesson level as well as unit level. I like to use questions as the structure for learning intentions at the beginning of a lesson. It may be a question that we are working with over several weeks or it may be a question pertinent to that lesson. For example, you might say:

Over the last few weeks we have been investigating the question 'What makes a great story?' I want to share another story with you now. This is told without words. It relies on the illustrations to communicate. This book won the 'children's book of the year' prize two years ago. The judges said it was indeed a great story! So, as we share it, think about what might make this – in their opinion – 'a great story'. Another question we might ponder as we share this is, 'How do pictures help communicate feelings?' Take a moment to think about how you would answer that question now, and then we'll come back to it after I've shared the book and see if you have further thinking to add.

THE QUESTION MATRIX

Weiderhold's (1991) Question Matrix helps teachers and learners create and select a range of questions using different question starters and word combinations. Questions in the bottom right quadrant will often yield deeper thinking than those in the top left quadrant, which are more simple.

	EVENT	SITUATION	CHOICE	PERSON	REASON	MEANS
PRESENT	What is?	Where/when is?	Which is?	Who is?	Why is?	How is?
PAST	What did?	Where/when did ?	Which did ?	Who were?	Why did?	How did?
POSSIBILITY	What could?	Where/when could ?	Which can?	Who can?	Why can?	How can?
PROBABILITY	What would?	Where/when would?	Which would?	Who will/would?	Why would?	How would?
PREDICTION	What will?	Where will?	Which will?	Who will?	Why will?	How will?
IMAGINATION	What might?	Where/when might?	Which could?	Who might?	Why might?	How might?

LINKING QUESTIONS TO A 'CYCLE' OF INQUIRY

Teachers who draw on a broad cycle of inquiry to inform the design of learning experiences can enhance their practice by using questions that prompt the thinking and strategies common to each 'phase'. While not exclusive to a stage of the cycle, certain questions can help ensure that learning purposes are clear.

PHASE (NOT STRICTLY LINEAR) AND PURPOSES	KEY QUESTIONS
Framing the inquiry • establishing the context and a compelling question • making links with the system/school curriculum • identifying understanding goals • identifying key skills and dispositions • identifying possible indicators of understanding	What do these students want and need to learn and do? What do we want them to come to understand and be able to do? What are the students revealing to us in these initial conversations? What is important to learn about this? What are the big ideas? Why is this worth doing? *Is* this worth doing? How can we connect this with our students' lives? What do we know/think/believe about this?
Tuning in • gathering data about students' existing thinking, knowledge, feeling and understanding • helping students make connections with the key concept/s • providing purpose, the big picture and authenticity • motivating, exciting, engaging students	What are you wondering? When you see this (image/question/word/object), what does it make you think about? What does this remind you of in your own life? What connections can you make? I wonder what you are thinking about this? What do we already think/feel/know about this? What do we need to know or think more about? Why might this be worth learning about? Let's figure out what we already think about this. Let's see what we can work out first. What's interesting about this? What do we need to get better at doing as learners?
Finding out • gathering new information to address the compelling question • developing the research skills that are required • learning how to organize and manage the process of finding out • having some shared experiences that will allow us to talk and share our thinking with others • stimulating curiosity through new experiences and information • learning how to record information gathered in efficient ways	What would be the best way to find out more? Who could we ask? What could we do? What would be the best way to remember what we find out? What is this telling us? How is this connecting to what we already knew? How do we know whether this is reliable information? How can we check this? Where has this information come from? How is this making us feel? What skills will we need to use?

PHASE (NOT STRICTLY LINEAR) AND PURPOSES	KEY QUESTIONS
Sorting out • comprehending – making meaning of the information gathered • revealing new thinking and deeper understanding • answering questions • reviewing/revising early thinking – synthesizing • interpreting the information and communicating with others	How is our thinking changing? What patterns are you seeing? What does this mean? What questions does this make you want to ask? What are you noticing? What questions have we answered? Now what? What's the best way to explain this to others? What connections are we making? How is this making a difference to us? How are we using what we are learning?
Going further • opportunities for students to pursue questions and interests arising from the journey so far • learners to work more independently on their investigations	What are you most interested in finding out about now? How could you take this further? How might you go about this investigation? What new questions do you have? Is there something you think you could *do* with this information? How can you achieve that? What personal learning goals can you set during this task? What do you need? What do you need to do?
Reflecting and acting (activated throughout the cycle) • to help students apply their learning to other contexts – to put the learning to use • to enable the students to reflect on what and how they have learned and set goals for the future • to assess final understanding and growth in skills	So what? What can we say now that we couldn't say then? What do we think is the most important thing we have learned about/to do? What have we noticed about our thinking along the way? What is in our tool kit as a result of this investigation? What should we share with others? How? How has this changed us? Now what? What questions are we left with? What have we learned about ourselves? About learning?

REFERENCES AND FURTHER READING

• Bain, K. (2012) 'Deep Learning: Pursuing Questions That Are Important, Intriguing or Just Beautiful', Project Information Literacy, 'Smart Talks' no 13, October 2012 (www.projectinfolit.org).

• Biggs, J. and Collis, K. (1982) *Evaluating the Quality of Learning: The SOLO Taxonomy*, Academic Press, NY.

• Carson, R. (1965) *The Sense of Wonder*, Harper and Rowe, NY.

• Chouinard, M. (2007) 'Children's Questions: A Mechanism for Cognitive Development', *Monographs of the Society for Research in Child Development*, 27(1), vii-1x, pp. 1-126.

• Costa, A. and Kallick, B. (2008) *Learning and Leading with Habits of Mind: 16 Essential Characteristics for Success*, ASCD, Alexandria, VA.

• de Bono, E. (1985, 1999) *Six Thinking Hats: An Essential Approach to Business Management*, Little, Brown, NY.

• Dewey, J. (1938) *Experience and Education*, Kappa Delta Pi, NY.

• Engel, S. (2011) 'Children's Need to Know: Curiosity in Schools', *Harvard Education Review*, vol. 18 (4), winter, pp. 625-45.

• Engel, S. (2013) 'The Case for Curiosity', *Educational Leadership*, vol. 70 (5), February, pp. 36-40.

• Gallas, K. (1994) *Talking Their Way Into Science*, Teachers College Press, NY.

• Godinho, S. and Wilson, J. (2004) *How to Succeed with Questioning*, Education Services Australia.

• Harris, P. (2012) *Trusting What You're Told: How Children Learn From Others*. Bellknap Press, Cambridge, UK.

• Lehmann, C. (2013) in Quillen, I., 'Why Inquiry Learning Is Worth the Trouble', retrieved from http://blogs.kqed.org/mindshift/2013/01/what-does-it-take-to-fully-embrace-inquiry-learning/

• Ritchhart, R., Church. A. and Morrison, K. (2011) *Making Thinking Visible: How to Promote Engagement, Understanding, and Independence for All Learners*, Jossey Bass, San Francisco, CA.

• Shultz, K., 'After the Blackbird Whistles: Listening to Silence in Classrooms', *Teachers College Record*, available at http://www.tcrecord.org/library/abstract.asp?contentid=15795.

• Traver, R. (1998) 'What Is a Good Guiding Question?', *Educational Leadership*, vol. 55 (6) pp. 70-3.

• Wolf, D. P. (1987) 'The Art of Questioning', *Academic Connections*, winter, pp. 1-7.

THIS IS YOUR WONDER JOURNAL!

It will help you wonder while you wander! You can put something in it any time at home, at school or on holiday. You might take it with you in the car or on a long journey, or keep it in your pocket when you walk the dog. You might have to jot an idea down at the dinner table or even draw a picture from a dream you had overnight. Many things can live in this wonder journal and it will be fed by your curiosity, your imagination and your *awe*someness. Your wonder journal is a like a researcher's notebook. You can use it to build your own investigation.

You might include:

Questions – Big, small, funny, serious…any questions that come to mind that make you want to find out more.

Photos – Have you found something intriguing? Take a photo and paste it in here!

Pictures – Sometimes it's easier to draw our wonderings than it is to write them.

Words – Have you read something that puzzled you or a quote that inspired you? Pop it in here.

Observations – These can be the best seeds for inquiry.

WANDERING AND WONDERING...
SOME IDEAS TO GET YOUR WONDER JOURNAL OFF TO A GREAT START

TAKE A LOOK DOWN

Next time you are out walking, notice the ground beneath you. What's there? Can you find something beautiful? Something intriguing? Something unexpected?

CAPTURE SOME COLOURS

Colour is everywhere - in the natural *and* the built environment. Choose a colour - maybe your favorite one - and write down all the things you do with that colour. What do you notice?

SHAPE UP

Choose a shape. Now see if you can find lots of examples of that shape in the environment. It may be in the least expected places! Take some photos and sketch your findings.

HEART OF STONE

Once you start looking, it's amazing how many things you can find that are heart shaped. Leaves, stones, clouds...start a collection. Make an art work.

LISTEN UP

Take the five minute listening challenge. Find a place outdoors where you can sit, alone, for at least five minutes. Now listen very, very carefully. What do you hear? What's close by? What's far away? Make a list of the sounds. Are there any mysterious ones? Record them.

WALKING WONDERS

People are simply fascinating. Have you ever stopped to watch the different ways people walk? Find a place where you can observe this closely. What do you notice? Why *do* people move differently? What does it make you wonder?

LOOK AGAIN

There are many things we see every day, but never look at closely. For example, take some time to look really closely at some coins and notes. Use a magnifying glass if you can. What do you notice? What do you wonder? Do you have money from other countries? How does it compare? What other everyday objects could you examine more closely?

PET DETECTIVE

It's amazing what you notice when you take time to really observe your pet closely. What *do* they do all day? How are they like and unlike humans? What is their favorite place to be? How do you know? Do you think they have emotions? Do they think? How do they communicate? Record your findings in any way you like.

DIZZY HEIGHTS

What's the tallest tree in your neighborhood? The tallest house? The highest fence? What are the tallest buildings in your city? Country? The world? How tall are you? How much have you grown since you were a baby? How tall do you think you will be when you are an adult? Take some time to explore height.

LOOK UP

The sky is the most amazing place to study if only we take the time to look up. What do you see when you look up? What does it make you wonder? Go outside in the early morning, at dusk and at night. How does the sky change? How does the light change?

WHAT'S IT MADE OF?

Everything in the world is made up of matter. What kind of matter are the things around you made of? Can you find examples of solids, liquids and gases around you? Are there some things that seem in between?

SAME, SAME BUT DIFFERENT

Make a collection of examples of the same thing - e.g. shells, feathers, rocks, keys, bottle tops, seeds, leaves or petals. Lay them out next to each other and notice how different each item is, even if they are all the same thing.

QUESTION PROMPTS

TO REMEMBER
- How many…?
- What is/was…?
- Can you name…?
- When did…?
- When was…?
- What happened after…?
- Who spoke to…?

TO PROMPT DEEPER THINKING
- How would you explain...?
- What do you think might happen next...?
- What was the main idea...?
- Can you clarify...?
- Can you show how...?
- What is a different way of saying…?
- What was this *not* about?
- What patterns are you noticing in…?
- Can you see a relationship between….and…?
- What's the difference between…and…?
- What new information did we get about….?
- How does this confirm what you already know about…?
- What is missing from…?
- What's wrong with…?
- What examples can you find to show…?
- What is the main message here?

TO PROMPT TRANSFER
- How could we use this again?
- What does this remind you of?
- Can you make a connection between…?
- If…had not happened, how might this have been different?
- Where is…?
- Can we use…?
- How does this connect to…?

TO PROMPT REFLECTION
- What's the most important thing about…?
- What makes you say that?
- How would you justify…?
- What would you have done differently?
- How do you know?
- How is your thinking changing? Why?
- What is your point of view?
- What might…think/feel/know about this?

TO PROMPT CREATIVITY
- What might you do with what you have learned about…?
- What new ideas can you contribute to…?
- What might happen if…?
- If…did not happen then how might…?
- What would you have done instead?
- What alternative strategy could you use?
- Is there a different way to do/think about/ say…?
- Can we see this from a different point of view?

LEARNING
TO ASK DIFFERENT KINDS OF
QUESTIONS

A question about
CHANGE

How and why has the game of football changed in the last 20 years?

A question about
HOW IT WORKS or
HOW SOMETHING HAPPENS

How do birds build their nests?
How does our voting system work?

A question about
HOW IT CAME TO BE

How did the pyramids get built?
How are guitars made?

A question about
WHY IT IS IMPORTANT

Why are polar bears important?
Why do we learn about fractions?

A question about
HOW TO DO SOMETHING

What do you have to do to make a kite?
How can you best throw a tennis ball?

A question about
WHAT PEOPLE THINK/OPINIONS

What is the best way to stay fit?
Have mobile phones made our lives easier?

A question about
WHAT IS NEEDED

What can we do to help people without a home?

A question about
IMPROVEMENTS

How could we help stop bullying in the playground?
How could we reduce traffic on our roads?
How could I change my sleeping habits?

A question about
CARING/LOOKING AFTER

How do you look after babies?
How do museums preserve memories?

A question about
FEELINGS

How do people feel about asylum seekers being detained for long periods?

A question about
POSSIBILITIES/PREDICTIONS

What if we had a rubbish-free lunch policy?
What would happen if we planted bird-attracting plants in the school grounds?

I am a scientist and I am investigating what happens to .... when I add ....

To carry out an investigation, I can only have one variable: 1 thing that will change or vary. For this investigation, the variable is ....

However, it is important to make the test fair. To make this test fair, I ....

....

My hypothesis, what I
think will happen, is
that ....
....

because ....

....

*'If the structure
does not permit dialogue
then the structure
must be changed'*

(Paulo Freire)

~ C H A P T E R ~

five

Finding our way:
WHAT ROLE CAN FRAMEWORKS AND MODELS PLAY IN SCAFFOLDING INQUIRY LEARNING?

It is essential that all
other conditions remain
the same because
otherwise, I wouldn't
if it was the ....
or something else that
making the difference

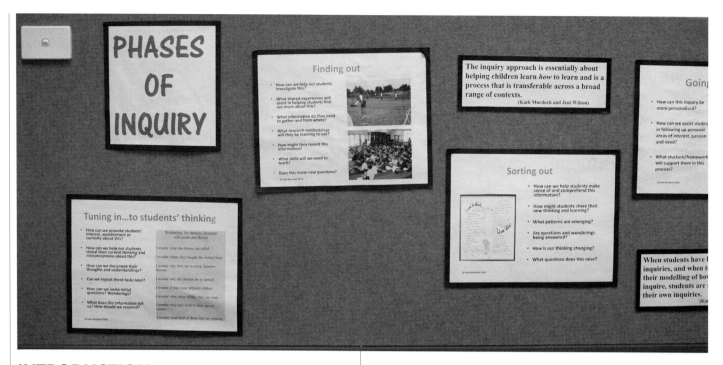

INTRODUCTION

Inquiry is about what learners *do*. It involves numerous connected skills, dispositions and processes. It is fluid, sometimes messy and complex. For this reason, it is challenging to represent as a written 2D model or framework. It is all too easy to reduce inquiry to a recipe comprising neat steps that are worked through in a linear fashion. This, in turn, belies the nuanced and organic nature of the process as it emerges between teachers and students. Without frameworks, however, it is similarly easy for an inquiry to become a kind of montage of activities that lack clear intent or thoughtful design. The challenge, then, is to acknowledge the way we can scaffold our planning and teaching by referring to a process *without* the process becoming overly prescriptive.

I have previously published several books that share a cycle of inquiry and the kinds of learning engagements that we might design within such a cycle. I have seen hundreds of interpretations of this idea in classrooms. Many have been gratifying and exciting.

Teachers who honor its true intention, understand its complexity and invite their students into the learning work beautifully towards helping students achieve deeper understanding. I have also seen (and heard) many bewildering versions or iterations of the cycle that are a long way off the original conceptualization and intent.

While frameworks do have an important place, particularly in informing the design of learning experiences, they can become problematic when they are treated simplistically or are slavishly adhered to. Rigid use of a cycle for its own sake can actually impede rather than enhance inquiry.

THE USE OF AN INQUIRY CYCLE TO SUPPORT PLANNING AND TEACHING

Articulating a model or framework for inquiry can support and guide our thinking and practice. The intention of the 'cycle' is to guide the teacher's (and learner's) thinking beyond simply coming up with activities and *towards a more thoughtful process that assists students to move from the known into the unknown and to engage in fruitful dialogue.*

When designed and used well, frameworks for planning and teaching should scaffold thinking. They help the teacher and learners design tasks that support the brain's inclinations to wonder, notice patterns, seek new information, connect to prior learning, create and transfer. There are many versions of a 'cycle of inquiry' and it is well worth exploring several in order to help you deepen and broaden your thinking about the approach. Here are just a few:

- **Short and Harste's inquiry cycle** – see Short, K. Harste, J. *et al*. (1996) *Learning Together Through Inquiry*, Stenhouse, Portland, ME.
- **Stripling's model** – see Small, R., Arnone, M., Stripling, B. and Berger, P. (2011) *Teaching for Inquiry: Engaging the Learner Within*, Neal-Schuman Publishing, Chicago, IL.
- **Eisenberg and Berkowitz's Big 6** information literacy scaffold – see http://big6.com/.
- **Kuhlthau and Todd's guided inquiry model** – see Kuhlthau, C. (2007) *Guided Inquiry: Learning in the 21st Century*, Libraries Unlimited, Santa Barbara, CA.
- **Trevor Bond's 'SAUCE' model** – see http://ictnz.com/index.htm.

The challenge, then, is to acknowledge the way we can scaffold our planning and teaching by referring to a process without the process becoming overly prescriptive.

In more recent times, the 'design thinking' movement has offered us new ways to think about the process involved in identifying problems and generating solutions. Design thinking emphasizes action and problem solving and broadly reflects the essence of all good inquiry.

In a design-thinking model, phases are typically described as:

- immersion/research
- synthesis
- ideation
- prototyping/testing/feedback
- implementation/sharing.

For more information on design thinking models, go the work of Ewan Macintosh and colleagues at www.notosh.com

That there are multiple ways to describe inquiry processes is healthy and affirming. While each model has its own emphasis and language, there are plenty of shared characteristics. These include:

- activation of a need or purpose for inquiry – e.g. an interest, curiosity, uncertainty, tension, a problem to solve or a task to work toward
- identification of current thinking, prior knowledge, understandings and misconceptions
- generation of questions/areas for investigation
- planning for and carrying out investigations and gathering information
- meaning making/analysing/sorting
- sharing/presenting/acting/using/transferring
- reflecting/reviewing/evaluating.

A cycle of inquiry can help us plan and teach with intention and it gives us some shared 'meta' language to use with students and colleagues.

ONE APPROACH TO DESCRIBING AN INQUIRY CYCLE

This articulation of an inquiry process draws on the early, visionary work of Keith Pigdon and Marilyn Woolley, first published in the book *The Big Picture* (1993, Eleanor Curtain). The model has been modified and reshaped over the years but not dramatically so. It is designed, as closely as possible, to support the teacher's thinking as they guide students in their learning and it is also useful in giving students a way of thinking and talking about their own inquiry journeys. The model on the next page attempts to outline a flexible, rather than fixed, framework. Broadly speaking, this process is common to many disciplines. Inquiry by its nature is, as already noted, cyclical, with new discoveries leading to new questions and so on. But this is much neater on paper than it is in practice! True inquiry can be messy and recursive. We gather and sort, then realize we have new questions so we return to some more gathering. In the cycle I use, I place great emphasis on the role of 'tuning in' to students' thinking to establish pathways for investigation. While it often sits at the start of the process, students and teachers return to 'tuning in' regularly. These are phases more than they are stages, elements more than they are steps. Having a relatively simple iteration of it in the form of this cycle can help us think more clearly and actually better manage the messiness without getting overwhelmed.

OVERVIEW OF AN INQUIRY JOURNEY

PHASE AND INTENTION	TYPICAL TEACHER AND STUDENT ACTIVITY
Framing the inquiry • establishing a worthwhile context and compelling question • identifying conceptual underpinnings • making links with the system/school curriculum • identifying understanding goals • identifying key skills and dispositions • identifying possible indicators of understanding	Teachers gather initial student ideas, questions and suggestions. Here, teachers are in the initial design phase, framing up possibilities and clarifying the big picture. They refer to curriculum standards, whole-school guidelines and other elements that inform their programming. Students share, with the teacher and each other, their views on what the inquiry may entail. Depending on their readiness and on the context for inquiry, students may sometimes attend, or provide advice to, planning meetings. Teachers at this stage are in dialogue about the higher purpose of the inquiry. They need to be able to see the horizon at a conceptual level, even if the journey towards it remains unknown.
Tuning in • provoking interest, curiosity, tension or uncertainty • gathering data about students' existing thinking, knowledge, feeling and understanding • helping students make connections with the key concept/s • providing purpose, the big picture and authenticity • motivating, exciting, engaging	In this phase of an inquiry, the teacher is essentially tuning in to the students' thinking (and so too are the students tuning in to their *own* thinking). The teacher takes a very active role as inquirer, with student thinking being the focus of their inquiry. Students are typically making their thinking visible in a range of ways, through play and structured tasks. They are producing evidence of their early theories, possibly beginning to ask questions and becoming more aware of how this inquiry links with their lives and what they will be learning more about and learning to do. Increasingly, students are able to identify and share their early ideas confidently and in a range of ways. They are aware that their ideas are tentative and are likely to change through the course of the inquiry. Depending on the nature of the inquiry itself, this may be a time when students are challenged with a project or task that they will be working towards or a problem they will be addressing. Importantly, the information teachers are gathering at this stage helps inform subsequent planning.
Finding out • gathering new information to address the compelling question • developing the required research skills • learning how to organize and manage the process of finding out • having some shared experiences that will allow us to talk and share our thinking with others • stimulating curiosity through new experiences and information • learning how to efficiently record information gathered	Typically, students at this phase are involved in the process of planning for and researching new information. What they do depends on the manner in which they will be finding out. They may be experimenting, surveying, searching the web, watching clips, emailing or Skyping experts, asking their parents or others, making phone calls, reading texts, viewing images, listening to podcasts, stories or speakers, examining artworks or working through a trial and error process. They are also recording what they are finding so they can refer back to it when they take their thinking deeper. They may also add to their wonderings or wonder for the first time: *I think we could/should…* *Maybe we should search for…* *How about we ask…* *I found out…* *Oh, now I know…* *This makes me wonder about…*

OVERVIEW OF AN INQUIRY JOURNEY (CONT'D)

PHASE AND INTENTION	TYPICAL TEACHER AND STUDENT ACTIVITY
Sorting out • comprehending – making meaning of the information gathered • revealing new thinking and deeper understanding • answering questions • reviewing/revising early thinking and synthesizing • interpreting the information and communicating with others	This is a critical phase in the assessment of understanding. In this phase students are typically analyzing and sharing their discoveries. They may use math, art, language, graphic organizers, drama, dance, music etc. to process and respond to the information they have. They are talking, responding, sharing and processing. They are revealing a new and deeper understanding of the concept and noticing patterns and trends. New questions may emerge as a result of this processing of information. **Verbal evidence** *I used to think… but now I think…* *I can answer some of my questions* *I wasn't expecting to find out that…* *I can connect this with…* *I have learned that…* *This means/I think this means…* *This tells me that…* *Now I'm wondering…* *I'm learning how to…* **Other evidence** *art works* *written pieces* *digital products* *graphic organizers*
Going further • opportunities for students to pursue questions and interests arising from the journey so far • learners work more independently on investigations	This phase typically involves teachers releasing more responsibility to students. They may be working on projects/investigations that are more independent and focused on aspects of the inquiry they need to find out more about or have become most interested in. Students are also applying some of the skills they have been learning in the shared inquiry to a more personalized context. *I want to find out more about…* *Why/who/what/where/when/how…?* *Can we/I…?* *I think I should/could….* *I'm confused about….* *I still need to know/do….*

PHASE AND INTENTION	TYPICAL TEACHER AND STUDENT ACTIVITY
Reflecting and acting • helping students apply their learning to other contexts – to put the learning to use • enabling students to reflect on what and how they have learned and set goals for the future • assessing final understanding and growth in skills	Typically students are engaged in tasks that put their learning into action in some way. This action might be individual or collaborative. It might take place at the end of the inquiry or during it. Students are also reviewing, revising and reflecting on what and how they have learned. They are involved in tasks that provide some closure to the inquiry but are also mindful that new questions have arisen and further investigation is possible. Importantly, students are sharing their awareness of *how* they are learning. *I used to think…but now I think…* *I can use this when…* *I /we should…* *I/we have learned to…* *I have learned more about…* *Next time I need to…* *I wish I had…* *I have got better at…*
Evaluating • reviewing the inquiry to identify strengths and weaknesses • identifying recommendations for future planning	Using feedback from students, assessments of learning and their own reflections during the journey of inquiry, teachers now pause to review the effectiveness of the whole. They look back over the learning and ask themselves how students' understandings, skills and dispositions have been strengthened and what needs further attention. Reflections on the inquiry are recorded and many will prompt thinking ahead for the next journey of inquiry.

The cycle should inform and guide planning but, as previously stated, this does not mean a completed cycle can or should be devised before the learning begins. Planning emerges over the course of the inquiry in response to teachers' assessment of students' needs and the students' own interests and questions.

USING THE ARC OF INQUIRY IN A SINGLE LESSON

When applied to planning processes, an inquiry-based approach has most often been associated with extended units of study. In these units, the phases of inquiry are encountered (and re-encountered) over several weeks. The phases of an inquiry journey can also be experienced over a much shorter period. A cycle may be complete within a morning or even within a lesson. When we take a more nuanced, flexible approach to this basic process it becomes a useful way to frame any investigation, whether short or long term.

Over the past few years, my work has increasingly involved modelling instructional strategies in classrooms. This work has strengthened my own understanding of inquiry as a pedagogy and of the way my understanding of inquiry learning processes can help me design a single lesson (which may be part of a larger inquiry). The following framework is one I find helpful when designing or re-designing a lesson so students are more engaged as inquirers. Essential to this structure is the emphasis on giving students more time to see what they can find out/ work out for themselves before I step in with more direct instruction. I want students to be actively involved in figuring things out for themselves, and then my role becomes one of stepping in and providing direct instruction at the point of need.

- Consider a quick **provocation** – something to spark curiosity/raise a problem/establish a question/ engage interest.
- Share the lesson's **intentions** with students as questions. Create a '**split screen**' set of intentions: one that links to conceptual understanding and the other that links to skills/dispositions.
- Create **success criteria** if appropriate. What should we all be looking for/doing?

- Give students an opportunity to **connect with their prior learning** and current thinking (theories/predictions/hypotheses/current views/wonderings). Share it with each other and record it.
- Provide an **opportunity for exploration** –this challenge may be open-ended or quite scaffolded. The key is to give students a chance to figure out what they can do on their own or in small groups, using resources/texts/materials. Use this time to prompt, question, scaffold and observe. Try to use strategies that can be used again (such as thinking routines, visual organizers).
- Ensure there is some **element of choice** in the lesson (about what, where, with whom, how…etc.).
- Pause to **reflect** at some stage, notice the learning and link back to intentions.
- **Provide input** as required (to individuals and small groups) to help students strengthen understanding, go deeper, and address misconceptions.
- Reflect on both the **content and process.**
- **Connect** to other learning.
- **Clarify the purpose and relevance.**
- **Re-visit prior learning** and predictions – how did thinking change?
- Identify **new questions.**

LESSON SAMPLE

A Story for Bear by Dennis Haseley and Jim LaMarche (Koala Books, Sydney, 2002)

This book was shared with young students as part of a wider inquiry into friendship.

Setting intentions

Share the two key questions driving the lesson and invite students to respond.

- How do we sustain friendships?
- How can inference help us better understand a text?

Tuning in

Share the front cover with students. Ask them to predict what they think this book might be about? What makes them say that? What *questions* do they have about this story before they hear it? Document their ideas under the heading 'We think this story will be about…' Pose the challenge 'How might this story connect to our investigation into how friendships work?'

Finding out

Students listen to the story as it is being read, regularly pausing to check against predictions, and ask 'Now what are we thinking?' 'Does this make us want to ask some new questions?'

Sorting out

Ask 'Can we answer any of our questions about this story?' 'Does it raise new questions?'

Display around the room copies of some of the key illustrations with text. Students are given Post-it notes and are invited to make 'text to self' and 'text to text' connections (see chapter 10 for more on this strategy), placing the Post-it notes on the relevant pages from the text. They are encouraged to link the text to data they have already gathered about the nature of friendship.

Drawing conclusions and reflecting

Ask students to share their connections with each other and note similarities and differences. Reflect on the questions 'What did you notice about how your thinking about this story has changed?' and 'How might this help us add to our thinking about lasting friendships?'

Acting

Some students may be interested in transferring the structure of this text to their own narrative about friendship. Their ideas may be recorded in their writer's notebook for later use.

USING QUESTIONS TO SCAFFOLD LEARNING WITHIN AN INQUIRY LESSON

As discussed in the previous chapter, the questions we pose to students have a vital role to play in nurturing the inquiring mind. I often think of my questions as a form of scaffolding, and when I take time to really think about the placement of those questions throughout a learning sequence, I support students to think more widely and deeply as they move through an inquiry cycle.

Questions in anticipation of a task
- How might we go about this task?
- Why are we doing this?
- What kind of thinking might we need to activate to get this done?
- Can you close your eyes and visualize yourself doing this learning task (turn and talk about what you 'saw')?
- What will you need to do/say/think/believe to help you with this?
- How might we find out? Who would be best to help us? How might we organize for this to happen?
- What would be the best system for gathering this data?
- How might we record/present/share what we find out?
- How will we know if we have been successful?
- What are some of the possible pitfalls with this?
- What kind of groups might work best for this? How might we organize them?
- How will we help make sure the group gets the job done?
- What do we want to achieve?
- How might we achieve this?
- What will we need to avoid or be cautious about?
- What do you feel least prepared for?
- What personal goal could you set yourself?

Questions during the learning task

- What are you noticing about your thinking?
- What strategies are you using?
- How are these strategies working for you?
- What other tasks does this remind you of? Are you using some strategies you have used before?
- What has surprised you?
- What are you struggling with? What do you need to change/address/re-think?
- How is your progress towards your goal? How do you know?

Reflection

- What did you learn about yourself as a learner?
- How did this compare with your predictions?
- What strategies did you use?
- How could you use these again?
- What are you most proud of? Why?
- What would you like to strengthen and improve?
- What would you do differently if you were to use this approach again?
- What didn't work?
- What would you say to yourself next time?
- What would you advise others?
- Why did we do this? Why are these skills useful?
- What if we hadn't…?

PLANNING AND DOCUMENTATION

Framing a worthwhile journey of inquiry

As I have already stated in chapter 3, it is possible for students to inquire into just about anything. The worth of an inquiry, however, is determined partly by the degree to which students can gain a deeper, transferable understanding of the way the world works and strengthen relevant skills through the process. *It is largely through the teacher's grasp of the generative potential of an investigation that the true worth of an inquiry journey can be experienced.* The teacher themselves needs to see beyond topics and tasks and keep their eye on the bigger picture. In many ways, a good inquiry teacher is like a cartographer: they work at keeping a kind of 'aerial view' of the learning pathways available to the students.

Whether the focus of an inquiry journey is carefully planned ahead or the product of an 'in the moment' need or interest, this big-picture thinking is essential. I think of this as 'framing' the inquiry and it is when teachers (and indeed students) have their most important planning conversations. Where we once put most of our effort into coming up with lots of activities about a topic, our primary purpose in meeting to plan is now to discuss the learning students might gain from their inquiry experience.

Bringing an inquiring disposition to the planning table is the key to successful framing. I usually find it most useful to ask a series of questions to help us establish this big picture and avoid the trap of planning at 'activity' level. These questions keep us focussed on process rather than product and they stop our planning from becoming didactic and fixed. The questions below are useful ones to return to throughout an inquiry journey. The scaffolding for inquiry is not built all in one sitting! It is a work in progress.

PAINTING THE BIG PICTURE – SOME QUESTIONS TO GUIDE OUR CONVERSATIONS

- **Why** *this* inquiry for *these* students?
- What **concepts** might underpin this inquiry? How can we use this inquiry context to explore the concept of…?
- How does this connect with the **lives of our students** now and in the future? Why is this worth working on? Why does this matter?
- What are our students **already saying**/thinking/wondering/hoping about this?
- What do *we* as **teachers understand** about this? What are our questions, perceptions and views? How might our way of seeing influence our work with our students? Do we need to engage with experts in the field? What's out there? Who's out there?
- How can we facilitate this with authentic, meaningful resources? Can students access **people, places, objects or texts** that might assist them to take their thinking further?
- What **skills and dispositions** might this inquiry demand of our students? What might they need to be able to *do* as researchers, collaborators, communicators, self-managers and thinkers? How can we support the development of these skills?
- What might students come to **understand** through this inquiry? What are our understanding goals?
- What *might* this understanding **look like?**
- How might this inquiry connect with our system-level **curriculum framework?**
- What connections can we see to other aspects of our program? Is there **integrative potential** here? How can we foster deeper connections? Are there other staff/community members that we can involve?

DOCUMENTATION

How do we record the plans we make? The vexed issue of documentation has plagued inquiry schools ever since I began working this way. I have often felt as if the perfect planner was the holy grail of the inquiry teacher. Of course, there has never been and will never be a perfect way to document all that we plan and do as inquiry teachers. Working this way is complex and layered. When I first started teaching, my documentation consisted of neat, handwritten folders for each subject area that outlined my 'course of study' for the year. I designed this course before I even met my class! The courses took hours to write and were then dutifully submitted to the principal before being stored on my shelves for the rest of the year. I, like most of my colleagues, rarely looked at them. What we *did* use were our work programs – a double-page spread where I would write the activities planned for each session of each day for the week. It was neat, organized and a very satisfying ritual in which I engaged each Sunday evening in preparation for the next week. Anyone could have picked up my program and carried out the various activities I had planned for that day. I'm not sure they would have been clear about the learning intentions behind many of the activities. I'm not sure that I always was!

Our rather simplistic approach to planning and documentation back then pales into insignificance when I think of the level of intellectual engagement with planning I now witness in inquiry schools. Around the planning table, teachers wrestle with key concepts, curriculum standards, data from assessment, available resources, student interests, targeted skills and dispositions, designing authentic and engaging contexts. Is it any wonder the act of recording all this remains challenging?

Keeping some records and documentation of our planning is important. At the very least, it helps keep us accountable to the various stakeholders in students' learning. But when it works

well, documentation can also scaffold our thinking. Schools can design proformas so they prompt teams to consider important elements in planning for learning. As I write this book, an increasing number of schools are using web-based platforms such as Google Docs for their documentation and planning. The potential of these more flexible, collaborative, interactive and hyperlinked forms for inquiry is powerful.

Regardless of whether you are still planning in hard copy or through digital means, documentation needs to be fluid and ongoing. A journey of inquiry cannot be planned in minute detail from start to finish. Teachers learn to plan and document in new ways: on-going, responsively and collaboratively. Craig Dwyer, an inquiry teacher working in international schools, puts it this way:

> '*The physical document* of the planner is a powerful tool of self-reflection and gauging the narrative of the story that has passed so far. If it truly is to be a living document, it needs to be updated and interacted with daily. From the list of possibilities, I start to pull out the activities that I have actually completed and insert them into the planner. As the unit unfolds, so does the planner. They co-evolve together and they both help shape and focus the unit. In essence, the planner itself is an emergent phenomenon.'
> (Dwyer, C., 2012: 8)

EVALUATION: THE CRITICAL BUT OFTEN NEGLECTED PIECE

Guiding students through a journey of inquiry is a satisfying but often demanding task. No inquiry ever really 'finishes', but most come to some kind of closure – albeit with some questions unanswered and new questions having emerged. In an inquiry classroom we may have several investigations proceeding at the same time. Some will continue on for the year while others will have their 'time in the sun' before they give way to a new cycle. As major inquiry journeys wind down, it is important to take time to evaluate their effectiveness and to consider the implications of this evaluation in future planning.

On the following pages is one example of a proforma that can be used to scaffold a detailed evaluation. Criteria can be modified for your own use.

DOCUMENTING A SHARED INQUIRY

- *This is a sample planner only – modify it to suit the needs of your own school/team.*
- *The structure can be applied to a collaborative digital platform (e.g. google doc).*
- *The planner is useful for accountability/reference and sharing purposes.*
- *Documentation is ongoing and evolving. The planner should be refined and modified through regular assessment and evaluation.*
- *The planner should guide discussion – use the questions to prompt teacher thinking.*
- *Note where student input is suggested.*
- *Tasks documented in this planner are not linear.*

SAMPLE PLANNER

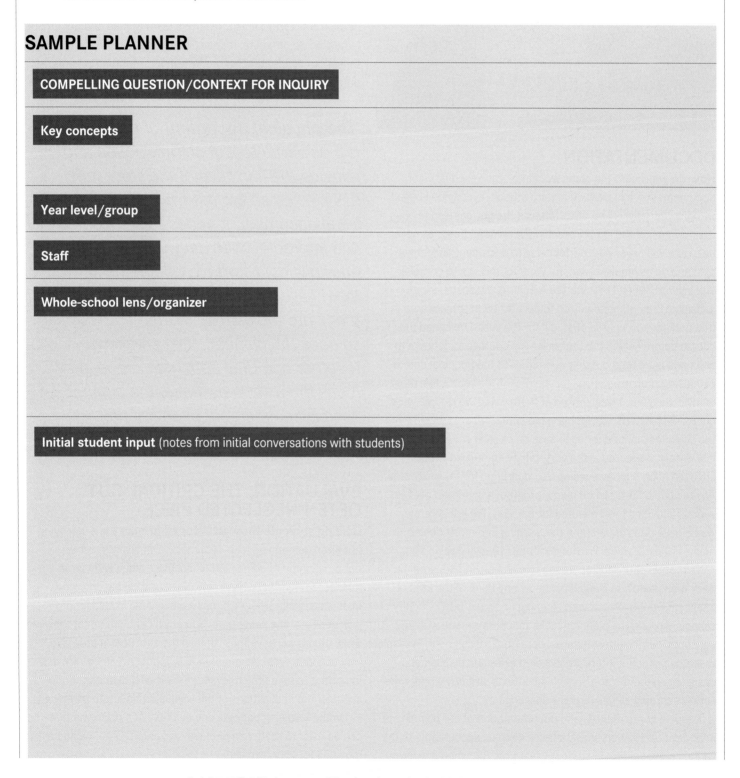

COMPELLING QUESTION/CONTEXT FOR INQUIRY

Key concepts

Year level/group

Staff

Whole-school lens/organizer

Initial student input (notes from initial conversations with students)

SAMPLE PLANNER (CONT'D)

UNDERSTANDING GOALS

- What do we hope students will understand by the end of this inquiry?
- What is important and relevant for these students?
- How might students demonstrate these understandings?
- What criteria might guide our assessment?

Understandings (2–3 maximum, written as statements)	Possible evidence of understanding (to be fine-tuned as the inquiry progresses)

System-level curriculum connections (cut and paste here or include links)

LEARNING ASSETS What do we want our students to be able to do/be?

as thinkers	as communicators	as researchers	as self-managers	as collaborators

SAMPLE PLANNER (CONT'D)

TUNING IN (BASELINE DATA)

- *How can we assess students' prior knowledge and experience in relation to this context? How will we record this information for later assessment?*
- *What can we do to provoke interest/enthusiasm/curiosity/ motivation?*
- *How can we assist students to make 'conceptual connections' and see relationships to and links with their own lives?*

REVIEWING TUNING IN DATA

What did the tuning in tasks reveal to us about students' interests and needs?

SHARED INQUIRY

Finding out – investigating/gathering
What experiences/resources/ activities could be used to assist students to gather information in relation to our planned understandings?

Sorting out – analyzing/explaining/sharing
How can we help students make sense of the data they have gathered? How might they process, sort out, organize and present their ideas?

SAMPLE PLANNER (CONT'D)

GOING FURTHER: PATHWAYS AND POSSIBILITIES (INDEPENDENT INQUIRY) • *How can we cater for individual and small-group pathways as they emerge during the unit?* • *How will we facilitate students' personal inquiries?* • *How can we encourage students to make choices about what and how they will learn?* *(Note: individual teachers will need to add to documentation of the unit once personal inquiry pathways have been established)*	
REFLECTION AND ACTION • *How can we empower students to act on what they have learned? How can we assist students to pull it all together and reflect on their learning?* • *What structures can we put in place to encourage ongoing reflection?* • *What local/global actions might connect with this inquiry?*	

RESOURCES

Useful websites/links/clips; books; people; organizations; materials – add to this throughout the inquiry.

EVALUATION

CRITERIA	HIGH	MED	LOW	EVIDENCE	IMPLICATIONS FOR FUTURE PLANNING
A. The compelling question, understanding goals and skills were engaging, challenging and developmentally appropriate for this group.					
B. Planning was informed by student input/ideas/prior knowledge both initially and throughout the inquiry. Feedback from the students was regularly sought.					
C. Students helped make some decisions about how the inquiry would proceed. Plans were modified and adjusted accordingly.					
D. The inquiry was linked to 'real world' issues/contexts/situations.					
E. Students gathered information from primary and secondary sources. They worked as researchers, both collaboratively and individually.					
F. Students had regular opportunities to make their thinking visible.					
G. Students had opportunities to identify their questions and explore avenues of interest/need in relation to this inquiry.					
H. Students had opportunities to act on/apply their learning to their lives.					
I. Learning engagements were sufficiently open-ended, varied and differentiated to allow for diverse needs and interests.					
J. Skills and processes were explicitly embedded into, and taught during, the inquiry.					
K. Digital technologies were effectively harnessed to enhance the inquiry as a means of gathering/sorting/communicating/creating.					
L. The inquiry allowed for useful, genuine connections to be made across learning areas (including specialist teachers).					
M. Students helped design assessment criteria. They were involved in self-assessing their learning.					
N. Students showed increased mastery of the relevant skills and learning dispositions.					
O. Students showed an understanding of the broader key concept/s that framed the unit.					
P. Students showed engagement in and enthusiasm for their learning.					

AN INQUIRY CYCLE FOR STUDENTS

(May support the *Going Further* phase)

TUNING IN

What do I already think, know and feel about this?

Do I have questions at this stage? What are they?

How can I show what I think about this already?

What am I expecting to find out/do with this?

Why is this important to do/learn about?

What else does this remind me of?

What puzzles me about this?

FINDING OUT

What do I need to do?

Where do I need to go?

Who could I talk to?

How could I investigate this?

How will I record/document what I find out?

What skills do I need to use to find out?

What will help me learn more?

What do I need to organize?

THINKING
COLLABORATING
SELF-MANAGING
RESEARCHING
COMMUNICATING

EVALUATING

How valuable was this inquiry?

What were my strengths as a learner?

What did I do well?

What do I need to work on?

What might I have done differently?

What do I need to remember for next time?

SORTING OUT

What information is useful?

What patterns and connections am I noticing?

How is my thinking growing and changing?

Are my questions being answered?

Do I have some new questions?

How could I share this with others?

Do I need to go back and find out
some new information?

What is confusing? Challenging?

REFLECTING AND ACTING

What have I learned about learning?

How can I use this learning elsewhere?

How has my thinking and feeling changed?

What might I do with this new understanding?

How can this learning make a difference to
my life or the lives of others?

What questions remain?

How do I feel about this learning?

AN OVERVIEW OF INSTRUCTIONAL STRATEGIES AND RELEVANT APPS FOR USE WITHIN AN INQUIRY CYCLE

STAGE OF INQUIRY	SAMPLE STRATEGIES RELEVANT TO THIS PHASE
TUNING IN • gathering data about students' existing thinking, knowledge, feeling and understanding • helping students make connections with the key concept/s • providing purpose, big picture and authenticity • motivating, exciting, engaging	• concept mapping, flow charts, Y charts and other visual organizers • true/false statements – sort into what you think now • structured brainstorms (e.g. 1–3–6; hot potato) • labelled diagrams/drawings, art works • listing, bundling key questions • structured discussions (e.g. using talk tokens, paired interviews, piggy back brainstorming or round robin brainstorming) • using visual texts – analysis/captions/see–think–wonder • talk to the picture – what does the picture tell you? • writing/speaking about relevant experience • interviewing each other (e.g. using a donut strategy) • post box – collecting data about the class's prior knowledge • sharing objects, photos and other artefacts from home • posing problems or challenges associated with this topic – how would we go about solving this now? (compare later) • initial definitions (e.g. using think–pair–share) • exploring related objects – what do we know about these? How are they linked? (placemat to record thinking) • mind maps • open-ended play-based learning centres – teacher interaction and observation used to assess prior learning and interests • NSEW: need to know, suggestions for finding out, excited about, worried about **Apps** • *Poplet* • *Inspiration* • *Ideassketch* • *Mindmash* • *Mindmeister* • *Socrative* • *Picsforlearning* • *Padlet*

AN OVERVIEW OF INSTRUCTIONAL STRATEGIES AND RELEVANT APPS FOR USE WITHIN AN INQUIRY CYCLE (CONT'D)

STAGE OF INQUIRY	SAMPLE STRATEGIES RELEVANT TO THIS PHASE
FINDING OUT • gathering new information to address the compelling question • developing the research skills required • learning how to organize and manage the process of finding out • sharing experiences for collaborative analysis and reflection • stimulating curiosity through new experiences and information • learning how to record information gathered in efficient ways	• working with/learning from real people in the community with expertise in the field • simulations to experience the concept • experimenting/trial and error/tinkering • observing and recording real events and behaviors (e.g. school ground, community) • conducting experiments (long and short term) to gather data • composing questions and defining terms • listening to, reading and analyzing song lyrics • using literature and picture story books to extend experience of the concept • viewing videos/film, photos, paintings and other visual texts as resources • interviewing a range of people to seek opinions or gather data • creating and conducting surveys • reading a range of print material (fiction and non-fiction books, pamphlets, maps, charts, etc.) to gather information • Skype/FaceTime/email/Edmodo etc. – using digital means to connect with experts • note taking and other record keeping to document research • learning from each other – individual or small-group presentations on an aspect of the inquiry • web searches, use of websites, wikis, clips, YouTube, simulations etc. **Apps** • *Livebinders* • *Access my Library* • *www.nationalgeographic.com* • *www.edted.com* • *DuckDuckGo* • *Infotopia* • *Kidtopia* • *Wonderopolis* • *Mashpedia* • *Quintura for kids* • *Search-Cube* • *SlineKids (20 search engines for kids)* • *Polldaddy (create surveys and polls)* • *SurveyMonkey* • *QR code readers* • *Podcast/audiobook apps* • *AppleTV*

AN OVERVIEW OF INSTRUCTIONAL STRATEGIES AND RELEVANT APPS FOR USE WITHIN AN INQUIRY CYCLE (CONT'D)

STAGE OF INQUIRY	SAMPLE STRATEGIES RELEVANT TO THIS PHASE
SORTING OUT • comprehending – making meaning of the information gathered • revealing new thinking and deeper understanding • answering questions • reviewing/revising early thinking – synthesizing • interpreting the information and communicating with others	• artistic representations – show what you have found out across all modes of visual arts • musical composition – instrumental, vocal, using existing pieces and making a soundscape, raps, chants, songs, podcasts – there are a variety of apps for music making • movement and dance – mime, freeze frame, short skits • mathematical forms of visual representation, mapping, graphing, Venn diagrams • writing across genres • reading comprehension tasks, e.g. Text to Self, Text to Text, Text to World • data charts and other graphic organizers to help sort and represent thinking about the topic • using photos for visual and written records and responses – photo editing tools to add to students' capacity to share understanding • drama activities, e.g. role play, conscience game • writing statements of generalization • consequence wheels • de Bono's Thinking Hats • revisiting early work (tuning in) – how has our thinking changed? • using metaphor and analogy • diagrammatic representations of the concept • tug for truth • matching cause and effect • compare and contrast (with related concept) • creating digital texts – web pages, Excel, PowerPoint, Publisher, Prezi etc. • mind maps and other visual organizers that emphasize sorting and connections • true/false statements **Apps** • *Diigo* • *Piktochart* • *WordPress or* • *Evernote* • *Vimeo* *Edublogs for* • *Lino* • *iMovie/iMovie* *blogging* • *Photobucket* *trailers* • *Voicethread* • *Dropbox* • *Microsoft Movie* • *Explain* • *EasyBib* *Maker* *Everything* • *Videostar* • *Pinnacle Studio* • *Dragon Dictation* • *Animoto* • *Book-making* • *Minecraft* • *Audacity* *apps (e.g. Book* • *Airsketch* • *Blogger* *Creator for iPad,* • *Google SketchUp* • *Balbberize* *Blurb)* • *Animation* • *Glogster* • *Xtranormal* *Creation*

STAGE OF INQUIRY	SAMPLE STRATEGIES RELEVANT TO THIS PHASE
GOING FURTHER • opportunities for students to pursue questions and interests arising from the journey so far • learners to work more independently on their investigations	• wonderwall, wonder boxes: following up new lines of inquiry. Creating small interest-based inquiry groups • individual and/or small-group contracts with a range of choices for students • individualized inquiries • alternative 'finding out' experiences – new texts, contrasting experiences • research tasks focused on unanswered questions or interests • individual or small-group work leading to culminating task • learning centers/research centers • Jigsaw – expert groups • blogging for a real global emphasis • Quad Blogging – making links with three other schools from around the world *Apps from the previous three stages can be used here.*
REFLECTING AND ACTING • students apply their learning to other contexts – to put the learning to use • students reflect on what and how they have learned and set goals for the future • assess final understanding and growth in skills	• exhibitions of learning to school and community. What and how can we teach others? • making or continuing to make models/objects • completing design options for a system/structure • performances to promote a cause or celebrate learning • social or environmental action projects – working with local and global communities to make a difference • creating pamphlets and other texts to promote, persuade, encourage and inform • personal goal setting and action plans • publishing writing to celebrate the inquiry throughout the unit • learning logs/research journals/thinking books – various self- and peer-assessment tasks • reviewing and responding to questions asked during the inquiry *Apps from the sorting out and sharing phase can also be used here.*

REFERENCES AND FURTHER READING

• Dwyer, C. (2012) http://dwyerteacher.wikispaces.com/file/view/Unit+Planning+as+Emergence.pdf.
• Friere, P. (1970) *Pedagogy of the Oppressed.* Herder and Herder. NY.
• Pigdon, K. and Woolley, M. (1993) *The Big Picture.* Elanor Curtain Publishing, Melbourne.

*'Learning should not only
take us somewhere;
it should allow us later to go
further more easily.'*

(Bruner, J., 1960)

~ C H A P T E R ~

Six

Assets for life:

HOW CAN INQUIRY NURTURE SKILLS AND DISPOSITIONS FOR LIFELONG LEARNING?

INTRODUCTION

If there has been one stand-out shift in the way I work as an inquiry teacher, particularly in the last decade, it has been the emphasis I now place on inquiring into *how* learning is taking place alongside *what* we are learning. The digital revolution has meant that schools are no longer the place students need to go to find things out, nor are teachers the 'knowledge keepers' they once were. Information is available almost anywhere, any time. With the devices we more frequently carry in our pockets, we have 24-hour access to a vast and ever-changing body of information in the most unprecedented and exciting way. It is now commonly accepted that simply 'knowing' falls a long way short of a valid learning outcome. If I want to know something, I can so often simply Google it. Activities that focus only on gaining and regurgitating information are no longer valid in today's classrooms – they have little to do with real learning. Inquiry is about coming to understand and learning how to get there.

In what is often described as the information age, teachers now have a much greater responsibility to help students build a repertoire of skills and dispositions that enable them to more effectively locate, access, understand and critique ideas, as well as design, create and share their own. When teachers use an inquiry approach to designing learning experiences for students, they provide an excellent opportunity to develop those very skills and dispositions critical for 21st century living. These skills must be developed for students to be able to inquire independently. While the significance of skills needed for inquiry has long been acknowledged, it has often been relegated to simplistic checklists. Skills have not received sufficient, explicit attention in planning, teaching or assessment.

Contemporary system-level curricula in various countries highlight the increasingly important role of learning skills and dispositions. In New Zealand, the Key Competencies are central to the curriculum. At the time of writing, the Australian curriculum, still in development, featured a set of 'general capabilities' that highlighted such skills as critical and creative thinking, self-management and social skills. The International Baccalaureate Program has long recognised the importance of such elements. In the Primary Years Program (PYP), the 'transdisciplinary skills', learner profile and attitudes ensure that the teacher's attention is not only focused on what students are learning but on *how* they are learning – and the kind of learner they are becoming. These are described as 'approaches to learning' in the IB Middle Years program.

Several educators concerned with developing students' understanding of learning processes and of themselves as learners have heavily influenced my thinking about skills and dispositions for inquiry. The work of Guy Claxton, in particular, reminds us that our ultimate goal as teachers is to help young people become better learners, both in and out of school:

> **'Today's schools need** to be educating not just for exam results but for life-long learning. To thrive in the 21st century, it is not enough to leave school with a clutch of examination certificates. Pupils need to have learned to be tenacious and resourceful, imaginative and logical, self-disciplined and self-aware, collaborative and inquisitive.'
> (Claxton, G. 2011: 2)

Claxton's work on 'building learning power' has taught us a lot about the need to focus very explicitly on what it means to 'do good learning'. I thoroughly commend his work for a detailed approach to helping students and teachers develop qualities for successful learning. Art Costa (2000) has been similarly influential in developing this emphasis on the learning process itself. His renowned 'Habits of Mind' provide a powerful framework of dispositions held by effective learners and he encourages us to, again, focus explicitly on these habits – to explore them and apply them across the curriculum. In more recent times, Carol Dweck's (2008) fascinating work has given us more insight into the impact our 'mindset' has on the way we learn. Her research reveals that people's beliefs about intelligence and about the nature of learning strongly influence the way they go about learning. Dweck's work with young people has shown that when we teach them *about* learning, especially about the ways in which our capacity to learn can be continuously strengthened rather than being 'fixed', their learning improves.

Helping students inquire into *how* they learn can require a significant change in teachers' priorities and a new way of thinking. Many of us have not given much explicit thought to this ourselves. Learning, ironically, has been a process rather taken for granted. What we know now is that spending time exploring such things as how we think, how we collaborate and how we self-manage helps us become more mindful, effective learners.

When we turn our attention to the 'how' and 'why' of learning (not simply the 'what'), something shifts in our teaching. We begin to pay attention and to notice the learning challenges and opportunities within tasks rather than focusing on the end-of-task outcome. The wonderful educator Elliot Eisner suggests that teachers can strengthen their work by adopting

Through thinking **routines** students are enculturated into thinking, developing both their ability and their inclination to think.
Ron Ritchhart

dispositions and ways of seeing aligned with the arts. He reminds us that 'form and content are inextricable – *how* something is said is part and parcel of *what* is said'. While this relationship of form and content is most vivid in the arts, it is something that the expert inquiry teacher notices and works with. In simple terms, this means we help students not only prepare an oral presentation but attend to the *form* of that presentation; not only listen to the story but consider how the story is *composed*; work on a collaborative project while simultaneously reflecting on how the *act* of collaboration itself is working.

'The good teacher, like the good short order cook, has to pay attention to several operations simultaneously, and they do.'
(Eisner, 2002: 7)

DEVELOPING LEARNING ASSETS – SKILLS AND DISPOSITIONS

When we consciously engage young people in inquiring into how they learn, we are developing skills and dispositions that act as important assets to them as learners – across the curriculum, in school and beyond. I have used this term 'assets' to describe the broad skill sets that are commonly required of the inquirer: thinking, collaborating, self-managing, researching and communicating. Each of these broad assets includes

multiple, specific skills. The metaphor of a tool kit is a useful one. If we think of each of the five assets as a compartment in the tool kit, the specific skills are contained within each of those compartments. Alongside the skills in this tool kit is what many describe as dispositions. The distinction between these terms is somewhat vexed and can be quite subtle, but it is important to consider. A simple way to conceptualize it is that skills are more about what the learner is 'doing' whereas dispositions are more about what the learner is 'being'. Dispositions can be seen as having a 'tendency' towards behaving in certain ways. Many argue that without dispositions, skills are carried out much less effectively. One can, for example, be skilled at formulating a rich question for inquiry, but without curiosity to want to find out, courage to go beyond the known and an open-minded attitude about the information gathered, then the skill of asking questions is of little real value.

There is no definitive list of skills, qualities or dispositions but there are hundreds of examples available. The table on pages 102 and 103 offers one framework for skills and dispositions for the inquiry learner. It is deliberately simple in scope and is one I have used over the last few years with many schools with which I am associated. My intention is to make the framework manageable for teachers and accessible to students from K-6.

DEVELOPING LEARNING ASSETS IN THE
INQUIRY CLASSROOM – A FRAMEWORK

We are
RESEARCHERS

We can formulate questions and locate and use a wide range of sources and techniques to investigate problems, interests and issues. We think critically about the information we gather and we are careful to acknowledge our sources.

curious
courageous
resourceful

We are
THINKERS

We can think logically, creatively and reflectively. We think about *how* we use our thinking and have different strategies for making our thinking visible to others. We remain open-minded and know that our thinking changes as we learn.

open-minded
flexible
persistent

We are
COLLABORATORS

We can work with others on shared goals, questions and challenges. We know how to be a constructive part of a team, to use different roles for different tasks and to actively listen to and respect other people's views. We understand how our behaviour affects others.

empathic
compassionate
reliable

We are
SELF-MANAGERS

We can learn independently and can make wise decisions about our learning. We know ourselves as learners and can set and work towards personal goals. We know we can continually improve as learners.

resilient
responsible
reflective

We are
COMMUNICATORS

We can communicate ideas confidently in different ways and for different purposes. We listen thoughtfully to what others communicate to us. We can adapt our communication style to different contexts.

confident
responsive
respectful

STRENGTHENING LEARNING ASSETS IN THE INQUIRY CLASSROOM – STRATEGIES FOR SUCCESS

The learning assets are transdisciplinary and generic and, therefore, not the sole the responsibility of the generalist classroom teacher. All teachers can be involved in explicitly supporting the development of learning assets. The following strategies help ensure that the assets become more than a set of 'signs on the wall' and instead remain consciously embedded in the learning life of each student.

1. USE AND TEACH STUDENTS SPECIFIC LANGUAGE TO ACCOMPANY THE ASSETS

It has long been argued that the language we use in classrooms plays a significant role in mediating children's learning experiences and cognitive development (Feuerstein, 1980; Costa and Marzano, 1987). When children are able to 'label' the more specific processes they are using as learners, they develop a greater understanding of the nuanced differences between the skills and strategies required to achieve a task. When language is used in this way, a number of important instructional strategies such as providing feedback, self-assessment, peer assessment and goal setting become more effective, as teachers and learners can converse about the process with greater understanding. Terms like 'thinking' and 'cooperating' are used extensively in classrooms but too often our discourse is vague. The following table provides some of the terms that are useful to include in dialogue with students of all age groups:

Talking about COLLABORATING	Talking about SELF-MANAGEMENT	Talking about COMMUNICATION	Talking about THINKING	Talking about RESEARCH
take turns	plan	eye contact	analyze	proposal
share	organize	body language	synthesize	search
compromise	persist	audience	create	skim
negotiate	self-talk	message	innovate	scan
debate	control impulsivity	volume	question	key terms
team	consequence	tone	wonder	critique
respectfully disagree	reflect	product	imagine	resource
empathize	goal	explain	hypothesize	reference
role	responsibility	inform	evaluate	source
feedback	initiative	engage	reflect	primary data
agreement	independence	convince	sequence	secondary data
disagreement	choice	argue	connect	trustworthiness
protocol	self-assess	debate	empathize	judge
affirm	time management	props	compare	expert
encourage	persistence	visual	contrast	method
unite	risk taking	curate	strategy	fact
confer	resourceful	contribute	predict	opinion
moderate	leadership	dialogue	clarify	evidence
consensus	motivation	impact	contemplate	recording
consult	intention	declare	construct	information
equity	awareness	disclose	deconstruct	probe
participate	mindfulness	argue	evidence	permission
structure	conscious	digress	justify	scrutinize
collaborate	unconscious	counteract	fact	evaluate
	resilience	debate	opinion	author
	focus	text	infer	compose
		gesture	assume	edit
				publish

2. REVEAL YOUR PURPOSES:
A) MAKE LEARNING INTENTIONS CLEAR

Learners tend to learn more effectively when they are clear about their purpose. Knowing where you are going does not mean having to have every task mapped out in detail but it does mean clarity of purpose. Recent research has confirmed the value of sharing learning intentions with students, focusing not on what they will be 'doing' but rather on the *learning* that is taking place through the doing (Hattie, 2012). Even when teachers share the learning intentions with students, they can be too specific to the task and lack important transferability. For example, the teacher might say:

'We are learning how to design questions to interview our visiting scientist.'

In fact, the learning intention would be better phrased as *'We are learning how to design questions for an interview'*. The context in which this intention is being met is the interview with a scientist, but it is the skill of designing questions that becomes the *transferable intention*.

One effective strategy for sharing learning intentions, with the assets as the focus, is to adopt Claxton's 'split screen' teaching approach. I often use this when facilitating inquiry workshops for students and find it a great way to help ensure we have shared clarity about the learning focus of the session. Creating a 'split screen' learning intention reminds us all that we are continually focusing on learning to learn while we are learning 'about' a concept or exploring a question. The 'split-screen' metaphor acknowledges learning as layered and complex.

In keeping with an inquiry-based mindset, learning intentions can be formulated as questions rather than questions or statements. For example:

---

* instead of: *'We are learning how to disagree respectfully when working in teams.'*
  try: *'How can we disagree more respectfully when we are working in teams?'*
* instead of: *'We are learning about the impact of early explorers on the Australian landscape.'*
  try: *'How did the early explorers affect the Australian landscape?'*

The split screen idea can then look like this:

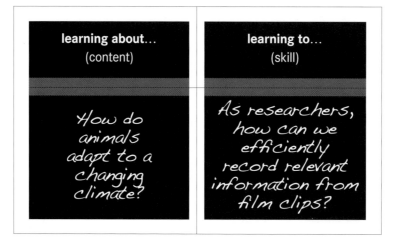

Or a triple split screen that identifies the 'content', skill and disposition central to the learning task, like this:

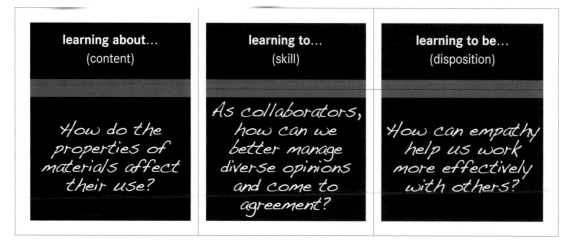

2B) LEARNING INTENTIONS AS QUESTIONS

The intentions we have for students' learning should be clear. They are not teachers' secret business. However, instead of documenting an intention as an inevitabity, ('We will learn'…) an inquiry teacher may pose the intention in the form of a question ('How might we?'…). In effect, the process of inquiry helps reveal the answer.

Students themselves can be involved in creating the learning intentions linked to a task. Using the language of the learning assets, ask the students to suggest what skills and dispositions they think will be needed/strengthened by the task.

As learning assets are explored and worked on over a year, more and more specific 'tools' are added to your students' inquiry repertoire. Keep a record of the skills you have focused on. Students may use these as checklists or menus for themselves. You may also devise some kind of digital bank of skills you have highlighted, create a booklet or other easy 'go to' resources or simply use a set of anchor charts to refer to on the wall.

However you choose to do this, it is important that students are aware of what they have learned to 'do' and 'be' and are able to refer this repertoire in subsequent inquiries. It is only through practicing the skills and using them across contexts that mastery can be achieved.

Supporting students in selecting assets they want to build for their own tool kit means that we need to know them as people as well as learners. Through observation, conversation and consciously taking the time to reflect on the strengths and needs of each student, we can make useful suggestions about areas for improvement. Effective teachers know the students who need to strengthen their collaborative skills, who find it difficult to take risks or who need to work on organization and self-management. The following tables provide a menu of specific sub-skills for each of the learning assets. These menus can be:

- used to help formulate learning intentions for planning purposes
- used to help develop self-assessment checklists
- used by teachers and students to help shape personal learning goals and provide feedback
- compared with similar lists in system level curricula and adapted accordingly.

LEARNING ASSETS FOR INQUIRY: (LOWER PRIMARY)

Collaboration	Self-management	Communication	Thinking	Research
• think and talk about our feelings with others • help each other in different ways • take turns • share our ideas with others • talk about how we can play/learn together • look after and share materials with others • look after the materials we use • listen respectfully to others • show others we are listening to them • use our manners when working and playing with others • record or retell what others have said • respect the rights, feelings and efforts of others • do our fair share when we are working in a group • learn and play with different people • do different jobs when we are in a group • share ideas about what our group could do • tell others about what our group has done / is doing • think about what we can do to help our group do a great job • choose sensible places to learn/play together • use words to solve problems	• think and talk about our feelings • come up with ideas for our own learning • think and talk about how we feel about our learning • make connections between what we know and new learning • stay focused on a task • express our new learning • use our mistakes to help us learn • ask questions to help us with our learning • get things done in time • set up and pack up for ourselves • think about and share what helped us learn best • think and plan before we start a task • think about the effect our thinking and behaviour is having on others • set ourselves a goal and work towards it • learn how to make a plan and follow it through • work things out for ourselves before we ask others • persist with our learning even when it is challenging • take responsibility for our things • listen to other people's feedback about our learning	• use our body and face as well as words to communicate effectively • re-tell what someone has told us • ask questions of someone else • confidently share our thinking and feeling • speak to others in a way that helps them understand • use objects/props to help us communicate more effectively • create digital texts to communicate ideas • understand the difference between a question and a statement • understand what people 'say' with their faces and their bodies • communicate to people respectfully • use the right voice and language for different situations • listen carefully to what we are hearing and show others that we are listening • listen without interrupting • ask questions to help us understand • share our ideas in different ways	• show and share our thinking in different ways • stay focused on our thinking • think of and share a question • think about and share how we have answered our questions • stay curious about what we are learning • reflect on what we feel and what we have learned • use visual organizers to show our thinking (e.g. Venn diagrams, spider diagrams) • find patterns • look for similarities and differences • make connections between ideas • think about and plan what we are going to do • talk about what we are thinking and share this with others • notice and explain how we are thinking and feeling • think about and explain how someone else might be thinking or feeling • talk about our thinking strategies • use our creative thinking to come up with new ideas and solve problems • challenge ourselves to take our thinking further	• talk about or show what we already know about something • decide what we want to find out • use our senses to find out about something • ask a question to find out information • come up with ideas for how to find out answers to our questions • use the internet to get information we can understand • use the internet safely • ask an adult/expert questions to find out new information • use non-fiction books to get new information • use photos/pictures to get information • use stories/picture books to add to our thinking about different ideas/ questions • use film clips/DVDs to get new information • observe things carefully to find out new information • share how our thinking has changed • record our new learning in words and pictures • find and contact people who can help us 'find out'

LEARNING ASSETS FOR INQUIRY: (UPPER PRIMARY)

Collaboration	Self-management	Communication	Thinking	Research
• share our ideas respectfully when we are working in a group • make wise choices when forming partnerships and teams • record or retell what others have said • respect the feelings and efforts of others • do our fair share when we are working in a group • compromise and negotiate when we don't get our way • give constructive feedback to others • encourage others to participate • devise an agreement before we begin a group task • use different roles when working in teams • seek and accept feedback from other team members • use strategies to deal with conflict when it arises in team work • be appropriately assertive and respectful when communicating with team members • manage time and stay organized as a team • understand and respect other points of view • question other people in a team to seek clarification, encourage participation and build cooperation • manage the influences that others have on us when we work in a team	• listen to and act on feedback from others • take risks and challenge ourselves • set short-term goals and reflect on them • manage our impulses and think before we speak • support ourselves when we feel uncertain or challenged by a learning task • look back over our learning and set new goals • seek feedback to improve our learning • make a personal plan to ensure that a task is completed on time. • identify how and when we learn best • devise an action plan to help us work towards a goal • seek feedback from others to improve our learning	• record the learning we gain from different kinds of communications • present our ideas and opinions to a range of audiences • evaluate the effectiveness of other presentations • express ourselves in new ways • design and use criteria to plan and assess our communication • select the right communication form for the purpose or context • persuade or convince an audience • keep an audience engaged when we are communicating our ideas • give appropriate feedback to others on their communication performances	• think about and explain how someone else might be thinking or feeling • talk about our thinking strategies • give reasons or evidence to explain our thinking • be flexible and consider how our thinking can change as we gather more information and experiences • think about the potential consequences of actions • think back over our learning and identify ways to improve • transfer thinking strategies to different situations • consider how beliefs and culture can influence people's thinking • analyze information gathered from different sources and look for patterns and trends • think creatively to solve problems • think about how we are thinking and how we can use our thinking to respond to a challenge or complete a task • record our thinking in new ways • plan ahead and think through a task before we begin it	• develop and refine questions to help us seek and gather information • seek and select the best source of information for the task • make a plan to systematically gather information • cite the sources of information we gather in appropriate ways • use both primary and secondary sources of information when investigating • record the information we gather in efficient and effective ways • be organized in our research • reflect on the information we gather • link the information we gather to the questions we have begun with • efficiently assess whether a text/source is right for us • judge the quality of information we gather using criteria • search the internet safely and protect ourselves • verify the source of the information we gather • understand the difference between fact and opinion • gather and use information ethically explain how and why our thinking has changed

3: BE EXPLICIT

As has already been suggested, the skills and dispositions needed for effective learning can make for engaging inquiry contexts in themselves. When we help students inquire into *how* they learn, we also have some great opportunities for explicit and specific teaching. A common misconception about inquiry learning is that simply exposing students to something or 'immersing' them in an experience will mean that they automatically 'discover' what we hope they will learn. Good inquiry teachers know that there is more to it than this. Yes, exposure and immersion are important; however, it is through quality questioning, deft 'noticing' and opportunities for reflection and feedback that deeper learning takes place. This is as true of skills and dispositions as it is of concepts.

If we want our students to, for example, develop their skills as collaborators, we need to do more than simply 'expose' them to experiences of working in a team. We need to layer the experience with explicit teaching that helps the learner uncover the techniques that work and don't work. This is true of all the assets.

Try the following techniques:

- **Model the behavior/skill yourself.** Ask students to reflect back what they noticed about the way you went about the task.
- **Break the skills down** and focus on specific 'micro' techniques for the students to practice. Instead of saying 'you need to manage your time better', inquire into the skill of time management and come up with some possible techniques to try out.
- **Provide strong and weak models.** For example show students what a powerful oral presentation can look/sound like and have them compare it to a poor one.
- **Invite students to talk to others** about their tips for successful collaboration/self-management/research etc. Ask older students, parents and experts in the field.
- **Identify particular students** who have strengths in certain skills. For example, there will be students who, as self-managers, are particularly organized and systematic. Ask those students to try to articulate what they do and how they do it.
- **Run short, focused teaching sessions** (or 'clinics') for students who recognize they need more support with particular skills.
- **Video students** for evidence of the skills in practice. Watch and analyze the films for self-assessment, feedback and peer teaching (particularly good for collaboration and communication).
- **Record conversations** and take notes, Apps such as AudioNote can be helpful for this.

4: USE THE LEARNING ASSETS AS THE BASIS FOR GOAL SETTING AND SELF-ASSESSMENT

When we invite students to set goals, we are giving them the message that they know something of their needs as learners and as people. We are respecting their self-knowledge at the same time as building it. Most importantly, we are giving our students one of the most useful gifts available to a human being, a sense of personal agency and control. Goal setting does not always have to be individualised. As a class, you can set a range of goals that build team spirit and cohesion and develop the language associated with effective learning. The learning assets are a useful platform from which students can design goals. Because the assets are cross disciplinary, they can be worked on across the day and in a range of subject areas. Students may select certain assets to work on as a result of feedback given to them by teachers, peers or parents. Assets may also be determined by the requirements of a task or project the student is working on. Interviewing students about themselves as learners can be a useful way to begin the process of personalising their goals – our job is to 'see' each of our students for who they are and to ask ourselves what we can do to help them become the best that they can be. This knowledge is gained in the way every teacher intuitively knows: through listening, observing, careful analysis of work samples and other data, stimulating talk and reflection and engaging with parents. The best goals are formed when we take time to confer with students one-to-one. Some questions that can assist this process include:

- What kind of learner are you?
- When do you like learning the most? When do you have the most fun?
- When do you find learning the least fun?
- What kinds of things challenge you as a learner?
- What do you think you are best at? What makes you say that?
- What is something you could teach others?
- What would you really love to be better at/know more about?
- Why? Tell me more about that.
- What do you think other people think you're good at?
- What is something you couldn't do in the past that you can do now? How did you learn to do that? What helped you?
- So, I can hear this is something you want to do/learn/be/ get better at – how do you think that will make a difference to you? What do you think it will look/feel/sound like when you have reached your goal?
- What do you think might get in the way? Is there anything you are worried about?

- How do you think you might help yourself work towards this?
- How will you know when you have got there?
- Is there anything you will have to do or change to help you reach this goal?
- Would you like me to share some of my thinking about this with you?
- Would you like some ideas about how to help you work towards this?
- What can I do to help you?

5: MAKE THIS EVERYONE'S BUSINESS!

In many primary schools, the role of the specialist or 'single subject' teacher remains somewhat removed or separated from the bulk of the students' daily learning experiences. It is still the case that students in most primary schools attend specialist classes (e.g. art, music, PE, library, languages) once a week. Attempts to integrate the learning that occurs in specialist and generalist classes have often been shallow and thematic, sharing a common 'topic'. We know now that concepts offer a much stronger way to help students develop deeper understanding through integration. But skills and dispositions can offer another powerful vehicle for quality integration. The learning assets outlined in this chapter are, in themselves, transdisciplinary. They belong neither to particular age groups nor to particular subject areas. They are about life-long and 'life-wide' learning. When specialist and generalist teachers work together to promote common skills and dispositions, students have the opportunity to practice these in different contexts. Inquiry teachers give careful thought to the exploration of learning skills and dispositions as they plan. Co-planning with specialists or single subject teachers is a powerful way to ensure that these transferrable skills are indeed transferred.

6: TAKE THE LEARNING ASSETS BEYOND SCHOOL

Not only are the learning assets transferable across subjects and from specialist to generalist classrooms, they are highly transferable to situations beyond school. Helping students to see the way they can use these skills in their lives outside the classroom is a significant step in consolidating the toolkit. Drawing the connection between home and school can have profound benefits that extend beyond this skill set. One effective technique is to put an 'asset' in the spotlight for a week/fortnight/term. For example, you might focus on self-management. Have the students compose something about this for parents in the newsletter, on the class blog or school website. Include articles about self-management for the parents. Have students brainstorm the circumstances when they can be great self-managers at home

and at weekend activities. Students can ask parents about the need for these skills and dispositions in their work place. Have students seek examples of people demonstrating the asset in the local community. Opportunities to strengthen learning assets beyond the classroom are plentiful. Have students work on an asset as a home learning task, as shown below.

STRENGTHENING MY LEARNING ASSETS AT HOME

Name: *Michael*
This week, I will focus on: *self-management*
I want to get better at: *managing my time*
Because: *I am always rushing and I don't get stuff done*
I plan to: *Write a plan for each day and allocate times for tasks*
Use my phone's alarm to time how long things take
Get out of bed 30 minutes earlier to do my chores
Signed by: PARENT_____ STUDENT *Michael*
Reflection:

FURTHER STRATEGIES TO HELP STUDENTS INQUIRE INTO LEARNING

INTENTION STARTERS

Provide students with sentence starters to help them formulate intentions for themselves as learners prior to a task, a day or a week by articulating what they hope they will remember to do or be as a learner. This encourages a mindful disposition and also gives the student something to reflect back on at the end of the session. The template on page 107 can be used to make a set of cards from which students can select. They may state their intention orally or record the remainder of the statement on a Post-it note, displaying it in their work area or on the wall.

WHAT'S YOUR STATE OF MIND?

Gather together a collection of images to present to students either on cards or on a screen. I often use photos of animals or scenes from nature. At any time during the day, ask students to choose the image that they believe best represents their state of mind. This can be a quick yet powerful way to gain insight into how a child is feeling and how 'learning ready' they are. Ask students to consider whether the state of mind they have identified is one that will lend itself well to learning, and if not, ask them to consider which image they aspire to.

REFLECTION STEMS

While they have been around for many years, reflection stems are very valuable in supporting students to think back over their learning and to articulate their thoughts more easily. Sample reflection stems are provided on page 106.

THINKING ABOUT YOUR STRENGTHS

ARE YOU...

CURIOUS?
Do you wonder about things? Do you want to find out more? Do you ask questions? Are you fascinated by things? Do you take time to observe the world around you?

COURAGEOUS?
Are you a risk taker? Are you willing to try new things? Do you challenge yourself?

OPEN-MINDED?
Do you allow your thinking to change? Do you consider other possibilities? Do you try to find out other points of view?

FLEXIBLE?
Are you willing to do things differently? Do you adapt to changing circumstances? Are you willing to compromise?

PERSISTENT?
Do you keep going even when you experience set-backs? Do you stay on task and focused? Do you try different ways to achieve a goal? Do you stick with things?

RESILIENT?
Do you bounce back? Can you accept critical feedback? Can you forgive or move on after a difficult experience? Do you try to see benefits as well as problems in challenging or confusing situations?

RESPONSIBLE?
Do you own what you say and do? Do you avoid blaming others? Do you stick to expected agreements and arrangements? Can you manage your own behavior?

REFLECTIVE?
Do you stop to think about what you do and say? Do you learn from mistakes? Are you self-aware? Do you take time to think? Do you ask questions and take time before making decisions?

EMPATHIC?
Can you stand in someone else's shoes? Do you consider how other people are feeling or experiencing something? Can you identify with other people's experiences and feelings?

COMPASSIONATE?
Do you care for others? Do you help other people even if it is sometimes at your own expense? Do you want to make a difference to the lives of others? Do you listen with your heart as well as your head?

RELIABLE?
Do you do what is asked or expected of you? Can others depend on you? Are you willing to lead others at times?

CONFIDENT?
Do you trust your own abilities? Can you describe your strengths? Are you aware of the things you need to improve? Are you comfortable sharing this with others?

RESPONSIVE?
Do you connect with others? Do you show and share how you feel and what you think? Do you contribute your ideas to a group? Do you give constructive feedback to others?

RESPECTFUL?
Do you listen well to others? Do you communicate in an appropriate and polite way? Do you acknowledge the achievements and positive qualities of others? Are you sensitive to cultural and other differences?

RESOURCEFUL?
Do you look for alternatives to help solve problems? Do you seek advice and ideas from different sources? Do like the challenge of trying to figure things out? Do you recognise and make the most of your skills?

SWITCHING ON TO LEARNING

I need to avoid…

SWITCHING ON TO LEARNING

I will try to…

SWITCHING ON TO LEARNING

I need to focus on…

SWITCHING ON TO LEARNING

I can help myself by…

SWITCHING ON TO LEARNING

I'll get more out of this by…

SWITCHING ON TO LEARNING

I hope I can…

SWITCHING ON TO LEARNING

One new thing I will try is…

SWITCHING ON TO LEARNING

I'd like to be more… because …

SWITCHING ON TO LEARNING

I'm looking forward to…

SWITCHING ON TO LEARNING

A skill I will need to use is…

SWITCHING ON TO LEARNING

I can help myself by thinking more…

SWITCHING ON TO LEARNING

I will challenge myself by…

SKILLS NEEDED FOR EFFECTIVE RESEARCH USING DIFFERENT RESOURCES

Finding out by…	Sample skills required
reading non-fiction books and other printed texts (pamphlets, posters, charts, magazines, reference books etc.)	• selecting a relevant book/article • skimming and scanning text and selecting relevant information • using structural features of the texts – headings and subheadings, content and index • critically evaluating the trustworthiness of the source • note taking and making notes • interpreting/comprehending the text • comparing and contrasting to other forms of information • organizing and displaying information gathered (using, for example, appropriate visual organizers)
direct observation (of phenomena, a demonstration, an object, during an experiment)	• clarifying what is being looked for • staying focused and avoiding distraction • designing effective methods to record observations • recording information in a quick and efficient manner • describing observations to others • noticing detail • reviewing the experience – identifying discoveries and wonderings
accessing information via the internet	• using search engines – narrowing searches to find the most relevant information • evaluating the trustworthiness of the site by identifying the author/source/sponsor • locating evidence of accountability (where does the author get the information from?) • making connections between information from multiple digital sources • articulating and summarizing information in own words • using a variety of apps to access information
interviewing someone to gather information (one-to-one, small group, listening to guest speaker, talking to a buddy; may be face-to-face or virtual)	• formulating appropriate questions (open and closed) • using respectful body language and eye contact • actively listening without interrupting • using probing and clarifying questions • recording information gained in an efficient and concise way • using protocol for interviews (gaining permission to use material etc.)
sending a letter/email/tweet to seek information	• using conventions associated with (for example) emails, texts or tweets • accessing and responding to blog posts • understanding digital etiquette • framing appropriate questions suited to the focus of the investigation • comprehending material sent in response
designing and conducting surveys (digital or hard copy)	• identifying the information that needs to be gathered • designing, producing and evaluating a format that will enable efficient and effective gathering of relevant data • analyzing data and looking for patterns • drawing conclusions based on data received • refining the survey based on trials • gaining permission for data use

SKILLS NEEDED FOR EFFECTIVE RESEARCH USING DIFFERENT RESOURCES (CONT'D)

Finding out by...	Sample skills required
conducting experiments/ simulations	• using materials safely • hypothesizing/predicting possible outcomes • identifying variables and designing a fair test • recording information gathered systematically (as a scientific report, for example) • analyzing and concluding based on observations or data gathered
viewing infographics / videos/ DVDs/film clips/photos/images/ artworks	• selecting a relevant visual text • skimming and scanning text and selecting relevant information • critically evaluating the trustworthiness of the source • identifying the text features used to communicate and privilege information – colour, sound, animation, casting, music etc.) • interpreting/comprehending the text • comparing and contrasting to other forms of information • noticing and recording detail
using real objects and artefacts	• *(see direct observation)*
listening to audio files (music, songs, broadcasts, podcasts)	• active listening for relevant information • recording and summarizing information gained • skimming and revising the text to review information • critically evaluating the trustworthiness of the source and the 'agenda' of the composer/producer • note taking and making notes • analyzing and comprehending information
reading literature (fiction)	• selecting texts appropriate to the concepts/questions being explored • identifying themes and ideas • identifying fact vs fiction • making connections between texts

REFERENCES AND FURTHER READING

• Claxton, G., Chambers, M., Powell, G. and Lucas, B. (2011) *The Learning Powered School*, TLO, NY.
• Costa, A. and Marzano, R. (1987) 'Teaching the Language of Thinking', *Educational Leadership*, October.
• Costa, A. and Kallick, B. (2000) *Exploring and Discovering Habits of Mind*, ASCD, Alexandria, VA.
• Dweck, C. (2008) Mindset: The New Psychology of Success. Ballantine Books, NY.
• Eisner, E. W. (2002) 'What Can Education Learn from the Arts about the Practice of Education?', *The Encyclopedia of Informal Education*, www.infed.org/biblio/eisner_arts_and_the_practice_or_education.htm.
• Feuerstein, R. (1980) *Instructional Enrichment*, University Park Press, Baltimore, MD.
• Hattie, J. (2012) *Visible Learning for Teachers: Maximizing Impact on Learning*, Routledge, NY.

'The heart of human excellence often begins to beat when you discover a pursuit that absorbs you, frees you, challenges you, or gives you a sense of meaning, joy, or passion.'

(Terry Orlick, 2007)

~ CHAPTER ~

seven

To each their own:
WHY MAKE IT PERSONAL?

INTRODUCTION

'Are we preparing kids to learn without us?' This simple but powerful question raised by educator and blogger Will Richardson got me thinking. He goes on to ask: *'How can we shift curriculum and pedagogy to more effectively help students form and answer their* own *questions, develop patience with uncertainty and ambiguity, appreciate and learn from failure and develop the ability to go deeply into the subjects about which they have passion to learn?'* (Richardson, W., 2012:23). **Providing students with** opportunities for personal inquiry is one way these questions can be addressed. At the time of writing, there is mounting interest in 'personalized learning'. More and more schools are rethinking the arrangements they make to cater for the needs and interests of each student and recognizing the possibilities of new technologies, in particular, to enable students to investigate those things in which they are interested. For the purposes of this chapter, I will define personal inquiry as that which generally arises from the student's own interest or passion. The inquiry is personal when the student identifies what *they* want or need to investigate and proceeds to plan (usually with continued teacher guidance) a personal pathway for learning.

Of course, inquiry-based learning is, by its own design, an approach that *already* includes strong student ownership. In inquiry classrooms, we invite students to contribute their questions and we negotiate with them about how the learning might proceed. Inquiry teachers already give learners a voice and provide opportunities to make choices. Having said that, even co-constructing a journey of inquiry does not guarantee that individual students will have opportunities for truly personal inquiry experiences. In the majority of classrooms in which I work, the contexts for inquiry are dominantly shared contexts, meaning that the class/cohort of students explore the same 'big idea', albeit with opportunities for individuals and small groups to investigate questions and issues they become interested in within that context.

I maintain that this shared, collaborative inquiry is a vital element of the classroom program. Through shared inquiry, students develop the skills of negotiation; they are exposed to multiple viewpoints; and they learn to co-construct tasks and criteria. Shared inquiry also helps students learn the value of constructing ideas and understandings *with* others and exposes them to avenues of inquiry they may never choose for themselves. Shared inquiry is generally more manageable for the teacher in terms of resourcing, facilitating teaching groups and integrating the curriculum. When teachers are guiding students through a shared investigation, they are helping put important 'tools' in their learning tool kits so they can be better equipped for their own inquiries. Shared inquiries can also trigger interests and questions about things that students may otherwise have never thought about. Shared inquiries build an important knowledge base that can be drawn upon for personal inquiries. These inquiries can truly take the learner beyond their realm of experience.

Great inquiry classrooms offer students a mix of experiences as inquirers: some whole-class, some small-group and some individual; some selected for them, some selected by them. I believe that it is not only possible to include both shared and individual inquiry in the classroom, it is desirable.

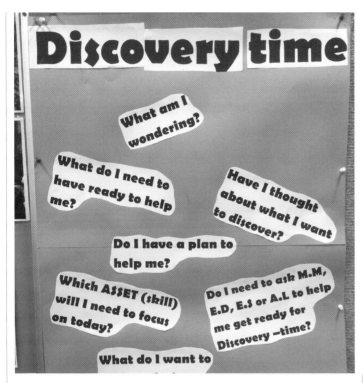

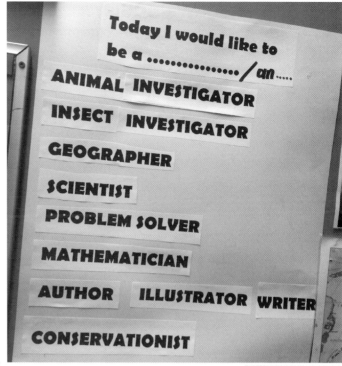

WHY THE NEED FOR PERSONAL INQUIRY OPPORTUNITIES?

Numerous, prominent educators support the idea of providing students with opportunities to focus on their interests *and* have time to learn more individually. Ken Robinson (2009) reminds us that we are often at our best when we are 'in our element' and that finding our passion can be one of the most transformative experiences in our learning journey. Daniel Pink's (2009) extensive research into motivation concludes that unless we feel we have some autonomy within a task/learning context, we don't feel ownership and are less likely to maintain commitment and energy. Susan Cain's (2013) fascinating research into 'the power of introverts' is a compelling reminder of the need to provide children with opportunities to be alone and to quietly pursue their learning without the necessity to collaborate. Collaboration itself often requires a degree of extroversion, including putting ideas forward, defending positions, negotiating and presenting. Cain argues that the opportunity for more 'solo' time not only caters for those children who prefer it but may also teach all children to get in touch with themselves and develop deeper thought and creativity. Mihaly Csikszentmlhalyi (1998) is well known for his work on the concept of 'flow', which describes the state in which the individual is completely absorbed in a task – so fully immersed in what they are is doing that they barely notice time passing or events around them. At a more fundamental level, we have all experienced the drudgery of being forced to read, write or find out about something in which we have absolutely no interest and to which we make no connection. Good teachers know how to bring new ideas and new contexts to students in engaging ways, but there is nothing quite so engaging as having the opportunity to explore something in which you are personally invested.

In summary, when they have opportunities to determine and pursue their own interests as a learner, students:

- are more **motivated** they are interested and feel their interests have value
- are more likely to stay **on task and focused**
- **can apply** the skills and strategies they have gained in their shared inquiry experiences, and can therefore demonstrate their facility with these skills
- are **less reliant** on their teacher or peers and so develop important **self-management** skills such as planning, organization, time management and goal setting
- learn by watching and listening to **peers** exploring a wide range of topics and interests
- **share their skills** and knowledge in their particular areas of expertise with others – building self-esteem and deepening learning by teaching others
- have opportunities to be **in their element** – to learn in a state of 'flow' and build on talents and passions
- gain confidence and self-belief
- have opportunities to **work and learn alone** rather than collaboratively. For some students this time is precious and when they feel most 'in their skin'.
- can often **make better connections** between their interests and the general classroom program or curriculum
- can **teach and inspire others** about new content or ideas.

WHAT IS PERSONAL INQUIRY?

PERSONAL INQUIRY IS NOT...	PERSONAL INQUIRY IS...
teachers getting on with other things while the students have free time	teachers working side by side with students to support their learning
a treat students get if they have finished all their 'real' work	real work: a rigorous and valued part of the program
about the product – such as producing posters, slideshows and art works	about the process – the product is part of that but is not the main focus
separate from the curriculum	a way of helping students see their passions in connection with the curriculum (and beyond)
for 'gifted' students or 'early finishers'	for all students
dependent on access to technology	about learning in all sorts of ways, using primary and secondary sources, digital and non-digital products
about content – learning about 'stuff'	about learning to learn while deepening understanding in an area chosen by the student
unstructured	well structured with clear routines and expectations
outside the assessment agenda	a great context for assessment of learning skills and processes
simply following a passion	possibly following a passion or an opportunity to explore something you know little about but are interested in
about always learning on your own	about learning independently *and* being a connected part of a community of learners

An in-depth personal inquiry is a great way to see what students understand about the process of designing a journey of learning for themselves as well as their understanding of the issue or content they are inquiring into.

SOME SUGGESTED APPROACHES

Providing students with opportunities for personal inquiry can be done in a range of ways. There is no one 'best' way to set up a personalized inquiry routine. The approach that will best work for you will depend on a number of factors, including:

- the students' and teachers' prior experience with and confidence in inquiry approaches
- the school's timetable and other logistical factors
- the students' age/developmental readiness
- the resources and physical set up of the learning environment.

THE PASSION PROJECT

Passion projects offer students an opportunity to inquire into something in which they have a high level of interest over a substantial period of time. A project may run for 4–8 weeks, allowing the student time to plan, investigate, create, share and evaluate. Students may collaborate around shared interests or work individually, but generally they work on their own. An in-depth personal inquiry is a great way to see what students understand about the process of designing a journey of learning for themselves as well as their understanding of the issue or content they are inquiring into. In the IB Primary Years Program, the celebrated 'exhibition' that occurs in the last stage of their primary schooling proceeds in much the same way. I have seen a number of powerful exhibition processes over the years and they always remind me of the capacity of students to step up when they are given the responsibility of designing and managing their own learning.

Passion projects tend to work most effectively when there has been explicit attention to the skills and processes required for effective inquiry in the lead up to the project. The project requires students not only to select an issue/question/problem/action to work on, it also asks them to design a pathway for investigation. They are much more able to do this when they have the language of inquiry and a conscious 'tool kit' of strategies. Without this, a passion project can be, at best, a matter of simply finding out interesting information about a topic (the kinds of projects we remember doing!), and at worst, a waste of precious learning time as children wander, lost, in a haze of uncertainty.

When students have some understanding of how to construct a journey of inquiry and when the classroom environment already favors independence and choice, then passion projects can be a great experience for everyone. There are several ways that teachers can design and support passion projects with their students. The following example is only one approach to the process.

DESIGNING A PASSION PROJECT

Stage 1: Reflect on the learning assets, skills and strategies that students have been developing. What can we do? What do we know about how to design an inquiry?

Stage 2: Spend time (if needed) identifying and sharing passions with each other. Talk to parents, teachers and other students about their passions and build lists of possible projects. Share examples of individuals who have inquired into or worked with their passions in some way.

Stage 3 (optional): Model your own passion project before or during this period.

Stage 4: Co-construct some criteria for selection of a focus. Consider the questions: 'Can we inquire into anything?' 'What would make something inappropriate or unrealistic?' 'How can we decide what will make a good focus for our passion projects?'

Stage 5: Have students select a focus and share a justification for it. Use a class blog or system that allows students to give each other feedback.

Stage 6: Brainstorm some possibilities for the elements of the process that might be important for everyone to include. The design of the investigations is largely up to the students, but there should be some agreed elements, such as identifying prior thinking/knowledge; using more than one source of information; sharing learning in an authentic way with a real audience; and connecting to the community.

Stage 7: Establish a system for regular conferring with individuals throughout the duration of the project. This is not an opportunity for teachers to vacate the space! Passion projects need teachers constantly moving around the room working side by side, tracking, monitoring, noticing, recording, questioning and helping kids stay focused.

Stage 8: As the projects develop, consider offering some 'tool kit' sessions when you notice there is a need. Small workshops can be offered to those who need it on the use of apps and other digital tools for researching, recording and creating or on ways to organize resources or credit sources of information. A team teaching set up, at least during passion project time, can be very helpful. As one person roves the room, another can be offering targeted teaching groups.

Stage 9: Consider how the projects will be shared and with whom. Develop some success criteria for students to use as they complete their project. Keep the audience as real as possible. Invite the community in. Upload to sites that allow for global sharing. Seek feedback.

Stage 10: Reflect and evaluate. This should be happening the whole way through the process but it is important to allow time at the end to have students identify what they learned – about their passion but also about themselves as learners.

iTIME – WEEKLY OPPORTUNITIES FOR PERSONAL INQUIRY

Providing regular opportunities for self-driven learning is often seen as having its genesis in the work of the extraordinarily successful company Google. Google's innovative 80/20 approach to work time meant that employees were given 20% of their work time as time to explore ideas that interested them, regardless of what their official role or area of focus was for the remaining 80%. The proviso was that the project they worked on had to be linked in some way to the company's overall work and it had to be shared with the company. This is essentially giving people time 'off' to be innovative, to foster creativity and to build a strong sense of ownership and motivation. It is said that many of the most successful apps and programs were born out of the 20% innovation time that developers were afforded.

When applied to the school setting, this approach can take numerous forms. The passion project (as explained) may be a significant portion of the school year, but by contrast, 'iTime' is a regular, weekly opportunity so becomes part of the fabric of school life throughout the year. It is variously described as 'iTime', 'genius hour' and 'oasis time', but the broad concept is the same. Teachers set aside a regular time each week for students to work on initiatives of their choosing. This may be in the form of a question they want to explore or a skill they want to develop or a product they want to create. Like passion projects, iTime sessions need systematic planning, record keeping and self-assessment. Itime is not 'free time'; it is focused and rigorous with high accountability. The content for iTime may stretch across the curriculum. For example, some students may be working on technology-based projects while others are working in the arts. Single subject teachers contribute to iTime as a resource for students interested in extending their skills in one of the specialist areas.

There is no single approach to iTime. Some teachers limit the number of sessions students can spend on a project, preferring them to experience a range of investigations over the year. Others allow students to negotiate timelines according to their current interest. Some teachers present iTime as an individual opportunity while others offer collaboration around common interests. The advantages of iTime are numerous and many have already been documented. At the time of writing, I am working with several schools who have set aside weekly opportunities for personal inquiry, and the response from both teachers and students is overwhelmingly positive.

PERSONAL INQUIRY PROJECTS: HOW DO THEY DIFFER FROM THE PROJECTS WE GREW UP WITH?

I still see them in corridors and classrooms in schools in 2015: brightly colored, large sheets of card on pinboards with carefully written headings such as 'Explorers of Early Australia', painstakingly written factual snippets glued to the card accompanied by photocopied pictures and, of course, a border. These were the projects of my childhood. They taught me more about how to use an encyclopedia and how to do bubble writing in my heading than they did about the long forgotten content itself. These projects have no place in the contemporary classroom.

Personalized inquiry projects need to go beyond the poster. The following table outlines some essential differences.

TRADITIONAL PROJECTS...	PERSONAL INQUIRIES...
are about a 'topic'	are driven by an authentic question/problem/purpose
are often done at home	are part of the school day
require the same presentation format for all	allow multiple forms of expression
are a collection and regurgitation of information	require analysis and evaluation of information
have few guidelines	are guided by co-constructed criteria
are teacher determined (although students may have chosen the topic)	are negotiated with the student through conferencing with teacher and peers
often lead to poor quality feedback	include specific and on-going feedback
entail limited use of (generally) secondary sources	use and cite primary and secondary sources

ONE APPROACH TO ITIME

At Elsternwick Primary School in Melbourne, Australia, teachers introduced iTime to their year 3/4 classrooms. At the time of writing, the iTime routine was still developing and being refined; however, some useful processes have emerged:

Project proposals: students devise a proposal for how they will use their itime. This proposal is shared with peers for feedback and then checked by teachers who can confer with students if they feel they need to refine their ideas in any way.

Charts and checklists: having them document and display their progress on a group chart encourages student accountability.

Not just learning about, but learning to do: A key element of the proposal is the inclusion of a learning asset goal. Students consciously work on skills and dispositions while they are exploring their question.

Create agreements: when students have the opportunity to learn in highly independent ways, those who find self-management and self-regulation difficult can be challenging. Working with students to create agreements about behavior in itime means there are clear criteria for goal setting, self-assessment and behaviour management.

Limit time: for this age group in particular, we have found that students tend to be more productive when they have a known time budget. Students in the year 3/4 cohort at Elsternwick have two iTime sessions to work on a project. If students need more time, they may continue to work on it as part of home learning, but this is not mandated. At the end of a three-week cycle, students share their work with each other (gallery style), provide simple feedback and then consider their proposal for the next cycle.

Avoid last session on a Friday: iTime needs to be given the same value as other aspects of your program. When this kind of learning is relegated to the final session of the week, it is positioned as potentially less important or significant than other learning opportunities.

Build in goal setting: passion-based learning is a wonderful vehicle for students to work on personal goals as learners. By including a focus on strengthening their learning capacity, we prevent this time from simply being about 'doing a project' and value it as another context in which to grow inquiry skills and capacities.

Invite mentors from the community: invite parents and others with passions/talents/skills to come along to iTime workshops. These guests can act as inspiration and a source of support for children working on particular areas.

INNOVATION DAYS

Written extensively about by American educator Josh Stumpenhorst (see http://stumpteacher.blogspot.com), Innovation Day is an alternative way to provide students with opportunities for self-directed, personal inquiry. A full day is set aside each year/term/month for students to use in pursuit of an interest, a passion or skill development. Like iTime, the student prepares a proposal for how they will use the day, conferring with peers and teachers to ensure they set themselves up for an effective day's learning. Students with common interests are often grouped and can then work in spaces set up to support their interests (e.g. a space may be set aside as an art studio, construction area, writer's corner, technology center, kitchen or science lab).

Once interest areas have been established, community experts and mentors are invited to visit the school for the day and offer their expertise as required. The timetable is suspended for the day so specialist teachers may also be available to support students in their learning. At the end of the day or the next morning, students showcase their achievements.

WRITER'S NOTEBOOK AS A VEHICLE FOR PERSONAL INQUIRY

Oh, how I love writer's notebook! While this is primarily used as an approach to teaching writing, it is highly compatible with the concept of personal inquiry. Teachers who use writer's notebook encourage their children to collect 'seeds' that might form the basis of pieces of writing. Like most authors, student writers need to learn to notice the world around them, to find the things that appeal to and interest them and often to explore them further in order to grow those 'seeds' into writing. Writer's notebook is a highly personal and learner-centered approach to teaching writing. As students craft their pieces, they are both inquirer and author. More information on using the writer's notebook approach can be found in Buckner, A. (2005) *Notebook Know-how: Strategies for Writer's Notebook.* Stenhouse, York, ME.

PLAY-BASED DISCOVERY WORKSHOPS

Perhaps the most pure form of inquiry occurs through play. Play is the vehicle through which children investigate their world, test their theories, explore and create. From the moment they are born, young children are natural inquirers. Curiosity and a desire to solve even the most simple of problems trigger daily opportunities for discovery as the child yearns to make sense of the world around them. Teachers in the early years are often mindful of the importance of maintaining opportunities for rich, sensory, play-based experiences for their students as part of the classroom program. The loss of open-ended, hands-on exploratory time is often a sad consequence of beginning 'formal' schooling.

In an inquiry school, the early years are vital in laying the foundations for future attitudes towards and confidence in the learning experience, and teachers play a crucial role.

Early years teachers set the scene for what school is all about, and even in the most subtle of ways, they determine the young child's view of themselves as a learner. Given the power and influence that we have at this level, it is vital that we treat our role with the careful consideration it deserves.

Routines that provide children with time to explore through play are an ideal way to nurture personalized inquiry from K to 6. While some inquiry occurs spontaneously through play, observant teachers prompt, question and challenge to extend exploration.

As, for example, the five year old drops objects into a water tray, he or she may begin to inquire into what makes some materials float while others sink. Materials provided for play may trigger more sustained investigations: for example, a child who spends time in the home corner, role-playing bathing a baby, may go on to find out about how other people bath their babies and how this is the same and different from family to family.

In a play-based or 'discovery' workshop, the teacher sets up materials around the room that act as stimulants for inquiry, and students also locate and organize materials to pursue their interests. Gradually, students come to take more ownership of the space and the way it is set up, bringing their own materials or innovating with the materials available to them in the classroom. The atmosphere in a discovery workshop is focused, lively and highly engaging. Children choose how to use their time and with whom they will learn (if they wish to collaborate). The time is highly interest based, although the teacher naturally generates interest in certain things merely through the provocations he/she chooses to place in the learners' path.

The following table outlines some common, general distinctions between what we might describe as 'free play' and a typical more inquiry-based workshop:

FREE PLAY	DISCOVERY TIME
Teacher sets up materials in the learning space.	Some materials may be set up; others are gathered by the children according to their planned tasks. Materials are often matched to the interests/questions of the children as established before the workshop.
Children can move freely between materials across the session.	Children make a plan for how they will use their time and often stay with that task for the session.
There is usually little or no explicit focus on skills and dispositions.	There is a very explicit focus on skills and dispositions.
Learning is less intentional.	Learning is intentional – children make plans for what they will do in the session/s. Learning is often in response to questions/wonderings.
Tasks are often 'in the moment' with a focus on manipulatives.	Children are encouraged to develop a project over time.
Emphasis is on hands-on engagement, play and social interaction.	Emphasis is also on investigation.
Children choose with limited teacher input.	Teachers are more proactive in guiding and supporting children.
There is informal observation of children.	Teachers observe and record for planning, analysis and assessment purposes.
Teacher planning may be minimal.	Planning for discovery sessions incudes a mini-lesson, reflection time and targeted foci for individuals and groups.
Focus may be on sharing what has been done – but less on reflection.	Sharing learning is an important part of discovery time where children are encouraged to share what they are learning and how. Reflective discourse is modeled and nurtured.

SIMPLE OVERVIEW OF A TYPICAL DISCOVERY WORKSHOP IN THE EARLY YEARS

This is a sustained learning session that allows individuals and small groups to conduct investigations of interest and meaning to them. The investigations usually involve interactions with materials and resources, but they may also be an opportunity to research a topic of interest. These investigations may last a session or may continue over weeks. Although it may appear to be rather loose and informal, the discovery workshop is highly structured and well planned.

PHASE	TASKS
Introduction	• Take a gallery style walk around the room to look at the materials/options available. • Revisit some of the projects begun in previous sessions. • Identify a focus (skills based) for attention in this session – e.g. 'today we are going to think about how we can be great collaborators and look for ways we can help others'. • Possibly demonstrate a technique children could use in the session – e.g. a graphic organizer. • Ask children to identify what they are going to work on today (they may place a name card at a photo or a table). • Identify a photographer/observer for the session and link their observations to a specific focus. • Let the children know about a table/area you might be working at if they are interested in that task (e.g. 'Some people were asking questions about colours yesterday. I am going to be over at the round table to see what we can find out about how to make different colours with paint and food dye'). • Possibly remind children about their personal goals if they have them.
Investigation	• Children move to the areas they choose to do their learning in today. There may be some time limits placed on them. • Teachers may be at particular stations for some of the time. • Teachers are generally moving around the room observing, note-taking, recording conversations, questioning, suggesting, taking video footage and photos etc. • There may be one moment in the investigating time when teachers will stop the class and gather for a quick 'mid-session' reflection or to ask the observer to report back on observations (linked to the intention of the session). • Teachers are highly active but are not directing the tasks; instead they are providing timely feedback and scaffolding.
Reflection and planning	• Students pack up materials or place a 'work in progress' sign against ongoing projects. • Teachers invite some students to share what they have been doing and what they have learned in discovery time. The teacher prompts, questions and provides feedback. • Sentence starters and other scaffolds are used to support children in thinking back over their learning. • A video or photo taken during the session may be shared, encouraging reflection on learning behavior. • Students may be invited to write about today's discoveries. • Some students may write captions for photos taken in the session. • Teachers invite children to think about and possibly record their plans for the next discovery time, encouraging children to work towards extended projects.

ZURICH INTERNATIONAL SCHOOL

MATERIALS FOR DISCOVERY WORKSHOPS

The materials placed around the room are critical to the success of discovery time and need to be thought about carefully. Some materials will be a regular part of the workshop and others will be deliberate provocations for a specific period of time.

Again, there is no one way to do this but some useful guidelines are:

- Collect materials linked with the current interests of the children.
- Aim for open ended materials that don't have a direct, narrow use (e.g. a puzzle that can only be solved in one way).
- If you have an overarching concept or shared inquiry question currently being explored by the class, then you may consider including some areas that connect with this.
- Ask children what they are interested in on a regular basis and use this to help you set up provocations.
- Avoid too many materials – clutter leads to chaos.
- Consider the presentation of materials – the aesthetic is important.

SAMPLE CENTERS/MATERIALS FOR DISCOVERY WORKSHOPS

- sequential **pictures** of things growing or changing that children discuss and put in order
- a wide variety of **seeds** that students can classify, create patterns with and eventually plant (avoid directed activities like making seed pictures – keep this open-ended)
- **freezing objects in ice** and timing how long it takes to melt – encouraging students to predict and to draw the change in shape over time
- **water with a variety of objects** that float and sink – introducing simple T charts to record thinking
- water with a variety of other substances to mix with it – some soluble, some not. Again, children should predict, test and describe each time. Include **various sized containers**, eye droppers, spoons, funnels and tea strainers.
- **paint charts/sample colour cards** to encourage children to match colour in natural objects with the paint cards
- **seed planting** and observation with magnifying glasses; photos and drawn records of growth.

- **collections** of different rocks, pebbles, shells, feathers and other natural materials to sort, classify, examine, draw and wonder about
- an overhead projector on a table, or a lightbox, with various objects that can be projected as **shadows**
- magnifying glasses, binoculars, microscopes and digiscopes, with **natural objects** to examine
- **boxes** of different sizes for creating and building
- objects that can be **pulled apart and tinkered with**
- **sensory materials** – clay, Plasticine, pipe cleaners, soft modeling wire, fabrics, buttons etc. (see also chapter 2)

FURTHER READING ON PLAY-BASED LEARNING

- http://www.discoverytime.co.nz – a useful resource in addition to the book by Brenda Martin and Gay Hay.
- https://www.facebook.com/SherryandDonna.at.irresistibleideas/photos_stream – a great Facebook page about play and learning.
- http://www.letthechildrenplay.net/2010/05/beautiful-learning-spaces-in-reggio.html – loads of great ideas.

Pinterest is a great source of images to help you think about classroom set-up. Try these pages:
- http://pinterest.com/cguerriero/inquiry-play-based-learning/
- http://pinterest.com/christaldoherty/inquiry-play-based-learning/
- http://pinterest.com/camtown/play-based-learning-ideas/
- http://pinterest.com/fcaratti/reggio-classroom-ideas/

SETTING THE SCENE FOR PERSONAL INQUIRY

Regardless of the approach you choose for personal inquiry, it's best to hasten slowly! There is a range of things you can do to build interest in and awareness of passions and interests.

- **Have students interview or survey others** about their interests and passions. Gather and share this information. Interview teachers, older students and parents. This will provide inspiration and potentially some ideas for investigation. Add these interests and ideas to the lists you create around the classroom.
- Provide students with **a set of images** that connect to different interest areas –for example, music, the environment, construction, the arts, technology, film, travel, science, different cultures, food, animals, design,

space, history, mapping/geography. Have them order the images from most to least interesting to them…. Ask students to share and compare their rankings.
- Email parents or ask them to share **their perspective on their child's interests and strengths.**
- Ask students to consider what they might be an **expert** on – something they know about and could share with others (looking after a certain kind of pet, using a particular app, drawing, dance, judo, soccer, another country, paper aeroplanes – *anything*). Invite each child to share their passion with the class in an 'ask the expert' segment.
- **Share your passions** with the students – what do *you* love learning about? Share your hobbies/interests/questions.
- Host an afternoon where you **invite people** from the parent or wider community who are experts in interesting things. Have them share their interests and passions with the students (keep it brief – this is all about stimulating curiosity).
- Share video clips that showcase young people's passions. Here are a few suggestions at the time of writing (see also, chapter 4 for ideas for stimulating curiosity).
  - http://mashable.com/2013/03/05/six-year-old-breakdancing/ – A six year old girl with amazing dance skills.
  - http://www.youtube.com/watch?v=faIFNkdq96U 'Caine's Arcade' is about a boy who makes an extraordinary arcade out of cardboard boxes. Caine shows creativity, patience and entrepreneurship.
  - http://www.youtube.com/watch?v=1cpBpIxYh7M – Ryan was only 6 when he decided he wanted to help people in an African village get clean water. He is 16 in this short clip and he talks about his foundation.
  - http://www.youtube.com/watch?v=V-bjOJzB7LY – A Ted Talk given by an amazing young girl who challenges adults about what kids can do.
  - http://www.youtube.com/watch?v=F7Id9caYw-Y – This 11 year old boy gives an impassioned speech about our food system.
  - http://www.youtube.comwatch?v=LPgJB P 17PJc&list=UUah2 qz4GmPiQTGfW4puTebQ&index=9 – A clip from the 'kids are heroes' website that profiles kids who have set out to make a difference to their lives.
  - https://www.youtube.com/watch?v=I-gQLqv9f4o – 'Kid President' gives a pep talk to students about their learning.

THE CHALLENGE OF LETTING GO

'Personalised learning means much more than adapting the presentation of the curriculum to learning styles and the different range of abilities of the students. To personalize the curriculum the school leader must build a strategy for teaching and learning that makes each individual a partner in the teaching and learning process.'
(Otero, G., 2011: 10)

True personal inquiry allows the learner to lead the way. In this chapter, I have described several different ways in which we can offer this opportunity to students, but none of them will be successful unless we truly believe in the right of our students to inquire into those things that are important to them. Personal inquiry does *not* mean we have to abandon the curriculum – far from it. Most of the things students choose to investigate can easily be connected to the curriculum, and many teachers, particularly of older students, invite their students to explore those connections by sharing the curriculum with them. Even when not directly curriculum related, the skills and motivation that results from these opportunities means that students are more likely to 'buy into' and engage in the contexts for learning that we bring to them.

Handing over choice and responsibility to students and allowing them power over what they will do means some letting go. For many of us this can be hugely confronting. We need to have open and honest communication with our colleagues about the way we feel and the challenges we face around our identity as teachers. And we need to be prepared for the 'messiness' and uncertainty that comes with shared power.

Over and over again, I hear teachers say that when they do 'let go', when they do learn to stand back and allow more voice and choice, they are humbled by what their students are capable of. Personal inquiry can give your students an opportunity to truly shine like they never have before. It also reveals gaps and challenges experienced by individuals that may be masked by collaborative and shared tasks. We can do our best teaching here because we are working with the inquirer as an individual right at the point of interest and need.

LETTING GO BUT 'HOLDING THE SPACE'

When we begin to offer more choice it is common for a few students to seem unmotivated or unable to use the time well. There are multiple reasons for this. One of the most common is that routines, systems and structures have not been sufficiently developed to support those students who find self-management difficult. While the inquiry teacher doesn't control the entire classroom, he or she remains a vital force in 'holding the space' and keeping students connected to their learning, accountable to expectations and, most of all, inspired.

One of the struggles we have as teachers is our own tendency to judge the choices that children make. We give them a choice but we can also make it pretty clear when we disapprove of the choice. Perhaps this is why some students can be tentative in saying what they really want to explore. Of course there will be some things that won't be appropriate for investigation, and criteria for that can be worked out with the class. But we need to be mindful not to shoot down their interests because we might not judge them worthy. The best teachers I see know how to take that desire to learn about something (e.g. soccer) and help the child develop a question or a focus for investigation that stretches thinking without devaluing their interest (e.g. 'How has the game of soccer changed in the last 50 years?' 'Is it a better game now than it was?' 'Why?') Using the concept list (chapter 3) with students can also help stretch out their focus and create a deeper study. Spending time in thoughtful conversation with children who need that extra support is vital. Just as we confer with students about their reading and writing, so too should we about their researching. This is not 'teacher free' learning!

We need to be like enthusiastic park rangers or deeply committed coaches. Our attitude towards this opportunity will be infectious, for better or worse. Talk up the students' learning and share it proudly with others. Show the students that you believe in them and that you are excited by their learning. Create and hold a nurturing and passionate space.

'Being around passionate people is the best way to become passionate. A passion-driven teacher is a model for her students. Teachers must be able to lead in the areas that they're passionate about (whether this be in the classroom or after school). They must demonstrate that they have lives outside of school and that they are well-balanced people. Being transparent with students and building relationships with them beyond the classroom can help drive learning – students work harder with people who matter to them.' (Vincent, K., 2011)

THINKING ABOUT iTIME

How might I find out?

- [ ] trial and error
- [ ] talk to an expert (email/Skype/FaceTime/face-to-face/phone call...)
- [ ] devise and conduct a simple survey
- [ ] watch some video clips/YouTube
- [ ] find good websites about the topic
- [ ] watch someone who knows how to do this
- [ ] look at photos/images
- [ ] read books, pamphlets, magazines, blogs
- [ ] devise an experiment to help me find out more or test an idea.
- [ ] have a go at it. Just get in there and do it – start making, building, creating, using trial and error
- [ ] use an app to help me (maybe finding out how to use the app is my project?)
- [ ] study an infographic, diagram or poster to help me understand more
- [ ] take something apart and study it more closely
- [ ] observe something carefully
- [ ] interview/survey people about it

How might I show/share my learning?

- [ ] blog about it
- [ ] design a poster/infographic
- [ ] create a slideshow
- [ ] design a pamphlet/booklet (digital or hard copy)
- [ ] make a video clip/documentary/news report
- [ ] give a short talk
- [ ] dance/role play
- [ ] use a graphic organizer using digital or hard-copy tools – a mind map, concept map, lotus diagram, fishbone, Venn diagram, T chart etc.
- [ ] compose a written piece – poem, story, report, letter
- [ ] produce photos, paintings – any form of art work
- [ ] record voice/podcast
- [ ] compose song/musical piece/music film clip
- [ ] make model (digital or 3D)
- [ ] plot a graph (using digital or hard-copy tools)

What do I need to do to be a successful, independent inquirer?

- [ ] figure out what I want/need to learn more about
- [ ] talk about my learning with others
- [ ] learn from my mistakes
- [ ] ask questions to help me learn
- [ ] plan ahead
- [ ] set a manageable goal
- [ ] stay focused on what I am doing
- [ ] try to work things out for myself
- [ ] persist with my learning even when it is challenging
- [ ] be organized and ready to begin
- [ ] ask other people for feedback
- [ ] take a risk and try new things

- [ ] go beyond the things I already know
- [ ] step outside my comfort zone
- [ ] think before I speak
- [ ] give myself encouragement
- [ ] use 'self talk' to help me through
- [ ] use my time efficiently
- [ ] be prepared to change my plan
- [ ] share my successes and failures
- [ ] explain how my thinking has changed
- [ ] use many different ways to find out
- [ ] know how to find relevant information
- [ ] use resources ethically and responsibly
- [ ] use the internet safely

- [ ] verify the information I gather
- [ ] share my learning in a way that is interesting to others
- [ ] share my learning in new and different ways
- [ ] offer my help to others
- [ ] give helpful feedback to others
- [ ] make sure I don't get in the way of other people's learning
- [ ] reflect on my learning and identify my strengths and needs
- [ ] keep my things organized and tidy
- [ ] stay curious
- [ ] enjoy my learning!

REFERENCES AND FURTHER READING

- Cain, S. (2012) *Quiet: The Power of Introverts in a World That Can't Stop Talking.* Crown Publishing, NY.
- Csikszentmihalyi, M. (1998) *Flow: The Psychology of Optimal Experience.* Harper Collins, NY.
- Juiliani, A.J. (2015) *Inquiry and Innovation in the Classroom: Using 20% Time, Genius Hour and PBL to Drive Student Success,* Routledge, NY.
- Martin, B and Hay, G. (2008) *Discovery Time.* Page Break Ltd, NZ.
- Orlick, T. (2007) *In Pursuit of Excellence.* Human Kinetics Publishing, Champaign, IL.
- Otero, G. (2011) 'Schools and Communities: Working Together to Transform Children's Lives'. Paper produced by the Centre for Relational Learning, March 22 2011.
- Pink, D. (2009) *Drive: The Surprising Truth About What Motivates Us.* Riverhead Hardcover, NY.
- Richardson, W. (2012) 'Preparing Students to Learn Without Us', Education Leadership, vol. 69 (5). pp. 22–6.
- Robinson, K. (2009) *The Element: How Finding Your Passion Changes Everything.* Penguin, London.
- Vincent, K. (2011) 'Nine Tenets of Passion Based Learning', http://blogs.kqed.org/mindshift/2011/07/nine-tenets-of-passion-based-learning/

MY iTIME PROPOSAL

NAME: _____

DATE: _____

I WANT TO USE THE TIME TO:
(discover more about/design/make/explore/test/prove/work out how to…)

because:

SOME QUESTIONS THAT MAY HELP ME DO THIS ARE:

I WILL NEED/USE:

THE LEARNING ASSET I NEED TO STRENGTHEN IN THIS iTIME IS:

THIS WILL S T R E T C H MY LEARNING BECAUSE:

_____   _____
Checked by a teacher (sign)   **Checked by a classmate (sign)**

PLANNING MY iTIME

NAME: _____

DATE: _____

TODAY I WILL:

I NEED TO REMEMBER TO DO/BE:

HOW DO I FEEL ABOUT MY LEARNING TODAY?

NEXT TIME I WILL:

TUNING IN TO MY PASSIONS

What am I passionate about?

Use these sentence starters to reflect on your strengths, passions and interests.

I **love** learning about

I am **most happy** when

My **favourite thing** to do is

I wish I could **learn more** about

I would love to **be better at**

I really **admire**

because

I would like to **make a difference** to

I am **curious** about

I get **inspired** by

I think I am **most creative** when

I often **find myself thinking** about

If I could do **one thing** all day it would be

Something I would like to do **in the future** is

ENDLESS POSSIBILITIES

What might I inquire into? Some examples to get you motivated!

- Why and how do birds migrate?
- What birds are in our school grounds? Which ones are native?
- Which animals can see in the dark and how do they do it?
- What volunteer work can kids do?
- What makes an ideal chicken coop?
- Why was Mandela such an important person?
- How can I make a great dessert?
- Can I compose my own song using GarageBand?
- What games did my grandparents play when they were young?
- How do people deal with stress?
- Why did the dinosaurs die out?
- What are the most popular sports in the world and why?
- How are soccer balls made?
- What do other kids eat for lunch around the world?
- How do you play the ukulele?
- How do you get into the police force?
- What and where are the countries in Asia?
- Who are some of the world's most famous ballerinas and why?
- What is Broadway and what happens there?
- What is yoga and why do people do it?
- What makes a healthy take-away meal?
- How does a skateboard actually work?
- Could I teach myself to write some Japanese characters?
- How do you make string puppets?
- What is patchwork quilting and how do you do it?
- How long would it take for a MacDonalds hamburger to decompose?
- What is the world's tallest building and what are some of its features?
- What does the RSPCA do?
- What can I learn about mixing colours?
- What plants grows best in this area – how should I care for them?
- How do you make earrings?
- How is money made?
- Where are Nike runners made? Why are they so expensive?
- How did Taylor Swift become so famous?
- Where are the best rock climbing places in the world?
- What is the best way to train for cross-country running?
- What dog breeds are best for city living?
- How can you train a dog?
- How safe is our school?
- How can science help me cook?
- How do volcanoes work?
- What is life like in detention centres?
- What does it take to become a doctor?
- What does Greenpeace do?

KEY ELEMENTS FOR SUCCESSFUL PERSONAL INQUIRY

FOCUS — know what you are inquiring into

PURPOSE — know why you care

CURIOSITY — stay open to possibilities

PLANNING — think ahead about how you might do this

PATIENCE — it may not happen the way you expect – stay calm and work around it

ORGANIZATION — keep it together, stay in charge

MINDFULNESS — notice yourself as you are learning

AUDIENCE — how might this be of interest/use to others?

RESPECT — your sources, the learning space, your fellow learners, your audience

TIME — keep your deadline in mind and keep it manageable

COURAGE — dare to do it differently

REFLECTION — keep asking yourself about your learning

QUALITY — aim for your best

COMMUNICATION — share in ways that engage others

HOW STRONG ARE YOUR LEARNING ASSETS?

Use the table below to help you reflect and challenge yourself to improve.

	I do this well when (example from school or home)	I find this challenging when (example from school or home)	I could strengthen this learning asset by
I am a researcher. I am curious, creative and critical.			
I am a collaborator. I am empathic, compassionate and reliable.			
I am a thinker. I am open-minded, flexible and persistent.			
I am a self manager. I am resilient, responsible and reflective.			
I am a communicator. I am confident, responsive and respectful.			

'Any fool can know.
The point is to understand.'

(Albert Einstein)

~ C H A P T E R ~

eight

Staying accountable:
WHAT DOES ASSESSMENT LOOK LIKE
IN THE INQUIRY CLASSROOM?

INTRODUCTION

In an inquiry classroom, teachers view much of what their students are doing and saying through an assessment lens. As discussed earlier, the inquiry teacher is regularly inquiring into his or her students as learners and asking 'What are they revealing to me?', 'How might I respond?' and 'What next?' Teachers who use an inquiry-based approach know that assessment is very much built in to the way they plan and teach. In an inquiry classroom, 'instruction' and 'assessment' are often two sides of the same coin and the relationship between them is continuous and reciprocal. *Formative* assessment is the dominant means by which teachers and students gather evidence of growing understanding and mastery of skills in order to give timely feedback and design new learning opportunities. Summative tasks certainly have their place but it is in the process of inquiring and the journey towards deeper understanding that the most useful assessments are made.

'I would come to know that teaching begins with understanding – not getting the children to understand, but rather about my understanding of each one of them – what they understand, know and care about and how they work in the classroom. I would realize that a significant aspect of teaching was listening to, honoring and responding to children individually.' (Avery, C., 2002: 4)

A SIMPLE FRAMEWORK

In recent times, we have come to see assessment in the following modes:

- Assessment *for* learning: this occurs when teachers use the information they gather and analyze about student learning to inform their subsequent plans.
- Assessment *as* learning: this is particularly relevant to self-assessment. Students reflect on their own learning and their progress towards their goals, and design or co-design a learning path in response. Many tasks both teach and assess simultaneously.
- Assessment *of* learning: this occurs when evidence is gathered about students' achievement (often at the end of a task/unit), which is often measured against standards.

Inquiry involves teachers and learners in each of these assessment modes with the central aim always being to inform both the student and teacher about where to next.

CONSISTENCY OF BELIEFS AND PRACTICE

The principles that guide the inquiry teacher (see chapter 1) apply to *all* aspects of the process, including assessment. More than any other aspect of our work as teachers, our assessment practices can reveal to students and parents what we deem to be most important. If, for example, we assess and report on students' mathematical understandings but neglect to report on their skills as collaborators, we are sending a message about what is the more important of the two. Mandated, system-level tasks such as standardized tests have less value in the inquiry classroom and can be inconsistent with inquiry learning's underpinning principles. Many teachers have no choice about the administration of such tests but they *can* make choices about the extent to which they devote classroom time or energy to them.

KEY PRINCIPLES UNDERPINNING ASSESSMENT IN THE INQUIRY CLASSROOM

- Assessment data **informs planning throughout** a teaching and learning sequence.
- Assessment practices **inform teachers' feedback** to students throughout a learning sequence.
- Assessment is **embedded within** teaching and learning tasks – and is **ongoing** throughout a learning sequence.
- Assessment strategies and evidence are **varied** to cater for the diversity of needs and ways of learning.
- Assessment tasks are as **authentic** as possible, allowing students purposeful contexts for demonstrating their learning.
- Students are active participants in **constructing what and how** learning is assessed.
- Assessment demonstrates to students (and parents) what is **valued** by teachers.
- Students are **clear about the criteria** against which their learning is being assessed.
- Assessment is **matched to teaching and learning goals** and intentions.
- Assessment **recognizes prior learning** and demonstrates student progress in relation to this.
- Assessment focuses on more than 'knowledge' – it provides feedback on skills and values/qualities, **addressing the whole of the learner**.
- Assessment encourages students to **think about, monitor and set goals** for their own learning.

> *'The inquiry teacher is regularly inquiring into his or her students as learners and asking 'What are they revealing to me?', 'How might I respond?' and 'What next?'*

KNOWING WHAT TO LOOK AND LISTEN FOR: THE KEY TO QUALITY ASSESSMENT IN INQUIRY

This may sound very obvious but unless we know what we are looking for in students' learning, the evidence we gather will fall very short of its potential to improve learning. The aim of the inquiry teacher is to help his or her students develop deeper understanding of the key conceptual threads underpinning the inquiry. We also want our students to demonstrate a more competent use of the skills and dispositions needed for inquiry itself.

If our aim is understanding, then it is *understanding* that we need to be looking for. But how do we know what understanding looks like? How do we know when they 'get it'? 'Understanding' itself is such a nebulous term and yet we use it constantly in our teaching discourse. Taking time to explore the nature of understanding itself can help teachers and students refine their assessment.

The literature exploring the complex nature of understanding sheds some light on what it looks like. Various frameworks and taxonomies are available to assist teachers to gather more valid evidence and to better determine the needs of the student. A selection of these frameworks is shared here. Each can help us examine student learning in a more informed way and together they provide useful ways to sharpen our focus and know what we are looking and listening for.

UNDERSTANDING UNDERSTANDING!

Wiggins and McTighe's excellent work on understanding has informed their well-regarded 'backwards by design' approach to planning:

'[An] important concept in assessment lies in our understanding of learning and the learning process and a recognition that learning involves much more than just taking in information and giving it back. It involves constructing meaning and making sense of things, seeing things from a different perspective and truly developing an understanding of what [students] are learning.' (McTighe in Cullen, 2011).

This work has helped teachers learn to structure tasks so they provide better insight into student learning and so they simultaneously promote understanding. Importantly, these ways of seeing and thinking about learning for understanding help us move on from simply assessing knowledge.

Assessment of knowledge is a fairly straightforward, black and white task. Generally, you either know it or you don't. I might, for example, know the names of the various organs and even systems within the human body and I might even sound like a real authority on the topic as I list them all, but this does not mean I understand how those systems work or what it is that I can do to help maintain the health of those systems. I may need some basic knowledge of components within the systems to help me get to the understanding. Simply assessing whether I can, for example, correctly label the parts on a diagram assesses my retention of information but not my understanding of the concept.

So, how can we design tasks and ask questions that move student thinking beyond simply 'knowing' and toward understanding? Wiggins and McTighe's facets of understanding, adapted for the following table, are a very helpful framework.

WINDOWS ON UNDERSTANDING *(Adapted from Wiggins and McTighe, 1998)*

WINDOWS ON UNDERSTANDING	SAMPLE QUESTIONING	SAMPLE TASKS / ROUTINES
Explanation *The student can provide justifiable accounts of phenomena, data, and events. Can describe the who/what/when/how/why of something*	Can you explain? How does that work? Why does this happen this way? Can you give me an example of…? What are some of the parts of…? How is this like…? What would happen if…? What would you tell someone who didn't know about this? How did this get to be this way? Why did this happen? What is the evidence for…? What makes you say that?	classroom expo/gallery/print walk create a product (clip, slideshow, diagram, model) to teach someone else consequence wheel concept map statements linking key words oral presentations/reports/small group interviews/podcasts 5 whys explanation game*
Interpretation *The student can show the idea in alternative ways and add a personal dimension/insight*	What does…mean to you? How would you illustrate that? What does this remind you of? Can you find something to symbolize that idea? How is…like….? Does this matter? Why? What's the big idea in this? How else could you show that idea?	creating and using metaphors and symbols art works (drawings, sculpture) mind maps and other graphic organizers freeze frames dance creating or locating suitable music to illustrate the concept writing narrative/poetry to explain the concept headlines*
Application *The student can apply what they have learned to a new context.*	How could you use this? Here is a problem – how could we solve it? What would you need to make this? To fix this? To complete this? To create this? How would you help someone in this situation? What would you do differently? What will you do now that you know this? Can you use what you know about…to do…? If we were in this situation, how could you use this? Where else would this be useful?	action projects – local and global expos models, art works problem-solving challenges personal goals/action plans community action campaigns creating websites using social media to spread the word

* Details of these thinking routines can be found at <u>www.visiblethinkingpz.org</u>.

WINDOWS ON UNDERSTANDING (CONT'D)

WINDOWS ON UNDERSTANDING	SAMPLE QUESTIONING	SAMPLE TASKS
Perspective *The student can see the bigger picture, identify what it is not as well as what it is, and can see how this connects to other things.*	What would…say/feel about this? What other views are there? What is the opposite of what you understand? What doesn't belong here? How might this look from…? Is there another way of looking at this? Why does…feel this way? Is there enough evidence? What are the positive and negative aspects? What was…trying to make you feel/see? What are the negative/positive ways of looking at this? What isn't this about?	role play question in role de Bono's 6 Thinking Hats debates PMI writing point of view articles circle of viewpoints* tug of war*
Empathy *The student can identify different ways of thinking about this. They can see it from a different viewpoint and can see the value in other viewpoints.*	What would…feel about this? What would it be like to be…? What is useful or valuable about this point of view? What do you think…is trying to make us see/understand? Why might they have said/done that?	role play simulations stepping in the shoes of others perceive, know, care about*
Self-knowledge *The student can identify how they have come to understand, where they might be biased, how their learning might be limited by their own views and what they still need to learn.*	How have your ideas about this changed? How has your thinking changed? What do you understand now? What do you still need to find out? How have you learned about this? How have you formed your views? How are your views different from others? Why? What has influenced your learning about this? What questions remain for you? Where are the gaps in your thinking?	revisiting and evaluating initial thoughts about the topic reflective journals learning journeys reflective blogs sentence starters paired interviews PMI I used to think but now I think* 3-2-1 bridge*

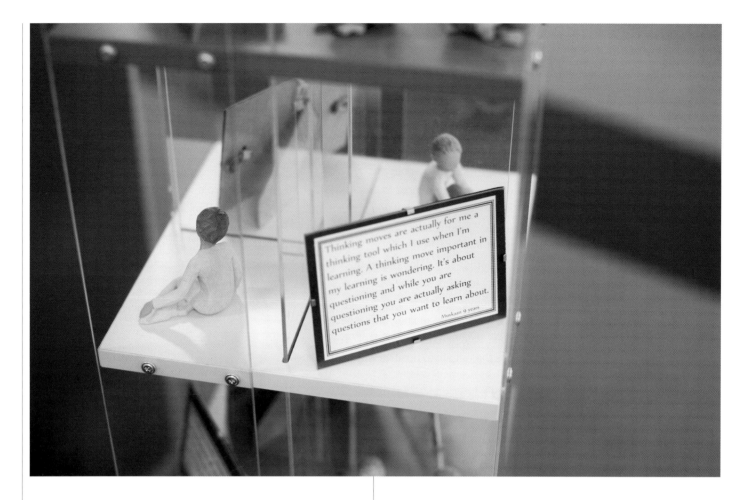

Thinking moves are actually for me a thinking tool which I use when I'm learning. A thinking move important in my learning is wondering. It's about questioning and while you are questioning you are actually asking questions that you want to learn about.

Muskaan 9 years

HOW ARE THE 'WINDOWS ON UNDERSTANDING' HELPFUL FOR US AS INQUIRY TEACHERS?

The elements described in the previous table can help us design and co-design tasks that build understanding, skills and dispositons. For example, when students are asked to take on a role to defend something they do not believe in, they demonstrate their ability to empathize with alternative points of view *and* build a deeper understanding of an issue. When we ask students to reflect on what they learned, how they learned it and the questions they still have, we are building self-knowledge *and* getting evidence of the degree to which they are noticing their learning (metacognition). These 'windows' can be used both formally and informally. As we observe students and listen to their utterances during discussion, we begin to recognize explanation or interpretation, for example. Further, we can ask questions that deliberately elicit understanding. We build and assess understanding at the same time.

David Perkins (1998) provides a similar set of indicators of deeper understanding. These indicators can be very useful when designing tasks for the development and/or demonstration of student understanding. An adapted list is provided here.

- **Explanation:** Can the student explain the idea and share its meaning?

- **Classification:** Can the student analyze and codify the idea/information?

- **Exemplification:** Can the students describe, model and illustrate the idea?

- **Transfer:** Can the student see and make connections between this idea and others?

- **Justification:** Can the student support their claims/ statements/answers with examples/evidence?

- **Comparison:** Can the student identify common and contrasting characteristics of the idea/phenomena?

- **Generalization:** Can the student see patterns and offer generalizations (rather than just facts) about the topic/phenomena?

- **Action:** Can the student put the idea into practice? Can they use it and apply it?

- **Metacognition:** Can the student identify how they know and what they need to know/do next to deepen understanding?

BIGGS' SOLO TAXONOMY

John Biggs' (1982) SOLO taxonomy sets out to describe increasingly sophisticated levels of student understanding of a subject. Teacher familiarity with this taxonomy can be enormously helpful in knowing what to 'look and listen' for, how to design quality questions and learning tasks, and also in the moderation of assessments with others. The taxonomy, which stands for 'Structure of Observed Learning Outcome', provides five levels of understanding that can be helpful when analyzing student learning.

PRE-STRUCTURAL	The student seems to have missed the point, the task/idea has not been understood or what is done lacks relevance or connection to the intended outcome.
UNI-STRUCTURAL	The student has included/responded to only one or a few relevant aspects of the idea/task. Responses are simple and obvious.
MULTI-STRUCTURAL	The student has responded to/included several aspects of the task/idea and made some connections but without explaining their significance.
RELATIONAL	The student shows multiple connections between ideas and can explain their significance.
EXTENDED ABSTRACT	The student has a higher conceptual understanding. Connections have been made to new topics/areas, and the work goes beyond the topic/idea.

HOW IS THE SOLO TAXONOMY OF UNDERSTANDING HELPFUL FOR US AS INQUIRY TEACHERS?

The SOLO taxonomy helps us think more deeply and carefully about what the student may or may not be revealing to us. It also assists us to create tasks that deliberately help students make connections between elements of an idea. In many ways, the SOLO taxonomy explicates the work of John Dewey, who wrote extensively about deep understanding arising from our capacity to see connections – to see ideas as part of a whole, not an end in themselves:

'To grasp the meaning of a thing, an event, or a situation is to see it in its relations to other things: to see how it operates or functions, what consequences follow from it, what causes it, what uses it can be put to. In contrast, what we have called the brute thing, the thing without meaning to us, is something whose relations are not grasped...The relation of means–consequence is the center and heart of all understanding.'
(Dewey, pp. 137, 146).

When we encourage students to think about how their discoveries connect to other concepts they have learned, we assist them to develop a higher level of understanding. When stated in simple terms, the SOLO taxonomy can also be shared with students and used for self-assessment purposes at any stage in an inquiry. Some examples of self-assessment questions are provided in the following table.

THE SOLO TAXONOMY FROM A STUDENT'S PERSPECTIVE

PRE-STRUCTURAL	I can't think of anything. I don't get it. I don't have any ideas about this.
UNI-STRUCTURAL	I have a couple of ideas about this but I need help to think of more.
MULTI-STRUCTURAL	I can think of lots of ideas about this and can give several examples.
RELATIONAL	I can give examples *and* make connections between different ideas. I can explain why this is important.
EXTENDED ABSTRACT	I can see how all of this connects to other things I know about. I can see the bigger picture and make predictions/inferences based on this.

BUILDING A PICTURE OF UNDERSTANDING IN PARTNERSHIP WITH STUDENTS

One of my favorite questions to pose to students is 'How do you know you understand something?' If we take time to think about that question ourselves or to discuss it with others, the complexity of understanding is quickly revealed. Within this complexity, however, common themes emerge. These common themes often resonate with the expert frameworks above. When I ask students to share what they believe to be evidence of understanding, I most commonly get the following responses:

You know you understand when…
- you can teach someone else about it.
- you can explain it in different ways.
- you can give lots of examples.
- you know what it is as well as what it isn't.
- you know how other people think about it.
- you know when there is an error or anomaly in an example.
- you can make links between it and other things.
- you know how you learned it and what you still have to learn.

I commonly use this exercise to assist students in being better able to demonstrate understanding to themselves, teachers and parents. When we agree on what might constitute understanding, we can design tasks or select evidence of progress accordingly. This is true for both teachers and learners.

The following checklist was developed in conjunction with a year 5/6 group in response to the challenge to show what understanding looks like. The checklist can be used to design tasks and also to collect evidence/artifacts for portfolios, student conferences or three-way reporting conversations.

SHARING EVIDENCE OF MY LEARNING

WHAT'S THE BIG IDEA?

(document understanding goal/s here)

WAYS I CAN SHOW MY UNDERSTANDING	✔	EVIDENCE (WHERE FOUND OR WHEN DEMONSTRATED)
I can explain/teach this to someone else.	☐	
I can give examples of this.	☐	
I can explain and justify how this connects to me and my life.	☐	
I can show this idea in more than one way.	☐	
I can use this idea to make/create/improve something.	☐	
I can explain what this is *not* as well as what it *is*.	☐	
I can share different points of view/opinions/perspectives about this.	☐	
I can make connections between this and other events/topics/ideas. I can show how this is the same as and different from other events/topics/ideas.	☐	
I can show how my thinking about this has grown/changed over time.	☐	
I know what I could find out more about. I know what I still don't know.	☐	
I can explain why this is important and how it can be used in different contexts.	☐	
I can transfer this to another context/situation. I can use this somewhere else.	☐	

HOW MUCH DO I GET IT?

A capacity matrix is another way to invite students to self-assess their understandings and share their thinking about their own learning. Students can colour in or tick where they see themselves along the continuum.

LEARNING OBJECTIVE:				
I have heard of this but I don't know what it means and I don't get it.	I get some parts of this but I am still confused and need help.	I need some help but I mostly get it.	I get it!	I get it and I can teach others how!

Webb (1997) similarly suggests a four-part framework to help distinguish between shallow and deeper understanding. Not dissimilar to Bloom's taxonomy, Webb argues that lower-level understanding is indicated when students simply recall. Understanding is increased as tasks demand classification, organization, strategic thinking, and finally 'extended thinking', where students are designing and creating in order to solve problems.

Such frameworks and taxonomies are important in informing our assessment of, as and for learning. They remind us that the tasks we construct for students, in themselves, can help or hinder the extent to which students reveal their learning to us. Assessment requires a well-informed repertoire of strategies and techniques and an understanding of understanding.

Being aware of the ways understanding can be demonstrated should not remain 'secret teachers' business'. Invite students into the conversation and build their capacity to select their own ways of sharing what they know and understand.

INQUIRY-BASED ASSESSMENT: NO SINGLE PATH

Over the many years I have worked in the field of inquiry-based teaching and learning, I have been privileged to witness various ways in which expert teachers weave formative assessment into inquiry learning journeys. These teachers bring an assessment 'disposition' to all they do: questioning strategically, listening carefully to student talk and consciously analyzing what students' work reveals to them. Their feedback to students then becomes more immediate and, ultimately, transformative. As I watch these teachers, it is obvious that no single assessment principle or practice is guiding their interaction with students. Rather, they have a 'suite' of practices that is activated throughout the inquiry process and these practices enable them to give students timely and specific feedback as well as inform their own subsequent planning.

PRACTICE
1
Clarify your learning intentions starting with the *why*.

PRACTICE
2
Involve students in the process.

PRACTICE
3
Activate and analyze prior learning.

PRACTICE
4
Keep checking in on learning.

PRACTICE
5
Include self and peer assessment.

PRACTICE

1

Clarify your learning intentions starting with the *why*.

SEE THE BIG PICTURE

Much has been made in recent years of the importance of sharing 'learning intentions' with students. An inquiry-based approach to this is discussed below. Before we can share our intentions (or even co-construct them) we do need to clarify what they are in our *own* heads. This might sound like a given but it is surprising how often, in the busy rush of daily classroom life, we can lose sight of *why* we are asking students to do what they are doing. Having a foggy idea of learning intentions can also result from the misconception that inquiry is simply a matter of 'letting the kids go' and allowing them to discover whatever they please. While there are certainly some moments when this very open approach is desirable, good inquiry-based teaching is informed by thoughtful consideration of the learning that students will be working towards.

Clarity of intentions doesn't mean having a watertight lesson or unit plan with every achievement standard and objective clearly mapped. It is actually about allowing time for our *own* thinking processes to reflect on the purposes behind our teaching plans. Clarity begins when we ask ourselves some simple yet powerful questions:

- Why is this important?
- Why are we doing this?
- How is this relevant and meaningful to our students?
- What do we hope students will come to understand?
- What skills and dispositions do we want to strengthen?

Establishing the big picture intentions for any journey of inquiry is the most significant conversation a teacher can hold with themselves and/or others. We may not know exactly how the students will get there (and our intentions may change along the way) but we must begin with purpose.

For most inquiry journeys, there are a few critical components to the broad learning intentions:

1: Conceptual understanding goals
Example: *Living things that share a habitat often depend on each other for their survival.*

2: Knowledge goals These may or may not be part of the assessment agenda. They are generally required to help build conceptual understanding but, in themselves, are lower-level facts.
Example: *Dead and dying trees can provide habitat for parrots.*

3: Skill goals
Example: *As researchers, students will learn how to better judge the 'worth' of a website by locating its author and triangulating the information (that is, checking to see whether the same information exists in at least two other locations).*

4: Dispositions
Example: *Students will have opportunities to demonstrate persistence in seeking and clarifying information online.*

Assessment of, for and as learning is more useful when teachers have spent time clarifying what it is the inquiry is really all about. Sometimes it helps just to capture the focus of the inquiry in one word, or one big idea. If the intentions become too detailed and complex, both teachers and students can become overwhelmed. Keep it simple and make sure you take time to talk this through with colleagues. When we are clear about what it is we want students to learn, we ask better questions, make more useful observations and provide more relevant feedback.

The feedback we provide to students based on our assessment should be:

- linked to intentions or goals
- tangible and easily understood by the learner
- specific
- able to be acted upon
- personalized
- timely
- ongoing
- consistent.
(Wiggins, G., 2012: 10)

through multiple lenses

A story of learning...through multiple lenses.

How does it change?

Understandings

Everyday materials can be physically changed in a variety of ways.

People use science and scientific thinking in their everyday lives.

Objects are made of materials that have observable properties.

How can water change?

SHARE YOUR INTENTIONS

Many past teaching practices have been akin to giving students a jigsaw puzzle without the picture on the lid of the box! When we make 'learning intentions' clear to students, they are more likely to make connections to those intentions as they engage in tasks. Knowing why they are doing what they are doing is critical to developing deep understanding and more valid assessment. Within an inquiry-based classroom, this principle can be applied in a number of ways. Constructing and displaying a powerful 'compelling question' (see chapter 4) acts as a focusing device and provides context. Displaying 'understanding goals' to students, in language that is accessible to them, also invites them into the purpose of the inquiry. Like the deepening of shades on a paint colour chart, students notice the gradual deepening of these understandings as the inquiry proceeds. Similarly, the intentions we have for students to develop particular *skills* as a result of the inquiry they are undertaking can also be made public and transparent to the students themselves (see chapter 6). When teaching and learning intentions are explicit, students are clearer about what it is they are expected to demonstrate through assessment tasks.

While it is important to have clarity about our intended learning outcomes and to be open and transparent with students, poor management of learning intentions can restrict the act of inquiry itself. Inquiry is about discovery. It is about the student experiencing the 'light bulb' moment when they make a connection or see a pattern. When teachers provide lengthy detail about what students 'will' be learning in a lesson, students could be forgiven for being less inclined to

want to investigate it. When learning intentions are broader (e.g. learning how to give everyone a fair go when working in a group), there is still plenty of room for discovery. Even better, if we frame the intention as a question ('How can we give everyone a fair go in a group?') we help focus student thinking and we encourage an inquiry mindset, and now this becomes a question to explore rather than an objective to be mastered. As students reflect on the question (during and after an experience) their discoveries help build criteria that can be used for subsequent self-assessment.

While inquiry teachers need to keep open to possibility and the unexpected in any lesson, they also need to have clarity about the bigger picture'. When they share this big picture with students, they let them in on the secret and ensure that assessment is not something done to students but rather with them.

The following table provides examples of learning intentions used for different classes, framed as questions. Each example pertains to a specific lesson within a broader inquiry.

These intentions are shared with students, and at times are *constructed with* the students. The intentions in the far right column are specific to that lesson, but often reflect a 'unit wide' focus of skill building.

SAMPLE 'SPLIT-SCREEN' INTENTIONS (LESSON LEVEL)

OVERARCHING, UNIT-LONG COMPELLING QUESTION	SPECIFIC LESSON FOCUS: 'CONTENT'	SPECIFIC LESSON FOCUS: 'PROCESS'
YEAR 1		
What can we learn by investigating other cultures?	How do children live in Japan?	**Researchers:** How can we ask people questions to find out information?
YEAR 4		
How does the human body work and how can we look after it?	What have we learned so far about body systems?	**Thinkers:** How can we use our thinking to make connections?
YEAR 5		
How and why is light so important in the natural and built environment?	What do we know about shadows?	**Communicators:** How can we explain and test out our theories?
YEAR 5		
How and why does the earth change?	How do naturally occurring events change our school grounds?	**Communicators:** How can we explain a science idea clearly and compellingly?
YEARS 3/4		
Why and how do humans explore?	What does the term 'exploration' mean to us?	**Thinkers:** How can we use images and symbols to make our thinking visible?
YEARS 5/6		
How do the media influence our choices?	What forms of media do we use?	**Collaborators:** How can we effectively negotiate with others in a group?
YEAR K/1		
How do living things grow and change?	What can we discover about the lifecycle of a stick insect?	**Researchers:** How can we observe something carefully and gather accurate information?
YEAR 4		
How and why do we preserve memories?	What are the purposes of museums and how do they communicate to the public?	**Self-managers:** How can we plan and manage our time when we are making and creating?
YEAR K/1		
Are we more the same or more different?	What is it like to grow up on a farm?	**Thinkers:** How can we compare and contrast information and show this to others?
YEAR 2		
Are we more the same or more different?	How do people around the world shelter themselves?	**Researchers:** How can we effectively summarize information?

Teachers who use inquiry–based methodologies have a firm belief in the transformative power of ownership. When students feel they are the ones 'doing the learning' rather than the teacher 'doing the learning to them' they are undoubtedly more engaged, and with engagement comes increased potential for learning.

PRACTICE

2

Involve students in the process

HAVE STUDENTS HELP TO DESIGN ASSESSMENT CRITERIA

'Instead of telling learners what is important or what 'should' be happening, we have learned that successful quality classroom assessment in support of learning occurs when students, teachers, school leaders, and system leaders are all involved and all engaged in using assessment to support their own learning – and the learning of those around them.' (Davies, 2013:1)

When we know the criteria against which something is assessed, we are more likely to stay focused on the task, to be clear about why we are doing what we are doing and to be able to regulate what we are doing accordingly. Not knowing the criteria leaves us confused and powerless – assessment is not supposed to be a guessing game. Many teachers address this issue by carefully constructing rubrics, checklists and sets of 'success criteria' to give to their students along with a task. This is a more transparent and fair process that empowers the learner as they know what is expected and have a clearer opportunity to demonstrate what they know and can do. While there is no doubt that having criteria is better than being left in the dark, when teachers make *all* the decisions about the task and the criteria by which they will assess it, students can

still have very little agency. Teachers who use inquiry-based methodologies have a firm belief in the transformative power of ownership. When students feel they are 'doing the learning' rather than having the teacher 'doing the learning to them', they are undoubtedly more engaged, and with engagement comes increased potential for learning.

One way to give students more ownership over assessment in inquiry is to involve them in the development of the criteria by which they will be assessed. For example, students undertaking an inquiry into the question 'What does it mean to live a healthy lifestyle?' may decide to create some kind of text to inform or advise others about healthy living. Before embarking on the task, teachers and students work together to build criteria by which the quality of this text will be judged. Whether in the form of checklists, rubrics or capacity matrices, these criteria both guide the students as they compose the text and become a basis for self, peer and teacher assessment. Developing 'success criteria' can itself be done through a process of inquiry. To determine 'What makes a high quality Power Point presentation?' for instance, students can examine and analyze the characteristics of high- and low-quality examples and gradually build a framework for what constitutes a highly effective product. This framework, in turn, becomes the basis for self, peer and teacher assessment. The process of designing success criteria is powerful even when criteria have already been determined at system level. Students can, for example, devise the criteria *they* would use to evaluate a narrative and compare what they come up with a centrally produced criteria list.

Work in the field of formative assessment by Black and William (1998) and Anne Davies (2011) suggests strongly that when students are involved in decisions about what is being assessed and how, then the quality of their learning improves.

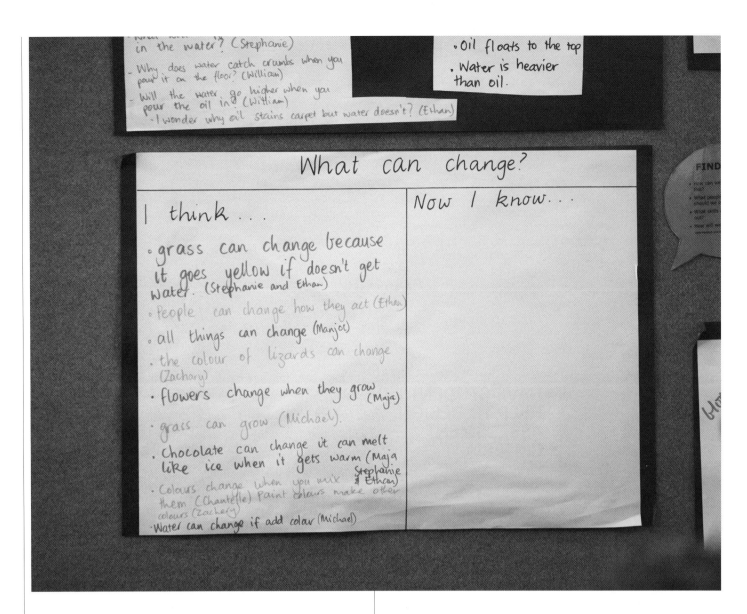

... in the water? (Stephanie)
- Why does water catch crumbs when you pour it on the floor? (William)
- Will the water go higher when you pour the oil in? (William)
- I wonder why oil stains carpet but water doesn't? (Ethan)

• Oil floats to the top
• Water is heavier than oil.

What can change?

I think . . .

• grass can change because it goes yellow if doesn't get water. (Stephanie and Ethan)
• People can change how they act (Ethan)
• all things can change (Manjot)
• the colour of lizards can change (Zachary)
• flowers change when they grow (Maja)
• grass can grow (Michael).
• Chocolate can change it can melt like ice when it gets warm (Maja Stephanie & Ethan)
• Colours change when you mix them (Chantelle) Paint colours make other colours (Zachary)
• Water can change if add colar (Michael)

Now I know . . .

FIND

PRACTICE

3

Activate and analyze prior thinking and learning

The early phase of inquiry is often glibly associated with the questions 'What do you know and what do you want to know?' Unfortunately, the real purpose of this phase is often lost in meaningless brainstorms, novelty 'hooking' activities or lists of random questions about which students may care very little. In rigorous inquiry, teachers spend time activating and assessing what it is students bring to the inquiry in terms of experiences, interests, understandings and misconceptions. The central purpose of this work is to gather information *about students' current thinking* in order to fine-tune plans made for subsequent investigation. Evidence of student thinking (in the form of work samples, recorded dialogue, video,

observation notes) should be brought to collegial planning meetings and analyzed. In true formative assessment we ask 'What is it that our students are revealing to us and what do we need to plan to do next?' The activation of prior thinking is even more powerful as part of the assessment suite when students regularly return to evidence of their initial thinking. Using the simple thinking routine, for example, of asking students to identify how their thinking has changed can give us evidence of growth at the same time as allowing students to recognize and articulate their own progress. It has long been understood that the activation of prior learning actually allows *new* learning to be better integrated into the learners' thinking. This is a perfect example of assessment *as* and *for* learning in inquiry. There are many ways we can activate and assess prior learning. (See the 'understanding check-ups' on the following page for ideas.) Data gathered about early thinking should be brought to the planning table and analysed in the light of the overall learning intentions. This information offers a baseline for assessment and helps refine plans for subsequent tasks.

As students move through an inquiry – whether it be a short, interest-based project involving a small group of five year olds or a sustained, collaborative investigation undertaken over a period of weeks by older students, teachers can glean an enormous amount of rich assessment data through the use of quality, layered teaching strategies. Even the way a teacher expects students to respond to questions in a group or class discussion can affect the extent to which students reveal their thinking. When students are constrained by larger groups, closed questioning, 'hands up' and little thinking time, discussions yield very little evidence of thinking. When most work is carried out individually and quietly rather than in groups with active, focused talk, again, there are limited opportunities for students to reveal their growing understanding or misconceptions. Focused and sustained talk, open-ended and challenging tasks and quality teacher questioning lead to more opportunities for students to reveal what they are thinking and understanding throughout an inquiry, and teachers can then use what they hear and see to plan for improvement. Reducing the amount of teacher talk and increasing the degree to which we can really listen to and observe our students as learners goes a long way to providing us with vital information about the progression of understanding throughout an inquiry. Teachers are increasingly aware of the value of reflection in helping students 'bed down' their learning into long-term memory and in helping students to become more aware of the learning they are doing. When structured reflection is a regular feature of the inquiry journey, teachers also gain another valuable opportunity to assess learning. The use of reflection strategies enables us to get a brief 'window' on thinking as the inquiry progresses and to make adjustments to our teaching in response. These reflections may be written or verbal. They may be simple responses to sentence starters (e.g. 'The most important thing I have learned so far is….') or more complex written entries in a blog. When teaching becomes an act of inquiry in itself we view learning through an assessment lens. Our planning is more responsive and our feedback more immediate and useful.

UNDERSTANDING CHECK-UPS

The following tasks can be used as 'reflective pauses'. They are relatively brief moments within a teaching journey but they can provide very rich data to inform both assessment of learning and evaluation of teaching. Once students are familiar with the techniques, they can be used even more efficiently. I describe them as 'understanding check-ups'. They are a moment to stop and think and share what we are learning and how our thoughts and learning skills are evolving. As you use these techniques, ask yourself 'What is this student revealing to me? And what do I need to do/say next?' Many of the techniques can be repeated throughout the inquiry and used to track progress, so the focus changes to assessing growth over time for each student. Use video, work samples, anecdotal notes, photos, journals etc. to keep a record of these assessments.

1: Think Pair Share

Provide students with a question/challenge/problem related to your targeted concept/skill. For example, 'What are some of the things you think we could do to help animals that are endangered?' Give students some time to think on their own – no talking to others, no hands up. They may wish to jot some ideas down. Now have them turn to a partner and share their thinking. I often suggest that they look for patterns/connections as they share. Finally, select a few pairs to share with the group. Or have pairs share with another pair and again look for connections. *Move among students and listen as they share.*

2: I used to think, but now I think

This is a simple structure for helping students think about how their understanding of something has changed. It can be done at any stage in an inquiry. Students can stand in a circle and take it in turns to share their thinking, for example. Changes in thinking may also be written and displayed throughout the inquiry.

3: 1st/2nd/3rd thinking

At the beginning of a lesson or unit have the students record a snapshot of their thinking about the concept. This may take the form of writing, a graphic organizer or an oral recording that can be reviewed later. Students repeat the task two or three times during the unit and reflect on the growth in their thinking or understanding as they do.

4: CSI

This technique stands for 'colour, symbol, image'. Ask students to think about the concept or topic you are working on. They then choose a colour, symbol and image (or picture) to represent that idea. There are obviously no 'right' answers to this; rather, it is an opportunity for students to share and explain their thinking using a very visual technique. As students share and discuss their CSI with each other, further insight into their understandings is possible. This technique has added value when repeated later in a unit to show changes in thinking. A final CSI can also act as a useful, brief summative task.

5: Confidence continuum

Create a continuum along the wall/board/ground. At one end, place a sign that reads 'very confident'; at the other end, one that reads 'not at all confident' or something to that effect. At the beginning of a lesson/unit, share the learning intentions with students. Have them stand/place their names along the continuum according to how confident they feel about their understanding of these intentions. A quick scan of the continuum will help you adjust questioning and differentiate more effectively as you teach. Return to it during and at the end of the lesson/unit and have students re-position themselves if appropriate.

6: Five whys (see chapter 4)

A powerful thinking strategy that helps students dig deeper into their understanding and demonstrate their grasp of a concept along the way. Give students a 'why' question that is central to your teaching focus. For example, 'Why is water such a precious resource?' Students then work with a partner to ask and answer a further four *why* questions that stem from this first one. The conversation pathway can be recorded and shared. Always ask students to reflect on what they noticed about their questions, their responses and their thinking during the strategy.

7: See, think, wonder

This can be done in response to a text or some specific experience or may be a more general reflection on a topic at any given time in the unit. The students may write, draw or say their response to the questions 'What did I see?', 'What did this make me feel?', 'What did this make me wonder?'.

8: Make a connection

The ability to connect one idea or experience with another is fundamental to understanding and is an excellent way to assess the development of thinking. When students can make connections, they are more likely to have a deeper and more sustained grasp of the concept. Making connections can be prompted through simple teacher questions such as 'Can you tell me something else that this reminds you of?', 'How is this like what we have just been learning about in…?',

'Can anyone make a connection to …'s idea?' Students can share their connections orally, or show the way they make connections through diagrams.

9: Forced association

This is a more creative way of making connections. Have students consider how a concept they are learning about is like something that might seem completely unrelated. For example, 'How is the human body like this apple?' The ensuing discussion quickly reveals understanding. As the unit progresses, have the students come up with their own metaphor for the topic/concept and share it with others.

10: Speed teach

This is a great way to get a quick glimpse of how students understand something. Simply ask students to form pairs or small groups. One student is 'the teacher'. In a short period of time (two minutes) ask them to explain something they have learned to the others as clearly as they can. As students 'speed teach' each other, their own understanding develops and there is an opportunity to 'listen in' to their thinking and assess accordingly.

11: Agree/disagree

Provide students with some controversial statements about which they need to form an opinion They can form a line, make a human graph, go to corners of the room or use any other means by which they can identify and then justify their point of view (e.g. do they agree or disagree?) Their justifications can give you an important insight into their understandings and their misconceptions.

12: 3-2-1

Ask students to write down three words that are important to them about the topic. They then work in pairs to reduce the list of six words they have together to two. Pairs then join to make groups of four and reduce their combined four words to one. The words can then be chanted around the class, performed as a 'freeze frame' or written on signs to be posted around the room.

13: Stand by me

In this strategy, understanding goals or skills intentions are written up on posters around the room. Ask the students to walk around the room and read them. They then move to the one they believe they understand the best and explain the reason why they have chosen to stand by that statement to others around them. The technique can be repeated, asking students which statement/concept/word they *least* understand. They then share their questions/uncertainties with others.

14: Thumbs up/down/sideways

This quick-check strategy simply asks students to use hand signals to identify how confident they are with what they have learned.

 I understand!

 I get some of it but need help on other things.

 I don't get it!

15: How is your thinking shaping up?

In this strategy, shapes represent a particular way of reflecting on a task/unit. Students can be given their own shapes to write in or a class set can be made as a prompt.

 What do you agree with? What did you already know?

 What is new learning for you?

 How are you feeling about this/your learning?

 What questions do you have?

16: Ticket of leave

At the end of a session, give students two Post-it notes each. On one they write an important thing they have learned, and on the other, they write a question or something they are still confused about. On the way out the door, they post the questions on charts or the whiteboard. They can be encouraged to loosely group them with others as they do so. Use the comments and questions at the beginning of the next session to help students see more connections in their learning. Digital alternatives such as 'Today's meet' can serve the same function.

17: Intention/reflection (see chapter 6)

Using various sentence starters, students identify something they hope they will understand more deeply or a question they believe they need answered. This intention is verbalized or written. The intentions are specifically returned to at the end of the session and students consider and share how well they have achieved that intention.

18: Sentence starters

Make a set of laminated sentence starters that prompt students to articulate their thinking and learning: for example 'An important thing I have learned is…', 'Something I could teach someone else about is…', 'I have a better understanding of…'. Distribute the sentence starters. They can be used for a round-the-circle share or in many other ways. (See chapter 6 for ideas)

19: Return to the question

Encourage students to regularly return to the compelling question and consider what they can add to the response they made to it at the beginning of the unit. Keep some records of the new thinking that is evident as the inquiry unfolds. I describe this process as 'looping' throughout a unit of study. We loop back to the original question and, each time, pick up more understanding along the way.

20: Metaphors and analogies

When students can create a metaphor to explain something, it generally suggests a deeper understanding of the concept. There are many ways to encourage students to work with metaphors. Having pictures or objects around the room to stimulate their thinking can be very powerful. Simply ask students to brainstorm all features that they believe the concept and their selected metaphor have in common. Students can also be presented with an analogy and can brainstorm the connections in groups. For example, 'How is the brain like the engine of a car?'

21: Tic-tac-toe

Prepare a grid with nine squares. The word in the center of the grid is the main topic/idea/concept you are working on. Students can quickly draw up their own, tic-tac-toe style. Teachers or students fill the remaining squares with relevant terms connected to the central concept. Students then draw a line through any three words, always including the central one. They must then create a statement connecting all three words. This is made more fun/challenging when there is a time limit applied to the creation of the statement.

22: Rocket write

Give students one minute to write down everything they think of when they think about this topic/concept/skill/idea. After one minute, they can share with others or post and do a gallery walk to compare and contrast.

23: One-word summary

At the end of a lesson or teaching sequence ask students to identify one word that best captures what they have learned. They can say it or write the word on a Post-it note and share.

24: Six-word stories

This is fun, creative and challenging. Ask students to sum up their learning by creating a six-word story. For example, a six-word story at the end of an inquiry into refugees might be: 'Displaced people may risk their lives.' (Examples of six-word stories can be found at http://www.sixwordstories.net.)

25: Pipe-cleaner gallery

Give each student a pipe cleaner. Ask them to create a symbol that represents what they understand. Have them hold up their pipe cleaners to make a 'pop-up gallery'. Call upon students to explain why they made what they made.

26: Collaborative quiz

If you need to assess students' recall or knowledge of something, then a quick, collaborative quiz can be energizing and effective and much better than a tedious pen-and-paper test. Organize students into small groups. Read out the questions and ask them to collaborate and agree on an answer. The team with the most correct answers wins each round. You can assess individuals by listening in and observing while they negotiate. Invite students to come up with their quiz questions for sections of the quiz.

27: ABC summary

Have students pick a letter out of a hat. They then have two minutes to come up with a word that has some connection to what they have been learning that begins with that letter. Quickly move around the room hearing each word.

28: Question me the answer

Provide small groups or individuals with a key word associated with what they have been learning. Small groups come up with a question to which that word is an answer. They then put the question to the class to see whether the response is their allocated word.

Good learners... also need to be aware of how their learning is going, and make strategic decisions about it... Good learners like taking responsibility for planning and organising their learning...they also monitor themselves – they have that little voice of self awareness that keeps their goals in mind.' (Claxton, G., 2002:33)

Inquiry is all about inviting students into decisions made about their learning. In an inquiring classroom, we expect students to be actively involved in thinking not just about what they are learning but how and why. Inquiry learners know themselves as learners and they question, reflect and goal set as part of their approach to investigations. It is essential to the process that we provide opportunities for students to assess their own progress as learners. As inquiry teachers, all the assessment we do is ultimately tied to growing the students' capacity to judge their own learning, to track their own progress and to set goals for improvement. An inquiry classroom without self-assessment is like a car without wheels: it is unlikely to go anywhere. While self-assessment is central to the inquiry classroom, it is not always handled effectively. To ensure that this is an effective, value-adding process, there are certain elements that need to be in place.

1: Teach students *how* to self-assess rather than assume that they can simply do it.

Judging one's own progress is a necessary but fraught skill. As with all assessment, we need to know what it is we are looking for and we need to have some kind of baseline to help us track growth. When we involve students in developing the criteria against which learning can be assessed, we better assist them to self-assess. Similarly, we can explore with students what might count as *evidence* of growth rather than simply asking them how they 'think' they might be going. Model the language of self-assessment to students. One of the most powerful things we can do is to take some evidence of our own learning (e.g. a blog post, a diagram or an art work) and show students how we might go about the process of appraising our own work in an honest and

constructive way. These 'think-alouds' can be done initially by teachers and then later by students themselves. Allowing students to listen in to the self-assessments of their peers can assist everyone in learning the skill.

2: Build capacity for self-assessment by promoting a growth mindset.

Our daily interactions with students can either nurture or stifle self-assessment. The language we use and the questions we ask on a daily basis have enormous influence on the agency students have in being able to think about and honestly comment on their own learning. Carol Dweck's work on the effect of praise on students' view of themselves as learners is salutary. If we want students to honestly assess themselves, remain open to challenges, strive for more and set and review goals, then we need to be mindful of the messages we give them as we respond to their learning. If, for example, we glibly say 'that's *fabulous'* when a student has completed a very ordinary drawing or tell them they are *fantastic* when they have simply tidied up their table and come to the floor, we are offering superlatives in all the wrong places. We want to teach our students how to attach appropriate value to effort. If everything is wonderful, there is not room for growth nor is there any need to go further. In addition, when we over-praise students' learning on a day-to-day basis, we give them the message that only we can decide whether their learning is worthy. When the teacher/s are the only ones 'passing judgment', we quickly set up a culture that is 'anti' self-assessment. When we ask students to share their own thoughts about what they are doing/learning, we give them the message that they can make such judgments for themselves. In an inquiring classroom, our first response should be to ask, not tell:

- This looks really interesting. Can you tell me about it?
- How do you feel about what you have done? What makes you say that?
- What does this tell me about your learning?
- What are you most pleased with?
- What would you like to strengthen in this?
- What are you finding challenging here? Why do you think that is the case? What might you do about it?

Once students have had an opportunity to share their view of their own learning, we can offer (if necessary) some thoughts of our own: *'I can see what you mean about this paragraph. Something else I noticed about what you have done is...'*

3: Provide feedback that not only supports and strengthens the learning but also models 'self' feedback.

Self-assessment is really about reflecting on what one has done and giving oneself feedback for improvement. To learn to do this well, we need to hear others give us feedback. We need to build resilience and to cope with feedback that is honest and constructive, so we can be that way with ourselves. John Hattie's widely respected work on visible learning cites feedback as one of the most influential forces in student learning. We give more effective feedback when we:

- Provide the learner with information about what they are doing well, e.g. 'This investigation is more convincing (than the previous one) because you have gathered your material from more than one source.'

- Avoid using feedback as a means of control (thereby diminishing learner motivation and confidence), e.g. 'You should have used more than one source for this investigation.'

- Link feedback to goals/intentions. Whether this is a shared intention or a self-generated intention, if students have clarity about the goal of the task, the feedback we give them will be much more useful and effective. Sometimes it helps to have students re-state the intention before feedback is provided. For example:

'Tell me about what you are doing.'
'I am writing a blog post.'
'What was your intention/goal?'
'To reflect on our science experiments and explain whether I think we designed a fair test.'
'Ok, so what do you think so far? Do you think the post is reflective? How do you know?'
'Would you like me to read it through and give you some feedback about that?'

When we share or co-construct learning intentions and success criteria with students, we make this kind of timely, informative and interactive feedback so much more possible.

4: Provide scaffolds that support students to self and peer-assess.

Like all assessment, self-assessment is more manageable when there are clear guidelines to assist the process. Rubrics, capacity matrices, checklists and other structures that support thinking about, and documentation of, student thinking about their own learning build the skills needed for honest and useful analysis. Again, when these are developed *with* students they become

more powerful as they are owned and better understood.

Peer assessment can be similarly powerful but requires even more careful framing than self-assessment. If we ask students to assess each other's learning in some way, then we need to be sure they are clear about the criteria they are looking for *and* the language they should use to focus on the learning rather than on the student themselves. Peer feedback is potentially negative and time-wasting if there is no explicit training in how to do it well. 'How can we give effective feedback to each other?' is a worthy process inquiry in itself. When it is used carefully, the value of peer assessment is that it can provide the assessor with insights into their own learning as well as develop a very important skill of honest and supportive communication with others. When the classroom culture has been developed to encourage trust, risk taking and honesty, peer feedback works beautifully. Taking on a 'teaching role' can be one of the most effective ways for students to learn. Hearing a student provide feedback to a peer can actually provide us with very useful information about that student's own understanding of the task. It can help build empathy and understanding and foster respectful relationships between students.

5: Ask questions that promote self-assessment

Self-assessment is something we want our students to do habitually rather than as an activity at the end of a learning task. Prompting students to regularly reflect on their learning and what they are noticing means they are more likely to get in the habit of thinking about their learning. The questions we routinely ask them can play an important role in this process:

- *What are you noticing about your thinking?*
- *How do you think you are going with this?*
- *How do you know?*
- *What would you like to see improved? How could you strengthen this?*
- *What are you going to do next? Why? How?*
- *What do you need to take this further?*
- *What do you think has improved since last time you did this?*
- *What would you like to work on next time? What goal might you set yourself?*
- *What will you need to do to achieve that goal?*
- *How will you know when you get there?*

6: Keep an inquiry mindset.

In many ways, inquiry teachers approach most – if not all – of their interactions with students from an assessment perspective. We ask ourselves, 'What is this moment/work sample/conversation/question revealing to me about this student's learning? And what might I need to do next?' Some simple strategies help ensure that assessment is never far from our thinking, including the following:

- talking less and listening more
- setting up routines that allow for more small-group/one-to-one conversations with students
- teaching students to be independent and self-managing to enable more one-to-one opportunities for deeper assessment
- using a variety of learning tasks to ensure that all students have opportunities to show their learning in ways that suit them
- stepping back, watching and really noticing what your students are doing/saying
- targeting a few students a day/week to observe closely
- regularly inviting colleagues to moderate evidence of student learning with you.

REPORTING TO PARENTS

Inquiry teachers often find they become increasingly uncomfortable with reporting formats and processes that emphasise achievement rather than progress and that focus on summative performances rather than the process students work through. In inquiry schools, sharing with parents is more a process of informing rather than reporting. While system-level requirements may well have to be attended to, schools can still make choices about how and what they will share with parents about their child's learning. Common reporting practices in inquiry schools include:

- student-led conversations about progress rather than traditional parent–teacher interviews
- annotated, portfolio-style evidence of growth over time across learning areas
- ongoing communication rather than twice-yearly reports. Many schools are using social media or purpose built apps to provide parents with learning snapshots throughout the year.
- sharing progress in relation to skills and dispositions, not just against content-based achievement standards
- including student self-assessment in what is shared with parents
- collaborative and individualized goal setting between teachers, parents and the student
- an emphasis on the progress of the student rather than comparison *between* students.

As I write, more and more schools are making use of digital technologies to re-think the way they report to parents. Some schools are using continuous reporting approaches where parents can more regularly access information on their child's learning through web-based systems. Artifacts of learning, such as videos, art works, writing and recordings, can be more easily uploaded and made available to parents as they happen and shared with their child at home. This suits the formative assessment focus in inquiry very well. Parents, teachers and students can more regularly communicate with each other throughout the year. With the increasing use of digital devices we may be seeing the beginning of the end of the twice-yearly report!

In many ways, inquiry teachers approach most – if not all – of their interactions with students from an assessment perspective.

REFERENCES AND FURTHER READING

- Avery, C. (2002) *And With a Light Touch: Learning about Reading, Writing and Teaching First Graders*, Heinemann, Portsmouth, NH.
- Biggs, J. and Collis, K. (1982) in Hook, P. and Mills, J., *SOLO Taxonomy: A Guide for Schools*, Essential Resources Educational Publishers, Invercargill, New Zealand.
- Blythe, T. *et al.* (1998) *The Teaching for Understanding Guide*, Jossey Bass, San Francisco, CA.
- Claxton, G. (2002) *Building Learning Power*, TLO, Bristol.
- Cullen, E. (2011) 'Did They Learn It?', an interview with Jay McTighe for Ontario Principal's Council, accessed at www.jaymctighe.com.
- Davies, A. (2013) 'Co-Constructing Success Criteria: Assessment in the Service of Learning', *Education Canada*, vol. 53 (3), http://www.cea-ace.ca/education-canada/article/co-constructing-success-criteria.
- Perkins, D. (1993) 'Teaching for Understanding', *American Educator,*, vol. 17 no. 3, pp. 8, 28–35.
- Perkins, D. (1998) *Smart Schools: Better Thinking and Learning for Every Child*, Free Press, New York.
- Webb, N. (1997) 'Criteria for Alignment of Expectations and Assessments on Mathematics and Science Education', *Research Monograph Number 6*, CCSSO, Washington DC.
- Wiggins, G. and McTighe, J. (1998) *Understanding by Design*, ASCD, Alexandria, VA.
- Williams, D. (2013) 'Assessment: The Bridge Between Teaching and Learning', *Voices from the Middle*, 21 (2), pp.15.

EFFECTIVE PRACTICES FOR ASSESSMENT IN INQUIRY: A SUMMARY

PRACTICE	IMPLICATIONS, EXAMPLES
Share learning intentions with students. Keep the focus conceptual rather than simply knowledge accumulation. *What do we want students to understand and be able to do? How might we know?*	• Clarify and document understanding and skill goals with the planning team. • Make these visible and accessible to students. • Keep intentions manageable and demonstrable.
Gather data about students' early thinking/understanding and skills. Use these to inform planning *and* to assess growth. *How will we find out what students currently think/understand about this?* *How will we find out what they can do in relation to our intentions?* *How will we keep records of this early data?*	• Use the 'tuning in' phase of the model as a time to 'access the known'. • Ask students to share their early thinking in a few different ways (visual, oral, written, performed). • Devise tasks that allow a range of understandings to be evidenced. • Revise learning intentions in the light of this data. • Consider how to cater for students with significantly limited or advanced understanding. • Repeat some or all of the tasks during and at the end of the process to gain comparative evidence of growth.
Use strategies that reveal thinking throughout the inquiry. *How will we question students during this task?* *What are we looking for?* *How is their thinking changing?*	• Use questioning techniques and thinking routines that probe beyond the surface. • Encourage lots of group work and talk-oriented tasks that allow you to 'listen in' to thinking. • Build in regular pauses to check up on understanding during the unit and don't wait until the end. • Treat each task as a potential assessment context, keeping the understandings and skills in mind. • Give students an avenue for revealing their developing understandings in an ongoing way (visual diaries, learning logs, reflective journals, mini-talks, portfolios, etc.).
Build in regular self and peer assessment opportunities into the inquiry journey.	• Have students self-assess against skills at the beginning of the inquiry and then again as it progresses. • Have students formulate specific goals for growth – self-assess against these. • Use co-constructed criteria for individuals to self-assess against. • Ask students to consider *evidence* to support their self-assessments (work samples, video clips, peer observations, etc.). • Vary self-assessment techniques, and combine them with quality teacher feedback.
Co-construct 'success criteria' for key tasks. *Which tasks may require specific criteria?* *What do we want to assess? How will we document and share the criteria – using rubric, capacity matrix or checklist?*	• Invite students to help build the criteria by which they will be assessed. • Provide the criteria to them as they are working on their tasks and also use to self, peer and teacher assess. • Use criteria from previous inquiries for repeated tasks and build on these. • Make criteria available to students when creating personalized inquiry.
Combine formative *and* summative tasks. *What does this task actually assess?* *What will the students be showing us an understanding of?*	• Ensure that assessment is not left until the end of the unit by gathering data throughout. • Summative tasks do not need to be overly complex or large; they may simply be a repetition of the 'tuning in' task to check growth. • Consider combining a summative task with independent inquiry and/or taking action. • Ensure that tasks actually demonstrate the skills and understandings you planned. • Consider opportunities for integrated assessment allowing several learning areas to be evidenced simultaneously.
Moderate and discuss student learning with colleagues throughout an inquiry.	• Tasks do not need to be the same across classes but concepts and key skills will often be shared intentions. • Use evidence of learning to help fine tune plans throughout the inquiry.

SAMPLE SELF-ASSESSMENT MATRIX: COLLABORATION

SKILL	NOT OFTEN	MOST OF THE TIME	ALL OF THE TIME	I CAN TEACH OTHERS	EVIDENCE WHEN DID YOU DO THIS? HOW DO YOU KNOW YOU DID THIS? (KEEP A RECORD.)
I wait my turn to speak.					
I contribute ideas to the group.					
I am willing to compromise.					
I encourage others.					
I listen well to others.					
I stay focused on the task.					
I can take on different roles.					
I can collaborate – even when I don't choose my team.					

THINKING BACK OVER MY LEARNING

REFLECTION STEMS

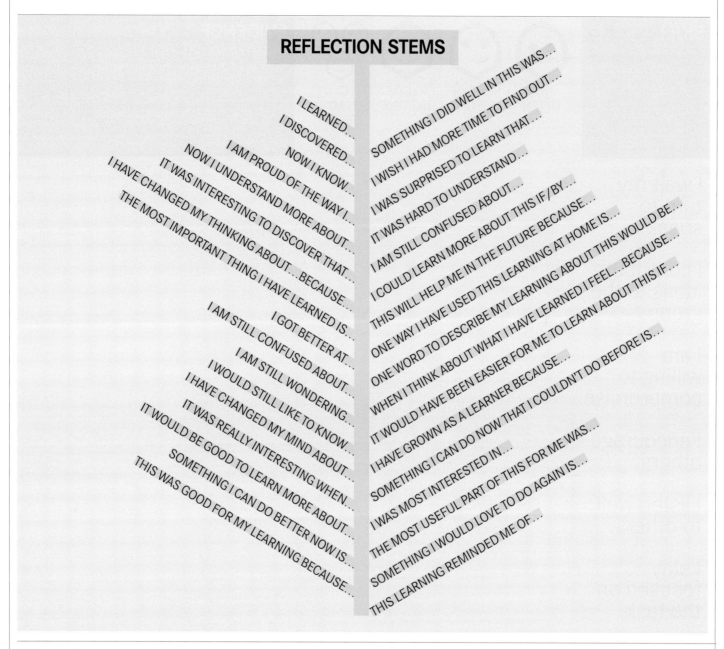

I LEARNED…
I DISCOVERED…
NOW I KNOW…
I AM PROUD OF THE WAY I…
NOW I UNDERSTAND MORE ABOUT…
IT WAS INTERESTING TO DISCOVER THAT…
I HAVE CHANGED MY THINKING ABOUT…BECAUSE…
THE MOST IMPORTANT THING I HAVE LEARNED IS…
I GOT BETTER AT…
I AM STILL CONFUSED ABOUT…
I AM STILL WONDERING…
I WOULD STILL LIKE TO KNOW…
I HAVE CHANGED MY MIND ABOUT…
IT WAS REALLY INTERESTING WHEN…
IT WOULD BE GOOD TO LEARN MORE ABOUT…
SOMETHING I CAN DO BETTER NOW IS…
THIS WAS GOOD FOR MY LEARNING BECAUSE…

SOMETHING I DID WELL IN THIS WAS…
I WISH I HAD MORE TIME TO FIND OUT…
I WAS SURPRISED TO LEARN THAT…
IT WAS HARD TO UNDERSTAND…
I AM STILL CONFUSED ABOUT…
I COULD LEARN MORE ABOUT THIS IF/BY…
THIS WILL HELP ME IN THE FUTURE BECAUSE…
ONE WAY I HAVE USED THIS LEARNING AT HOME IS…
ONE WORD TO DESCRIBE MY LEARNING ABOUT THIS WOULD BE…
WHEN I THINK ABOUT WHAT I HAVE LEARNED I FEEL…BECAUSE…
IT WOULD HAVE BEEN EASIER FOR ME TO LEARN ABOUT THIS IF…
I HAVE GROWN AS A LEARNER BECAUSE…
SOMETHING I CAN DO NOW THAT I COULDN'T DO BEFORE IS…
I WAS MOST INTERESTED IN…
THE MOST USEFUL PART OF THIS FOR ME WAS…
SOMETHING I WOULD LOVE TO DO AGAIN IS…
THIS LEARNING REMINDED ME OF…

THINKING ABOUT MY DAY

Choose from one of the prompts below to help you reflect.

- If your day were a colour/shape/animal/symbol, what would it be?
- What is one word you would use to describe your day?
- If your day were a newspaper headline, what would it be?
- Write a tweet that sums up your day (120 characters).
- ECG: emotion, cognition, growth. How do you feel? What did you learn? What next?
- Snapshot/freezeframe: what picture/photo from your day would best sum it up?

ASSESSING MY LEARNING ASSETS

	I don't really know how to do this.	I can do this but need help.	I can do this independently.	I do this and can teach others how to do it.
SELF-MANAGEMENT (For example, I can make a plan to help me manage my time.)				
COLLABORATION (For example, I can provide team mates with useful feedback.)				
COMMUNICATION (For example, I can ask questions for clarification.)				
THINKING (For example, I can think about something from a point of view different from my own.)				
RESEARCH (For example, I can design and conduct an interview to gather information from others.)				

'We must act as if our institutions are ours to create,
our learning is ours to define,
the leadership we seek is ours to become'.

(Peter Block, 2003)

nine

Together is better:
HOW CAN WE GROW AN INQUIRY SCHOOL?

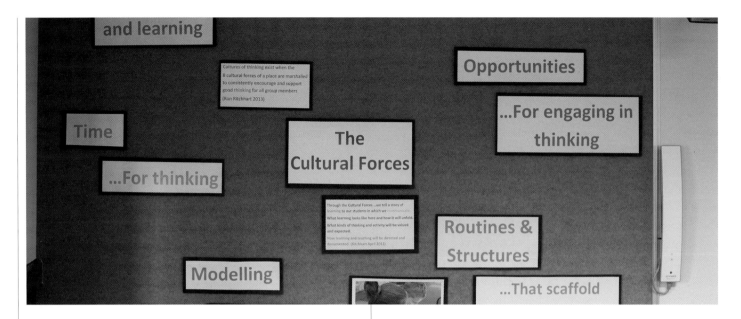

The Cultural Forces

- Time ...For thinking
- ...and learning
- Opportunities ...For engaging in thinking
- Modelling
- Routines & Structures ...That scaffold

Cultures of thinking exist when the 8 cultural forces of a place are marshalled to consistently encourage and support good thinking for all group members (Ron Ritchhart 2013)

Through the Cultural Forces ...we tell a story of learning to our students in which we communicate. What learning looks like here and how it will unfold. What kinds of thinking and activity will be valued and expected. How learning and teaching will be directed and documented. (Ritchhart April 2013)

INTRODUCTION

Much of this book has focused on empowering the inquiry teacher at classroom level and on the day–to–day, practical challenges and opportunities that present themselves when teachers and students meet in their learning spaces. I firmly believe that this is where the success of inquiry learning lies. It is, ultimately, in the skill of the teacher to facilitate learning in order to grow the capacity of each child as passionate, life-long investigators. This is possible for a teacher even when the school does not prioritise inquiry. I have seen some outstanding inquiry teachers work their magic in very traditional settings and I am sure the students in their classes, even for one year, are the better for the experience.

That said, inquiry learning is ideally nurtured in an inquiry school. When inquiry teachers work in an environment that supports their beliefs and that positions the teachers themselves as inquirers, powerful learning takes place. The best possible scenario is that inquiry teachers and learners are part of a community of inquiry and that students enter a school committed to their growth as inquirers from day one. All schools should be – at the very least – professional learning communities in themselves, as define nicely by Stoll (2006:6): *'An inclusive group of people, motivated by a shared learning vision, who support and work with each other, finding ways inside and outside their immediate community, to enquire into their own practice and together learn new and better approaches that will enhance all pupils' learning.'*

Growing an inquiry culture within a school is an exciting but by no means straightforward task. There is a wealth of literature on the complex subject of transforming schools. It is not the intention of this chapter to provide a detailed account of how this might be achieved in relation to inquiry but rather to provide a simple overview that can, I hope, begin or contribute to the conversation.

WHAT ARE THE CULTURAL MARKERS OF AN INQUIRY SCHOOL AND HOW CAN WE DEVELOP AN INQUIRY CULTURE?

'A school's culture is characterized by its deeply rooted traditions, values and beliefs – some of which may be common across schools and some of which are unique and embedded in a particular school's history and location. Culture informs the way in which 'things get done around here' and just as important, frames how change efforts are perceived'.
(Kruse and Seashore-Louis, 2009: 4)

How does the adage go? If we always do what we've always done then we'll always get what we've always got. Becoming an inquiry school means changing what we do. And changing what we do takes time, commitment, understanding, courage, energy and vision.

The vision is perhaps the most powerful place to start. What does an inquiry school look, sound and feel like? Knowing what we hope to become is surely critical to our success in getting there. So let's begin by identifying some of the basic characteristics of an inquiry school. In the following table, I refer to these as cultural markers – they indicate or illustrate deeper beliefs and values held by the school community.

CULTURAL MARKERS OF AN INQUIRY SCHOOL

MARKER	WHAT THIS MIGHT LOOK LIKE
Collaborative planning, teaching and learning lead to ongoing, open and honest dialogue.	**Teachers work in** collaborative, professional learning teams and time is given to the development of these and the avoidance of forced, inauthentic 'team work'. Teams meet regularly (weekly/fortnightly) to discuss, develop, document and evaluate plans for student learning. Teams may also be formed around shared professional inquiry questions/topics. Teaching is 'de-privatised', meaning there is a collaborative, open approach. This may mean some form of shared teaching in flexible learning spaces or other arrangements that foster a team approach to working with students. Each student's learning is seen as a shared responsibility. Building a collaborative culture does not mean denying teachers the opportunity for them to express their individuality in planning and in teaching. Far from it. In fact, great inquiry schools honor the strengths and contributions of individuals to the team. When thinking about the nature of dialogue in an inquiry school, I like the term 'courageous conversations'. Inquiry is about risk taking, and risk taking requires trust. In courageous conversations, individuals feel free to express their views openly and truthfully. Norms and processes are established to enable this to happen in respectful ways. Many would argue that the conversations we have in schools *become* the relationship between us; they certainly can point to the kind of relationship that exists. Mindful discussions are critical to healthy schools. Professional dialogue is critical for collaborative learning and growth.
Students and teachers use **shared language** and shared approaches.	**While acknowledging and** respecting individual teaching styles and strengths, inquiry schools are characterized by consistency in the language of learning that teachers use with each other and with students. This does not mean that each classroom has a 'cookie cutter' approach but that there are agreed broad structures that help students recognize, re-visit and deepen their grasp of inquiry processes as they move through the school. An example of this may be that teachers agree to use the same language to describe phases in the process, that they agree on a broad set of learning capabilities/assets, and that some of the tools and strategies students use as learners are shared and known across the school. Some schools also achieve this shared language by agreeing on shared features of documentation/planning proformas. Shared language, approaches and documentation ease conversation within and across teams. This is even more powerful if the agreed models/processes are developed with the staff themselves.
All staff see themselves as inquiry teachers regardless of subject or area of responsibility.	**Specialist and generalist** teachers engage in some shared planning. Specialist (or 'single subject') teachers use similar language and instructional approaches. There are plenty of integrative opportunities and there is a greater fluidity across learning areas. This means teachers find ways to plan collaboratively across generalist and specialist programs.
Students make strong connections to **local and global communities**.	**Particular attention is** given to opportunities for inquiry into authentic contexts and problems. The school grounds, local community issues and action projects feature as an important part of the school's program. At all grade levels, students experience some form of inquiry in a 'real life' context. The community beyond the school is used as a context for student inquiry, and students access expertise, mentors, information and community-based resources to support their research. Digital technologies are harnessed to access expertise, gather data, share ideas and connect with the world beyond the classroom. Parents are regularly informed about students' inquiries through, for example, school websites, class blogs and Twitter feeds. An inquiry school is invitational and open, and people can enter classrooms in a relaxed and informal manner. The students are used to visitors and teachers simply get on with their teaching. Students can easily talk about what they are doing and why.

MARKERS	WHAT THIS MIGHT LOOK LIKE
Students have a **voice** in decision making about their learning and about the school as a whole.	**Students are included** in decisions made about their learning and other events or elements of the life of the school. Students of all age groups are consulted and their views taken on board. Reporting happens via student-led conferencing where students learn to take the lead in sharing their progress and their goals. In an inquiry school, students can confidently talk about their learning with others. When visitors come to the school, it is the students who showcase what is happening, conduct tours and explain learning approaches.
Leadership is shared.	**In inquiry classrooms**, we invite students to share the responsibility of the day-to-day running of the program and to participate in decisions made about what, how, when and with whom they are learning. In the same way, inquiry schools are careful to **position their teachers as leaders.** Leadership is distributed rather than being 'top down', and teachers are invited to have a significant voice in the decisions made about the school.
There is **visible evidence** of inquiry as an approach to learning.	**In a classroom,** the walls and other physical features say much about what is valued by the teacher. The same can be said about the school as a whole. In an inquiry school, student learning is celebrated on the walls or as part of the physical space; artifacts that tell visitors about students' investigations are on display. Many inquiry schools deliberately display the current big questions they are working on in the most public part of the school. The school buildings themselves can invite inquiry by displaying provocations, questions, interesting news items and challenges. Parents can see the learning journeys their children are engaged in through the use of photos, displays, videos and other visible signage around the school. The learning spaces in an inquiry school are flexible and welcoming.
School grounds, the local environment and school events are harnessed for inquiry.	**The school grounds** and buildings are used as the context for ongoing research – for example, the gardens, energy use, the design and use of play equipment, canteen food, traffic management at drop-off and pick-up time, school performances/productions, art works, behavior management and peer mediation, school fêtes and fundraisers, cross-age buddy programs, special days/festivals and composting and recycling.
Professional learning is inquiry-based. Teachers are inquirers.	**Perhaps the most** powerful way to help teachers understand inquiry is to give them opportunities to use this approach in relation to their own professional learning as teachers. In an inquiry school, teachers see themselves as inquirers every day. They bring an inquiring disposition to all they do. The best professional learning happens when it is embedded within day-to-day practice and rigorously reflected on in collaboration with others. Inquiry schools expect all staff to be engaged in continuous inquiry as a part of their commitment to professional learning. This may take a variety of forms: <ul><li>action research teams formed around common areas of interest/need</li><li>data gathering and analysis as part of the professional learning team's planning process</li><li>spaced professional learning opportunities embedded in the school and encouraging classroom application and analysis</li><li>individual passion projects (20% time for staff) where each teacher selects a project to work on then share with the staff (under a broad shared vision)</li><li>the establishment of professional learning networks for each staff member – particularly through the use of online platforms such as Twitter, Facebook and blogs.</li></ul>

MARKERS	WHAT THIS MIGHT LOOK LIKE
	• classroom coaching, team teaching, observations and feedback • long-term, in-school partnerships with a critical friend • professional learning communities with an inquiry approach to their work While workshop days and one-off professional learning programs have value, this value is quickly diminished if it is not positioned in the bigger picture of the school's vision and improvement goals. Leadership must provide teachers with embedded opportunities to build capacity as inquiry teachers and to grow their skill base within the context in which they work: with their students in their classrooms.
Clearly articulated vision, shared principles and frameworks guide inquiry teaching and learning practices (see chapter 1).	**The success of** the inquiry school lies in what the individual teacher knows and does in his or her daily practice and this is enhanced when the overarching vision and underlying principles of the school as a whole are clear, transparent and well communicated. Great inquiry schools take pride in their work. They shout it from the hills and make it known in a range of creative ways. Shared frameworks for planning provide cohesion and direction without unnecessary prescription. Shared conceptual throughlines, a set of agreed skills and dispositions provide common language and a basis on which individuals and teams can plan.
Arrangements are made that allow teachers time for **collaborative planning,** inquiry and reflection.	**If collaborative planning** is expected and valued then timetabling must provide all teachers with the opportunity to meet regularly in their teams and, when needed to, have extended planning time (often early and late in the term). Some work also needs to be done on establishing norms and agreements that help teams work effectively. If we want teachers to be professional inquirers, they need the time and resources to do so.
A balance of personal and professional care ensures that staff feel valued and **relationships** matter.	**Throughout this book,** I have reiterated the importance of relationships as foundational to a successful inquiry classroom. In the same way, the relationships among staff and between parents and staff are crucial in helping build a sustainable culture of inquiry. Being an effective inquiry school means creating a climate of trust. Dissent and conflict are potentially useful contributors to growth, a culture of compliance can be stifling. Care for individuals as people as well as teachers is vital for wellbeing and the kind of positive energy needed for inquiry to flourish. This is where truly effective leaders shine. They take time to know and value individuals, to care about their lives beyond school, to connect with them even in small ways on a daily basis – and to balance personal care with professional care. Leaders who take time to care for their teachers' wellbeing model the kind of generosity and compassion we want teachers to have with their students. A stressed, negative, undervalued teacher is not going to take a risk or try something new. We also need to be very careful to avoid making assumptions about the skills each teacher might have in relation to inquiry. I have seen young teachers dismissive of older and very experienced practitioners because they see, for example, their lack of technological prowess as a failing. Being able to set up a Skype call on your interactive whiteboard does not make you an inquiry teacher. Each teacher in a school has gifts to bring to the learning experiences of their students. Seeking out and sharing those strengths and gifts is galvanizing and connecting. Without exception, the best inquiry schools I work with have leaders who ensure their staff feel listened to, supported, valued and trusted. You can feel it in the air.

CULTURAL MARKERS OF AN INQUIRY SCHOOL (CONT'D)

MARKERS	WHAT THIS MIGHT LOOK LIKE
Expectations are high.	**A pervasive myth** about the nature of inquiry learning is that it is loose, unstructured and without rigor. For some people, the term 'inquiry school' conjures up images of children choosing what to do whenever they want to do it and teachers acting as passive 'guides on the side', therefore avoiding any kind of direct instruction and allowing the chaos to swirl around them. Nothing could be further from the truth. The inquiry schools I work in are incredibly organized and hard working. The expectation that students will learn to manage themselves as learners and to gain deep understanding as well as mastery of skills is fierce. As we have already seen, the planning and teaching in an inquiry classroom is transparent and this is true throughout the school. This transparency also aids rigor and there is no hiding behind your private work program. In an inquiry school, teachers see their role as 'critical friends' to colleagues. Plans are shared and critiqued, questions are asked and evidence is required to support assessments. In an inquiry based planning team, teachers get used to being asked (and asking) 'why?'
Student learning is at the heart – the goal to nurture engaged, motivated, capable inquirers stays central.	**In an inquiry school,** teachers use evidence of student learning to inform planning and teaching across the day. Teachers regularly bring evidence fo student learning to the planning table and work hard to ensure that student learning is at the centre of their professional conversations. This practice in itself is a powerful means of learning about inquiry and assessment. What teachers do makes a difference to student learning but it is only in the analysis of that learning that we can determine what the best thing to do might be.
Technologies are embedded in the learning environment.	**The use of** digital technologies within the learning landscape is, in most contexts, no longer a matter of choice. Technology does not make inquiry happen, but it does widen the scope of what students and teachers can do and it can help personalize opportunities for both teacher and student inquiry. Today's students are profoundly connected through and to technology so it is essential to include this milieu in the landscape of a school. The trick is finding the right tools to enhance the learning experience rather focusing on the tools themselves. Inquiry is not simply about having one-to-one devices or the latest green-screen studio equipment. However, we know technology helps learning remain relevant to students' lives outside school, keep them engaged, help personalize learning and can enable learning in unprecedented ways. What students can now do – particularly in the creation and sharing of new learning should not be hindered by lack of available tools in our schools.

BUILDING A SCHOOL-WIDE CULTURE OF INQUIRY: SOME QUESTIONS TO ASK OURSELVES

Becoming an inquiry school cannot be achieved through attending a workshop, building a flexible learning space or buying a professional development 'program'. If there is one thing we know about schools it is that they can be notoriously slow to change and the change process is complex. There is no 'quick fix' and no recipe. I am a great believer in the power of conversation to begin the process. Opening a staff up to some honest and challenging questions about the school culture can begin a path towards change. When I think about moving a school towards a more-inquiry-based way of being, I see it in much the same way I see classroom inquiry: it's messy, non-linear and multi-faceted, but we need to have clear intentions and a clear idea of where we want to go. And we also need action. Too much talking and it is simply a conversation. The change process requires talking, doing and reflecting. The following questions can form useful starting points for individual reflection, small-group and staff-wide conversations:

- Are all staff invited into **decision making** about what happens in our school?
- Are **students and parents** involved in decision making about what happens at school (beyond the decisions made within their classroom)?
- Do we have a set of **shared principles**, values and school-wide goals that are consistent with an inquiry approach?
- Does our school have **connections with the community** (local and global) as part of student learning – through investigations, mentoring, providing feedback, etc.?
- Are our own curriculum **frameworks flexible** rather than fixed, and are they regularly reviewed?
- Are there 'big picture' concepts that drive our whole-school selection of inquiry contexts?
- Do teachers plan in **collaborative teams?** Are teams, in themselves, seen as contexts for professional discourse and learning?
- Is **open and honest dialogue** encouraged and questioning (and dissent) welcomed as potential for growth? Are norms and agreements developed to ensure courageous conversations can happen?
- Is there a genuine culture of **personal as well as 'professional' care** amongst staff? Do we know and care about each other as people as well as colleagues?
- Are parents and the wider community **welcomed into the school** regularly?
- Are our students involved in making decisions beyond the classroom? Do we seek their **voices** in matters related to the general running of the school?

- Are learning **spaces shared, open and flexible** (even if in a single classroom)?
- Can our students **confidently talk with others** about their learning? Do regularly we give them this opportunity?
- Is **feedback** from staff and students encouraged and welcomed by leadership?
- Are **leadership roles** shared? Do teachers have opportunities to take on a range of roles?
- Are there **time and opportunities** for staff to stop and reflect on their work at a deeper level?
- Do staff have an understanding of *how* to use inquiry based **pedagogy?**
- Do **planning** proformas or other expected forms of documentation reflect an inquiry approach? Do staff find them useful or burdensome?
- Do students **report on their own learning** to parents?
- Is **technology** easily accessible to students and teachers to add value to inquiry?
- Do teachers see student progress as a **shared responsibility?**
- Are the **grounds, buildings** and other structural aspects of the school included in problem- or project-based inquiry work? Is the school itself part of the inquiry landscape? Do students use the day-to-day life of the school as a context for research?
- Is the **timetable flexible?** Does it allow for sustained blocks of learning time and avoid fragmented and interrupted learning experiences?
- Are all teachers seen to be inquiry teachers? Do **specialist teachers** use an inquiry-based approach to their work?
- Are successes celebrated? Do we tell **stories of inquiry** to the community?
- Are there **rituals and ceremonies** that help connect the community and build relationships across age groups?
- Are teachers **recruited** with inquiry learning in mind?
- Are there staff members with **designated roles** around inquiry learning, supporting, resourcing and maintaining accountability?
- Is **professional learning** itself an inquiry process? Are teachers given opportunities to inquire into areas of interest as well as investigations connected to the school's vision?
- Are **parents** invited to participate in inquiry learning experiences? Are they informed and communicated with about the whys and hows of inquiry?
- Is inquiry '**visible**' to the community? Do student work samples, signs and other visible artifacts show inquiry at work? Are we using **digital technologies** and social media to facilitate this sharing?
- Do we give teachers/ourselves opportunities to **build our capacity** as inquiry teachers? Do we learn and share new techniques? Do we watch each other at work and share our reflections?

NURTURING AN INQUIRY DISPOSITION IN TEACHERS

As I have said numerous times throughout this book, effective inquiry teachers are inquirers. They bring an inquiring disposition to their work with students, and this can not only improve learning outcomes for those students but also contribute to an overall culture that is truly learning focused. Inquiry teachers are, in turn, supported by inquiry leaders – an attitude often illustrated by persistent, thoughtful questioning about why and how we do what we do, and how to make it even better. There are a range of strategies and approaches that work to nurture an inquiry approach to our work as teachers.

Learning walks

The idea of a learning walk (variously called 'walk-throughs' or 'instructional rounds') is that small groups of teachers walk through the school making brief visits to classrooms to gather a snapshot related to a particular focus or inquiry they have established earlier. For example, a group may set out to conduct a learning walk with a particular focus on collaborative learning. Once the 'learning walk' is complete, the group will share their observations with each other and then later with the staff, identifying quality practices and raising questions about possible areas for improvement. Learning walks are informal but powerful. They are a very 'inquiry based' practice, positioning the teacher as the researcher/observer (not evaluator), and allow questions to emerge from shared observation. For more on learning walks as a professional learning practice, see Cheryl Doig (2009).

Extended classroom visits – learning from each other

Although teachers spend their entire day surrounded by people, they can feel quite isolated, particularly if the design of the school does not easily allow for contact with other adults aside from at recess and lunchtime. Setting up systems that encourage teachers to spend time in each other's learning spaces, watching and learning from each other, can be a very effective way to inquire into practice. In this approach, we enter our colleague's space as a learner rather than a critic or judge. We ask ourselves, 'What can I learn from what I am hearing and seeing? What is this making me wonder?' After the observation, the visitor shares their thinking and learning with their colleague. This approach works best when the visitor to the classroom has a specific focus for inquiry. For example, I might visit a colleague's room to add to my thinking about questioning techniques. Most often, the information that we gather from watching a colleague and their children at work makes us question and re-think our *own* teaching. Reflections are shared in subsequent meetings with other teachers. Who to visit and what to focus on will depend on individual schools.

Some schools set up a roster system where teachers arrange visits among themselves each term; at other schools, teachers identify their questions/interests and are then matched up with colleagues with a similar interest. The most important element in this process is that everyone is clear about what classroom visits are and are *not*! They are not for judging or critiquing, although improved practice may emerge as a result of the reflections.

Asking others to spend time with us as we teach can be as beneficial to us as to the observer. When we are being watched we tend to notice ourselves more. We start to see ourselves through new eyes, listen to our talk more carefully and think about why we are doing what we are doing. This is a highly inquiry-based and reflective practice. When handled well, it also helps build a culture of collaboration, trust, empathy and respect for each other's skills.

Teacher research/professional-inquiry projects

When teachers are given an opportunity inquire into their own teaching and learning practices we truly become an inquiry school. The inquiring teacher is constantly inquiring into his/her practice, both formally and informally. But it is more than simply inquiring, gathering data, thinking and reflecting. It is *using* these discoveries to take action!

'*Effective teachers inquire into the relationship between what they do and what happens for students. But effective teachers do more than simply inquire (or reflect), they take action…to improve the outcomes for students and continue to inquire into the value of these interventions.*' (Aitken, G., 2010: 9)

Many inquiry schools provide teachers with opportunities to (and the expectation that they will) conduct professional inquiries related to classroom practice. To do this well, several things need to be in place:

- an identification of questions used to frame personal inquiries
- strategies for collecting evidence of student learning
- opportunities for collaborative analysis of the evidence (looking for patterns etc.)
- access to professional reading, further advice and research relevant to the inquiry
- forums in which to share learning with others.

Sample questions for inquiring into inquiry (teacher inquiry projects)

- How does our questioning impact on student responses?

- How does the use of personal devices (BYOD) impact on engagement in inquiry tasks?

- How can we use the questions students ask to more effectively inform our unit planning?

- How can we more effectively find out what prior knowledge students bring to an inquiry?

- How can evidence of prior knowledge be used to inform assessment?

- How can we assist students to work more collaboratively with each other?

- How does co-constructing success criteria impact on student learning?

- How can we structure the 'going further' stage of an inquiry to foster more independent inquiry?

- How can we make more genuine links between literacy workshops and our inquiry units?

- How can we give students more choices about the way they share their learning?

- What kinds of real-life contexts can the school provide for inquiry learning?

- What can we do to involve parents more fully in our inquiry learning projects?

- How can we encourage students to do more reflective thinking during an inquiry?

- How can we use literature more effectively as a source of experience and information within an inquiry?

- How can we more effectively assess the understanding students have gained during an inquiry?

- How can we better support students' self-assessment?

- What happens when students design their own criteria for assessment?

- How can we increase the role of social media in helping students access information and points of view as they inquire?

- What can we do to make better use of the local/global community during our inquiries?

- What can we do to improve the action component of our inquiries?

- How can we assist older students to design their own inquiries around an area of interest to them?

- How can we more effectively use play as context for our young students to inquire?

- How can we make our planning meetings more effective as a forum for teacher reflection?

- What effect does a collaborative, reflective journal have on students' understanding of the inquiry process?

- How can we assist children in using surveys and interviews as effective vehicles for inquiry/data gathering?

- How can we use blogs to help students track and share their inquiries?

- How can we enhance the role of the arts in inquiry?

- How can we increase the involvement of students in class discussions? What techniques invite more participation?

- How do 'understanding goals' impact on the effectiveness of an inquiry?

Innovation days/passion projects

In chapter 7, I highlighted the importance of giving students opportunities to explore the things that mattered to them. The same is true of teachers as learners. Of course there are times when non-contact days are used to engage with various experts, leaders, teachers from other schools and departmental representatives, but there are many other ways these days can be used and they can be even more productive. One strategy is to give the day over to teachers to use in pursuit of a professional inquiry of their choice. These inquiries are planned ahead of the day so that resources can be gathered or visits arranged to facilitate learning. Just as with students, teachers complete a proposal, set goals, identify resources, gather information and agree to share it with others with a view to adding value to the whole school as well as their own classroom. Such personal inquiry time can be incredibly empowering for staff, and they feel trusted as professionals and are often energized by the opportunity to delve deeper into their passions.

TEACHER INQUIRY PROJECTS:
WHAT MIGHT PUSH US TOWARDS SUCCESS?
WHAT MIGHT PULL US AWAY?

PUSHES	PULLS
Make sure your focus is a **tight** one, especially for each person in the team. For example, 'How do learning journals improve my students' reflective thinking skills?'	Avoid anything vague or broad, e.g. 'How can I improve reflective thinking?'
Make sure you choose something you can really do **as part of the work you do** in the classroom.	Avoid choosing something you can only really read about or talk about but not do much about.
Each member of the group should have their **own specific project** as part of a bigger, shared focus. This should be named and documented.	Avoid being too collective in your approach. The group is there to support individuals and to enable learning from each other. Each person needs to put in.
Get some **baseline** data. Make sure you have some evidence of what you/your students are doing now.	Avoid putting off the collection of some data. It's too late at the end of the project.
Plan a schedule of meetings with the project group. They don't need to be long but they do need to be regular.	Avoid simply meeting when it 'feels right' – it may never feel right!
Set an **agenda** and use a formal protocol to drive your meeting and sharing time. Focus on the questions 'What are we learning from our experiences?' and 'What do we need to do next?'	Avoid a 'talk fest.' Meetings can become little more than show-and-tell sessions. Keep the description to a minimum and focus on analysis and reflection.
Document everything along the way – work samples, conversations with kids and each other, photos, etc.	Avoid the temptation to talk about it but record little. Don't depend on others to record what's going on.
Encourage **action**. Focus on what you and your students are doing and collect some evidence along the way.	Avoid hesitation. Just do it!
Encourage **professional reading**. Check out journals, websites, books, Twitter, blogs and other digital sources. Share what you learn with your team.	Avoid simply doing what you have always done with what you have always known. Stretch yourself.
Share what you have learned with others. End with a bang, not a whimper.	Avoid allowing the project to simply fizzle out.

PEER COACHING

When carried out in a well-informed and collaborative manner, the strategy of observing and 'coaching' each other can be an excellent addition to the development of the inquiry teacher. There is a great deal of material available on setting up coaching systems (see the references at the end of this chapter) but, in summary, coaching differs from walk-throughs or other forms of observation because it comes with a specific intent to give feedback. While quality coaching is still regarded as a form of 'mutual conversation', it is based, generally, on self-assessed or identified needs of students and/or the teacher within that setting. For example, a teacher may have noticed that some students rarely participate in discussions and seem less engaged or involved than she/he would hope them to be. With an inquiry question in mind (such as 'How do my instructional strategies impact on the participation of my students?') another teacher is invited to observe the teacher inquirer at work. After an initial conversation, students and the teacher are observed, with the coach recording instances that may be helpful in follow-up conversations. Using the data gathered through observation, the coach provides feedback and together the coach and the teacher discuss strategies for improvement. This approach is very inquiry oriented but can easily be seen through the lens of performance appraisal. It needs to be deftly handled so the inquiry orientation is not lost. The concept of 'feedforward' (Goldsmith, M., 2013) can be powerfully integrated into this approach. Here, the emphasis is less on analysis of what has already occurred or been demonstrated and much more about how new goals might be worked towards in the future. Teachers can benefit from being asked about the teaching behaviour they would like to change or improve and then, together, colleagues can work to plan for improvement.

ESTABLISHING VIRTUAL PROFESSIONAL LEARNING NETWORKS

At the time of writing, the use of social media such as Twitter to form online professional learning communities is growing exponentially. More and more teachers are discovering the extraordinary resource base available to them at the swipe of a screen. A teacher in a small primary school in Melbourne, Australia, may be connecting with a high school teacher in India around their shared interest in how young people learn math. The online world is awash with enthusiastic bloggers who write about their teaching and share their reflections with the world. For someone with an inquiring disposition, such as myself, it's like being the proverbial kid in the candy shop! Never before has it been so easy to explore a question or issue of interest, to find like-minded educators, to satisfy an itch or to feed my curiosity. The online PLN (professional learning network) that sits in my back pocket is a very powerful form of continued and highly personalized professional development.

A virtual PLN can significantly enhance opportunities teachers have to inquire and to collaborate with others beyond their school. Because it is self-selected, the collaboration feels so much easier, as we tend to follow or link up with like-minded others. If things get difficult, we can simply 'unfriend' or remove ourselves from the conversation. I believe strongly that every teacher can benefit from this form of personal inquiry and professional collaboration, but that the skills needed for face-to-face collaboration and learning alongside those we don't necessarily choose to work with can only be truly developed in real time and face-to-face. An online PLN is generally a voluntary form of collaboration, unlike a school where collaboration is (and indeed should be) an expected norm. My hunch is that the opportunity to more easily connect with like-minded people online may mean we are more willing to do the hard work needed for in-school collaboration. Our personal needs are met through our PLN and our professional responsibilities are attended to at school. Ideally, the two are not mutually exclusive!

THE USE OF COLLABORATIVE TEAMS FOR PLANNING AND EVALUATION

As already identified, spending time collaborating with colleagues is a key component of the inquiry school. There is '*abundant research linking high levels of student achievement to educators who work in the collaborative culture of a professional learning community*' (DuFour, 2011: 59). Schools that organize teachers into 'professional learning teams' (as they are often referred to) provide opportunities for those teachers to grow their thinking through active collaboration with others.

Learning to collaborate well is in itself a key inquiry for teachers in schools. We know that simply putting people in teams does not mean the teams will function effectively. All teams, as noted by Lenconi (2007) are potentially *dys*functional. This is inevitable because they are made up of 'fallible, imperfect human beings'. Recognizing this is important because it reminds us that, just as in the classroom, we need to actively work on and consciously develop a mindful approach to collaborative tasks. We need to notice and name the skills required, endeavor to enhance them and construct systems and norms that help keep teams functioning constructively. Most professions require people to operate in teams of some sort and those teams are often not self-selected. Learning to collaborate effectively is as important for us as adult learners as it is for the children we teach.

> *'Collaboration is a means to an end. Collaboration alone will not improve a school, and in a toxic school culture, providing educators with time to collaborate is likely to reinforce the negative aspects of the culture and deteriorate into complaints sessions.'*
> (DuFour, 2011: 60)

COURAGEOUS CONVERSATIONS AT THE PLANNING TABLE: TALKING THE TALK AS INQUIRY TEACHERS

Collaboration requires communication. Just as the language we use in the classroom can powerfully influence students' perceptions of learning and of themselves as learners, so too does the language we use with each other shape our view of ourselves as teachers, our role, and even the way in which we see ourselves as part of the learning community. This is particularly important for teacher leaders and those in administrative roles where language can be used (consciously and unconsciously) to assert power.

Much of my teaching career has been spent in conversation with teachers. More often than not, I find myself at the planning table designing, planning, analyzing, reflecting and evaluating. I am acutely aware of how quickly the questions I ask, and the manner in which I ask them, can shut down or open up a conversation.

I am also aware of the way each person's 'talk' impacts on the group – what they say and what they don't say, how and even where they choose to sit and of course what they communicate non-verbally. It is powerful stuff. In an inquiry school, we aim to become mindful practitioners. The act of collaborating to plan or evaluate is always an opportunity for inquiry and, therefore, for learning. As an outsider coming into a school and as someone considered an 'expert' in the field, I have the additional challenge of breaking down the sometimes problematic barrier caused by people's perceptions that I am there to judge or critique their practice. This is also true of the teacher leading a team or a principal facilitating a staff meeting. In fact, one of the most important things we can do in working in and with teams is to examine how we see ourselves – and what we consider our role to be, whether we are a staff member, teacher leader or principal.

In an inquiry school, our aim is to foster the teacher as inquirer. This means being willing to take risks, share opinions, engage in dialogue, ask questions, admit confusion, critique and self-assess. Conversations grow relationships. Relationships grow culture and culture determines much of what goes on, or

doesn't, in a school. If collaborative conversations are part of the fabric of an inquiry school, then it is important we try to get them right. I have found certain questions/questioning techniques to be more positive and productive than others. These include:

- **Validating** – questions and comments that ensure the teacher feels heard and his/her experiences acknowledged, even if you might have a different perspective

'It must have been frustrating to feel like there was not enough time for your kids to investigate their own questions.'

- **Inviting** – lots of opportunities to share opinions, participate, and tell stories from experience. Sometimes this needs to be very direct.

'Jane, when you used that thinking strategy with your students, how did they respond? What did you notice?'

- **Valuing** – questions and comments that signal to the teacher that they have something of worth to say or contribute. This can be hard with very negative people but there is always *something* there.

'Your comment has really got me thinking about how we can best support students who are not engaged in this inquiry – thanks!'

- **Noticing and naming** – this is as important in meetings as it is in the classroom. It can be naming – as Glen Ochre (2013) describes it – 'the ghosts', the things that are affecting the conversation that no one will acknowledge, such as exhaustion, frustration, fear, resentment, excitement or confusion. Once named, these ghosts often evaporate.

'I am noticing that there is some real tension around this issue. There is some disagreement and some people have not commented at all. Is anyone else noticing that? Maybe we should talk a bit more about this so we can clear the air? How should we go about that?'

- **Challenging** – some of the best learning comes from the least comfortable place. Some questions are designed to push us out of our comfort zone and make us think differently. Good conversations help people 'sit in the fire' for a while and wrestle with discomfort. One of my challenges is to continue to ask questions that challenge, even when I am worried it might not be 'liked'. I also want teachers to ask me, and each other, challenging questions. Yes, we need to be validated, but we also need to be stretched.

'That sounds like a fun activity, but I am wondering about its purpose and about how it supports our big question? Can you explain that to us a little more?'

- **Summarizing/focusing/redirecting** – conversations around the planning table can too often go around in circles. Time is precious and we want to use it well and wisely. Summarizing people's thoughts or action agreements can be a powerful way to punctuate and move a conversation forward.

SAMPLE QUESTIONS FOR EFFECTIVE CONVERSATIONS

- Let's all remind ourselves what we were hoping to achieve (with this task/unit/meeting…). What's our main purpose?
- How do you think we are going (in relation to our goals)?
- How do we know? What evidence do we have to support our thinking?
- Why are we doing this?
- What are the students revealing to us?
- I would really love to hear more about….
- Can you tell us about…?
- What do you think about…?
- How did *you* find this? Did you have the same experience or a different one?
- What does it look like/sound like when…?
- You say it 'didn't work' – that's interesting. Can you tell us a bit more about what happened?
- What aspects went well?
- That's interesting – what do you think that might mean?
- Do you have a different way of thinking about/looking at that?
- I wonder what might happen if we….
- What is this making you wonder?
- What would help us/you do this even better?
- What's the most important decision you/we need to make? What's stopping us from making it?
- What's getting in the way of this happening?
- I wonder why…/Why do you think…?
- Ok, we've got a few possibilities here. What might be the most effective path to choose?
- Can you foresee anything that might get in the way?
- What could we do to remove those roadblocks?
- What do we need to make this work?
- What are you going to do next?
- What are you finding frustrating about this?
- Do we want to keep talking about this? Is this helping us achieve our goal for the meeting?
- I noticed that….
- I heard you say that….
- Can you say more about…?

SOME TRAPS TO AVOID

- **Unrealistic or no agenda** – even the most informal professional conversation should begin by determining its purpose.
- **Failing to be truly 'present' at the table** – agree to turn off phones, close the door, stay in the room and remain uninterrupted.
- **Failing to set start and finish time** – we all know what happens when we don't.
- **A room set-up that gets in the way of collaboration** – gathering around a shared table is best. Try to aim for a circular configuration.
- **Failing to keep a record of the conversation** – take notes/minutes. They keep people accountable and help prepare for the next conversation.
- **Getting off topic or allowing other things to hijack the time** – make the purpose crystal clear and stick to it.
- **Spending time on things** that could be sorted via email or in other forums.
- **Using the meeting to download/complain/gossip** – while it is important at times to allow someone to wear De Bono's 'black hat' and explore why things might not work or have not worked, some conversations go so far down the rabbit hole of negativity we never emerge.
- **Failing to express gratitude or acknowledge success**. When you are delighted, inspired, enriched by something your colleague has said or done, *tell them*.
- **Over-reliance on laptops/tablets** – which means there is little eye contact during the meeting. Lids down when the conversation requires real connection!
- **Failing to set agreements** – one of the most productive things a group can do is to take time to discuss not just what they want to talk about but *how* they might conduct their conversation. It is also useful to provide a few minutes at the end of a meeting to reflect on people's feelings about how the meeting went. All of this is about bringing an 'inquiry stance' to all we do: questioning our behavior, the success of a conversation, what we could do better and what we believe went well. Inquiry is a way of being.

LEADING FOR COLLABORATIVE INQUIRY PLANNING

To 'lead' a collaborative team may sound almost contradictory, but most teams benefit from having someone willing to facilitate the conversation around inquiry teaching and learning. In schools that practice 'distributed leadership', having someone take on this role for each team promotes efficiency without losing shared ownership. Successful inquiry leaders use the following practices:

1. Encourage reflective conversations.	*'How do people feel about the direction this inquiry is moving in?' 'Looking back on that task, I wonder if we could have improved it in some way?' 'How well are the children developing their understandings? How do we know?'*
2. Try to involve and include everyone.	Deliberately invite someone's opinion or suggestion. *'Diane, we haven't heard anything from you for a while. What do you think might be the best way to approach the task?'* Before a meeting, ask a team member to bring something to share that you have noticed in their room.
3. Record/monitor/track planning.	As the inquiry leader, you can help people keep accountable by recording plans (or at least organizing for them to be recorded!) This may be on chart paper, directly onto a hard-copy, digital or web-based planner. This is crucial in an emergent planning process.
4. Challenge thinking.	Team meetings are not as effective if they are simply about 'sharing' ideas and making plans. We can and should be each other's critical friends. As the inquiry leader, your job is to advocate for quality inquiry. If tasks are suggested that do not align with the principles of quality inquiry, question them. You can do this in an open and non-aggressive way: *'I am wondering how that learning task supports inquiry. I may be missing something but can we think about that a bit more? I need clarity'.* Own your question.
5. Provide support/ideas/resources.	As the inquiry leader, be on the look out for resources, websites, great blogs etc. Without going overboard, send your team things to read, an outline of a strategy etc. Build your own personal professional network through channels such as Twitter, blogs, online journals.
6. Ensure system/school/team congruence.	Help the team keep connected to the big picture. The inquiry leader often reminds people about the throughlines, concepts and curriculum links and about the way the assets can be blended within the process. Using the inquiry 'agreement', your job is to check this and to occasionally help the team get back on track to ensure alignment.
7. Keep the focus on student learning.	Encourage people to bring evidence of student learning to the planning table. Planning meetings are about planning for student learning. Make sure this drives the conversation.
8. Inspire/motivate/take risks.	You are the inquiry leader because you have an interest in and passion for this approach. Show it! Get excited and help the team avoid negative self-talk. Don't talk an inquiry down. Look for opportunities and positives and stay relentlessly optimistic about the possibilities.
9. Model and demonstrate good practice as the leader/planner/teacher.	The best teams have an inquiring disposition, so that means asking questions, exploring, observing and noticing. Try to use this kind of language in the planning: *'How could we…?' 'I wonder if…' 'Maybe we could see what happens when…'*
10. Celebrate success.	You can be the team's advocate and messenger. Celebrate successes of your team with the whole school community.

A SIMPLE PROCESS FOR TEACHER INQUIRY

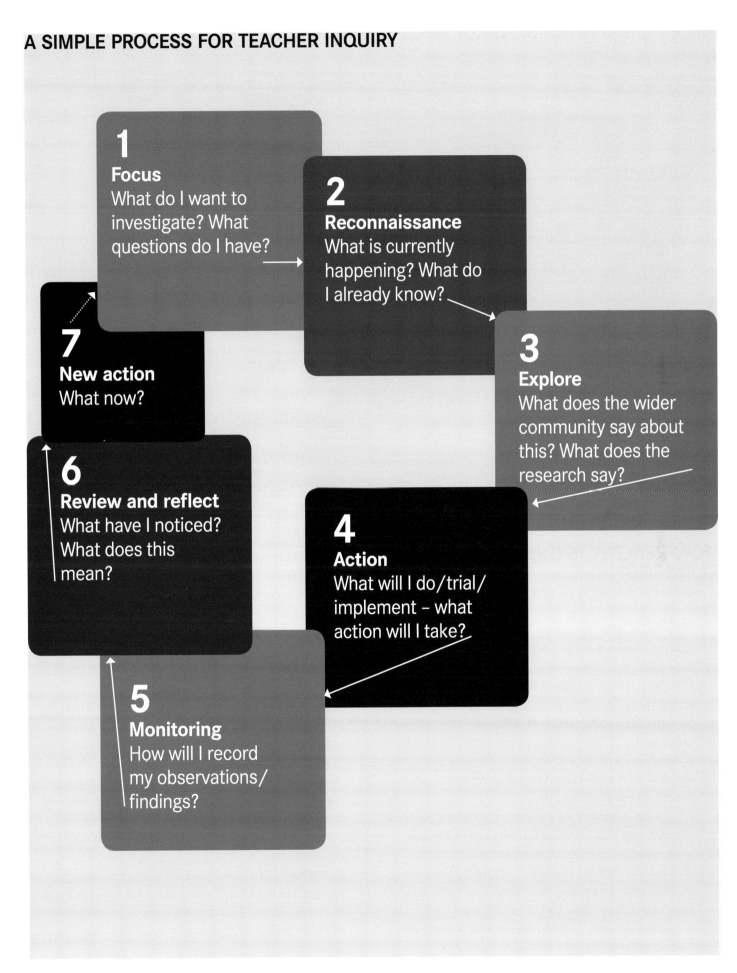

1 Focus
What do I want to investigate? What questions do I have?

2 Reconnaissance
What is currently happening? What do I already know?

3 Explore
What does the wider community say about this? What does the research say?

4 Action
What will I do/trial/implement – what action will I take?

5 Monitoring
How will I record my observations/findings?

6 Review and reflect
What have I noticed? What does this mean?

7 New action
What now?

HOW HEALTHY IS OUR TEAM PLANNING?

A checklist to consider when setting up or evaluating a collaborative team for inquiry planning.

- 1. We have **shared our expectations** of ourselves and of each other.
- 2. We have arrived at **explicit agreements** about the purpose of our meetings and how we will use our time and communicate and document, as well as the roles we agree to carry out.
- 3. We recognize that our planning meetings are a great opportunity for **professional learning**. We reflect and discuss our own thinking.
- 4. We **bring questions** and insights to the meeting and try to articulate what we are learning and thinking to each other.
- 5. We respect the **individual skills and talents** of each team member. We don't expect a carbon copy of a unit to unfold in each class but we do recognize the importance of some shared intentions.
- 6. We talk with students about our planning and **include them in the process.** We find ways to bring their voices (questions/theories/interests) to each meeting and use this to inform the next step. We keep **student learning at the center.**
- 7. We try to keep logistical and **housekeeping tasks out of** focused planning conversations.
- 8. The previous year's documents (if relevant) are used as a resource, but not until we have started with the needs and interests of this group of students (and this year's teaching team). **Every inquiry is a new inquiry.**
- 9. We allow **big ideas** to drive our inquiry. Even if our students are focused on investigating something very specific, we take care to consider the bigger picture beyond that focus. We care about transfer.
- 10. We take time to think about how our students will be learning and not just what. We use **'split screen thinking'** in our conversations and are careful to emphasize the skills and processes our students are gaining through their investigations.
- 11. **Authenticity and purpose** are really important to us. We want our students to see how this learning is real and connected to their lives now and in the future, so we try to situate their learning in authentic contexts using real people, real places, real objects and real actions.

Paper making

As learners we went on an excursion called CERES, relating to our inquiry 'How does Design Impact on the Environment'. There we participated in Paper Making, Sustainable Building Designs, E-Waste and Fair Trade. From our discoveries we have made at CERES, we will be recycling paper of our own at our school and will be making paper. These are some of the different textured paper we made.

- 12. We take time to discuss what **we understand** about this big idea – we know our own knowledge and experience about this topic will impact on our teaching.
- 13. We think about the **natural connections** we can help students make across learning areas. We use our core inquiry to ensure students can integrate their learning in other areas. We have dialogue with specialist teachers to enhance inquiry into both process and concepts.
- 14. We think carefully about how we can establish the 'known'. We want to get a good understanding of where our students are at in the early phase of the inquiry so we can use this to **inform our teaching and assessment.**
- 15. We are informed by, but not a slave to, a basic cycle of inquiry so the journey has some kind of **structure** and is not just a bunch of good activities.
- 16. We resist the temptation to fill our planner at the first meeting. We **document sparingly** at first and then add to the planner as the inquiry unfolds.
- 17. We see ourselves as **collaborative inquirers** with each other, with our students and even with others beyond our team/school.
- 18. We see reflective thinking and action as **ongoing**. We prompt both on a regular basis.
- 19. We include **transferable strategies** (such as thinking routines, graphic organizers) into our planning so we are building our students' toolkits.
- 20. We use **digital resources** to inform and document our planning and to assist students to research, create, record, share and act on their learning.
- 21. We have **courageous conversations** with each other when we need to, exercising both professional and personal care in our communication.

REFERENCES AND FURTHER READING

- Cheryl Doig (2009) 'Talking the Walk, Walking the Talk', available at http://www.thinkbeyond.co.nz.
- Kruse, S. and Seashore-Louis, K. (2009) *Building Strong School Cultures: A Guide to Leading Change.* Corwin Press, Thousand Oaks, CA.
- DuFour, R. (2011) 'Work Together: But Only if You Want To', Phi Delta Kappan, vol. 92 (5), pp. 57–61.
- Goldsmith, M. (2013) 'Try Feedforward Instead of Feedback', retrieved from http://www.marshallgoldsmithlibrary.com/cim/articles_display.php?aid=110.
- Lenconi, P (2007) 'Conquer Team Dysfunction', retrieved from http://www.tablegroup.com/pat/articles/article/?id=1.
- Ochre, G. (2013) *Getting Our Act Together: How to Harness the Power of Groups.* Groupwork Press, Melbourne.
- O'Sullivan (2011) in O'Sullivan, H. & West-Burnham, J. (2011) *Leading and Managing Schools.* SAGE
- Stoll (2006) Cited in O'Sullivan (2010) 'Developing a School as a Professional Learning Community'. Presentation to INTO Conference, Dublin.
- Timperley, H. (2011) *The Power of Professional Learning: Expanding Educational Horizons*, Open University Press, Maidenhead, Berks.

'I've had many teachers who taught us
soon forgotten things, but only a few like her
who created in me a new thing,
a new attitude, a new hunger'.

(John Steinbeck, 1955)

~ CHAPTER ~

ten

Building the repertoire
WHAT STRATEGIES HELP POWER UP INQUIRY TEACHING?

IT'S THE TEACHING THAT COUNTS

There is now ample evidence of the strong influence teacher quality has on student learning in the short and long term. Not all qualified teachers are equal. Given the impact of teacher quality on student learning, it makes a great deal of sense to put time and resources into building teacher capacity (Williams 1991). When teachers commit to being informed, self-aware and inquiring practitioners with a focus on continual improvement – and when they are prepared to adjust their practice in the light of data and student feedback – they can improve their teaching power enormously. Becoming a more inquiry based teacher can involve a seismic shift in the way we think about ourselves as teachers, the way we see students and the way we see the process of learning itself. This shift doesn't happen overnight. It takes time, experience, conversation and reflection. For many teachers, it is a gradual process of letting go old ways of thinking, being and doing and giving way to the new. It is an exciting, though challenging, journey and one I have been fortunate to witness many, many times. Looking back over this book, you will note the various shifts in thinking and practice that powerful inquiry demands. These include a shift from teaching 'topics' to developing conceptual understandings and a shift from using one-off activities to rich, layered strategies.

RISK TAKING AND RE-THINKING

Inquiry teaching means never becoming complacent. It is about bringing a passionate curiosity to all you do and rarely being entirely satisfied. It means remaining open minded and creative in your approach.

What would happen if…
- *we did this in groups instead of individually?*
- *I opened the task up and gave them more choice?*
- *I didn't show them but had them work it out?*
- *I stopped talking?*
- *I asked a student to lead this discussion instead of me?*
- *I just posed the question and challenge them to find out?*
- *I got them to devise the criteria?*
- *I took this outside?*
- *we just kept going – and did this for the rest of the day?*
- *I stopped right now and we use this question to steer the learning instead?*
- *I got the students to create the homework?*
- *I had some music playing while we did this?*

BUILDING THE REPERTOIRE

Throughout this book, I have attempted to provide numerous, practical strategies for classroom use. In this final chapter, I add to the repertoire by outlining several key techniques, routines and processes that I, and the teachers with whom I have worked, have found to be highly effective over our many years of working this way.

Of course, simply having a repertoire of effective strategies in itself will not result in strong learning outcomes for students. Inquiry, as already mentioned, is 'a way of being'. It is about the disposition we bring to the classroom. It is about what we think and feel as well as what we do. These strategies work best when carried out by a teacher who sees the very essence of their work *as* inquiry – a teacher who asks themselves 'What are my students revealing to me?' and 'What does this mean for where we go next?'

Strategies work when we know *why* we are using them. Learning how to use techniques for their own sake results in a kind of 'sham inquiry' classroom. It looks like inquiry, even feels a bit like inquiry but it isn't really inquiry. Without a depth of understanding, and a commitment to this way of seeing the learner and learning, the power of inquiry cannot be realized.

On the following pages I have outlined a range of strategies, and some of these can entail using digital tools. At the time of writing, these were apps and sites that were regularly used by teachers with whom I work but they are certainly only a small sample.

STRATEGY 1: THE WONDERWALL

Purpose

To generate, document and stimulate students' wonderings throughout an inquiry.

Procedure

- Invite students to write their wonderings on cards/Post-it notes and display them so they are easily shared, moved and revisited.
- Initially, there may be few questions but as the inquiry builds, more questions are added.
- Encourage students to group and classify their wonderings.
- Regularly return to the wonderwall and ask 'Have our questions been answered?', 'Are there new questions to ask?', 'Are there questions we want to modify or delete?'
- Have students interact with the wonderwall throughout the inquiry and keep it 'alive'. It should be a dynamic rather than static display.

Variations and suggestions

- Try 'wonder boxes' where each child has their own box into which they place wonderings. These are regularly shared.
- Use the wonderwall for generic wonderings, not necessarily for a single 'unit'.
- Add your own wonderings.
- Create a 'lift the flap' style display so answers or working theories can be documented.
- Make a set of laminated wondering cards that students can write on, rub off and reuse.
- Make a wonderwall for the staffroom or an area where parents congregate.

Digital tools

- Padlet
- Post-it Plus
- Popplet
- iBrainstorm

ST. FIDELIS PRIMARY SCHOOL

STRATEGY 2: IDENTIFYING AND SHARING FIRST THINKING

Purpose

To uncover early thinking in order to inform further planning and future assessment and to check in on misconceptions.

Procedure

There are so many ways to have students make their initial understandings of a concept visible to themselves, each other and the teacher. Here are some ideas:

- Provide students with a key question/problem/word or image.
- Ask them to write, draw or create a diagram in response.
- Record this in the 'first thinking' column.
- Students may then team up with others to share and compare their first thinking, establishing where they had similar ideas.
- The class can then create a 'first thinking' chart with their agreed, initial ideas recorded publicly, to be revisited and updated as the inquiry progresses.
- Have students return to their first thoughts at least twice.
- Ask students, 'How has your thinking changed?', 'what changed your thinking?'

Variations and suggestions

- Provide students with a set of key questions connected to the understanding goals for the inquiry. Ask them, 'How would you answer these questions now?'
- Invite them to share their initial responses in a way that suits them: a drawing, a written response, a voice recording, a diagram, etc.
- Set up a series of boxes in the room, each labelled with a key word or question. Invite students to place their responses to the questions in the boxes. Groups then work with a box each, sorting and analyzing the responses before presenting back to the group.

Digital tools

Any tools that allow students to make their thinking visible can be modified for use in the inquiry classroom. Some popular tools include:

- Today's Meet
- Google Drive
- Explain
- Padlet
- Scapple
- Popplet
- Wordle
- Edublogs
- Edmodo

STRATEGY 3: WHERE AM I AT?

Purpose

To have students think more deeply about their initial ideas about a concept and to help inform subsequent learning plans.

Procedure

- Give students time to record anything they 'think they already know'.
- Now invite the students to sort out the ideas they have brainstormed into the following categories:

I get this. I can explain it and defend what I know. I can give examples. This makes sense to me.	**I am not as sure** of this. I 'get' some aspects of it but need to clarify some things. I am on the way and can explain it in part.
I have heard of this, **but I don't know much** – if anything – about it. I would have trouble explaining it to anyone!	I am **interested** in finding out more about this.

This may be done individually and/or collectively. Have students notice patterns in the information they have analyzed about their own prior knowledge.

Variations and suggestions:

Have students explore their own thinking using the 'claim, support question' thinking routine (Richhart, 2011):

- I claim to understand that….
- I can support this with….
- A question I still have is….

STRATEGY 4: MAKING A STAND

Purpose

- for students to identify their position on particular issues and learn to effectively justify their thinking
- for students to develop greater empathy by becoming aware of other people's points of view
- for the teacher to gain more insight into students' thinking and understanding of issues central to the inquiry.

Procedure

- Using either statements generated by the students themselves (e.g. from a 'first thinking' session) or statements you have created, ask students to organize them according to those they *most* agree with to those they *least* agree with.
- Ask students to select one of the top statements and provide their reasons for prioritizing it highly.

- Similarly, they must justify their choice of the least important/agreed-with statement.
- Ask students to display and share the way they have ordered the statements and notice the similarities and differences between individuals' thinking.

Variations and suggestions

- Read the statements aloud and ask students to stand along a continuum according to how strongly they agree or disagree. Have them justify their position.
- Organize students into small groups and ask them to rate the statements as a group rather than individually. Statements that cannot be agreed on can be placed in the center. Have groups share their decision making process.
- Ask students to rearrange the statements according to how others might view them, for example:
  - *What might the prime minister think?*
  - *What might your parents think?*
  - *What might you have thought two years ago?*
- Keep a record of individual students' ranking. Revisit this later in the inquiry and ask them to consider whether their thinking has changed.

STRATEGY 5: MYSTERY OBJECTS

Purpose

- to provoke curiosity and a desire to discover more
- to generate interest and engagement.

Procedure

- Gather together some intriguing objects/artifacts. I have done this with random, unrelated objects and also with objects that are related in some way.
- Place them in the center of a table and cover with a cloth.
- Have students try to figure out what the object might be by feeling it through the cloth and looking at its shape.
- Once the object is revealed, use the following questions to invite further thinking about the object:
  - *What do you think this might be?*
  - *How might it work? What might it be used for?*
  - *What else does this remind you of?*
  - *What does it make you wonder?*
- Students can document their thoughts by making audio recordings, writing responses, using a 'placemat' graphic organizer or contributing to a large class chart.

Variations and suggestions

- Bring in an object each week and use the same questions to encourage students to explore what it might be.
- Ask students to bring in intriguing objects to explore with the class.
- Use powerful images in the same way.

STRATEGY 6: USING GRAPHIC ORGANIZERS

Purpose

To assist students to organize and share their thinking at any appropriate phase in an inquiry.

Procedure:

I always teach the use of graphic organizers as an inquiry in itself. Students gradually build success criteria as they engage with more and more examples of the organizer in use. They then use these criteria to adapt the organizer to their own purposes.

Once students have been taught how to use a graphic organizer (and been taught its purpose), add it to a class chart (or individual record) that can be referred to any time students need efficient ways to share their thinking.

Here are some examples of useful graphic organizers.

simple spider diagram

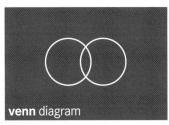
venn diagram

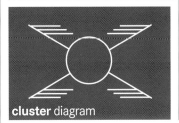
cluster diagram

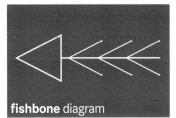
fishbone diagram

Digital tools

- MindMash
- iThoughts
- MindNode
- Idea Sketch

STRATEGY 7: FROM ME TO WE

Purpose

To generate ideas in collaboration with others, while maintaining high individual accountability.

Procedure

This technique generally works best in larger groups. Students may also find it useful to have some kind of personal recording device, pen, notepad or tablet.

- Share with students the challenge/question/prompt you would like them to think about. Remind them not to put their hand up or call out – they need to do their own thinking in silence.
- Give them a short but focused silent time to do their own thinking in response. Encourage them to record their thoughts.

- Now have them meet with 1–3 other students to share their thinking. You may ask them to:
  - *come to an agreed set of points as a result of their sharing*
  - *listen for similarities and differences*
  - *make a list that includes everyone's ideas*
  - *be ready to report on other students' ideas.*

Adaptations

- This technique can be carried out very simply (e.g. using the 'think-pair-share' technique).
- This technique can also be used in a much more complex way such as 1–3–6 consensus, when students must come to consensus on meeting with others, and small groups continue to merge their ideas.
- Teams may then report back, or the teacher may nominate certain students to share following the small-group discussion.
- Teams may document their thinking visually and then exchange it with other small groups for more idea building and comparison.
- Have students write their first response down, then invite everyone to move around the room, sharing their responses and noticing others had similar thinking. They record the names of those they made a 'conncction' with. When it is time to share, ask students to talk about the connections they made and with whom. The phrase 'think, ink, link' can be used to describe this sequence.

Digital tool:

- iCardSort
- post it Plus

STRATEGY 8: CONCEPT ATTAINMENT

Purpose:

This is a tried and true strategy founded on the work of Jerome Bruner. While it has been around for a very long time, it remains a technique that never fails to engage students in thinking for themselves. Having the students gradually work out the 'rule' that defines a set rather than simply telling them also captures the essence of inquiry teaching. In this strategy, it is the students who do the cognitive 'heavy lifting' as they look for patterns, test and revise theories, compare and contrast. Concept attainment is a powerful way to help students understand a new concept and often has a strong 'game like' quality to it.

Procedure

- Determine the concept you wish to teach (e.g. symmetry, living and non-living things, prey/predator, verbs vs nouns, mammals, odd numbers).
- Show students small selections of items that 'fit the

rule'. For example, to teach the concept of invertebrates, you might show them a picture of a spider, a beetle and a worm. Tell them that these things all belong together and are in the 'yes' group.

- Ask students to suggest something else they think might belong to that group. They may suggest a mouse, thinking it is a group of 'small animals'.
- Place this suggestion in the 'no' group (non-examples).
- Continue on, having students suggest what could be in the group. As more 'yes' examples are added, they begin to form theories and test these out with more and more examples. When the time seems right, ask them to share their theories with each other. What attributes do they think the 'yes' examples all share? Explain the term that is used to label the concept.

Variations and suggestions

Once students are familiar with this strategy, they can create concept attainment challenges for each other.

9: STRATEGIES FOR GROUP FORMATION

Inquiry classrooms are collaborative, social environments. Students learn to work with others in different ways and for different purposes. Often, but not always, tasks are carried out in small groups. Even when tasks are individual, meeting with others for feedback or simply to share learning is a common occurrence. There is no one 'best' grouping strategy. The key is variety. Students come to expect that sometimes the teacher will organize the group and the ways in which learning is shared. On other occasions, the students will be free to make their own grouping arrangements. Talking with students about why an arrangement might/might not work or did/did not work is a vital part of learning about the complex demands of collaboration. It is important to allow students to make suggestions and try out different groupings, and then reflect on their success. On the following page are a few ideas for group creation.

STRATEGIES FOR GROUP FORMATION

TECHNIQUE	PROCEDURE
clock partners	Give students a diagram of a clock face. Have them negotiate with each other to establish partners for each of the 12 'times' on the clock. For example, Ben and Olivia might decide they will be '11 o'clock' partners. They then record each other's names at 11.00 on the dial. Whenever a task calls for pairs, you can simply say, 'Meet with your 3 o'clock partner'. If more combinations are required, add some half-hour partners, such as 3.30. This strategy allows for quick organization into pairs and for a wide variety of pairings over time.
numbered heads	An oldie but a goody. Simply number students off to allow the group size you require.
word/picture match	Make a set of cards to allow for quick group formation. A simple one is colour (a class set of cards has three blue, three yellow, three red, etc.). Distribute them randomly, then ask children to find their matching colours. This activity can be done with a huge range of matching items: e.g. animal groups, number facts, simple sentences (each person in the group has a word) or sections of pictures. Make a few sets to keep the grouping interesting and varied.
line up – slice up	Have students form a line across the room using whatever criteria your imagination comes up with – e.g. biggest to smallest house numbers, birthdays earliest in the year to latest in the year, ages to the day. This is more fun if there is no speaking allowed! Once the line has been formed, simply 'slice up' into the group sizes required.
out of a hat	Simply having students pull names out of a 'hat' ensures that grouping is random and varied.

10: STRATEGIES FOR SHARING/ REPORTING BACK

In a typical inquiry classroom, students will often be working on open-ended tasks with varying outcomes or on different tasks. This diversity means it is often important for students to share their learning with others. While communicating learning is vital, it can be badly managed and result in a lot of wasted time. There is nothing quite as tedious as poorly prepared students taking it in turns to stand and share something with the class. The most benefit is felt by the one sharing while the audience can quickly lose interest. When we ask students to share their learning with each other, we need to have real purposes *and* use strategies that add value to the experience. Here are some suggestions:

Use very sparingly
- Have individual students coming 'out the front' to talk at length about what they are doing (a few at a time with strict time limits and success criteria).
- Have groups take it in turns to hold up a product and talk about it (as above).
- Go 'around the circle' and have every student briefly share.

Use more often
- **Learning walk:** Groups place their exhibits on the wall/screen/table. One member stays with the exhibit. Students walk the room, gallery style, and can listen to/ ask questions of the person at each exhibit.
- **Silent gallery:** A learning artifact (whatever it might be) is displayed. Students move around the room in silence, closely examining what they see.
- **50/50:** Half the class stays with their learning artifact. The other half moves around the exhibits, asking questions and making notes. The groups change roles and repeat.
- **Small group sharing:** Organize students into small groups (e.g. of four) and have them each share their learning. All groups are sharing simultaneously.

Variations and suggestions:
Sharing often becomes tedious when students go into lengthy detail and focus mainly on *what* they did rather than how and why, or when the audience is not sure what they should be listening/looking for. When we bring a more focused and purposeful intention to the sharing time, it is so much more valuable. Following are some possibilities:

- Create a simple list of success criteria before sharing what should we be looking/listening for. What will make a good report?
- Ask groups/individuals to summarize their report into no more than three main points. They need to decide what is the most important thing about what they have done/learned.
- Invite students to notice something specific, e.g. 'As you listen/observe, find one thing that connects to what you have been working on and be ready to share your connection'.
- As you look at the learning other students have done, ask yourself what you are learning from it. How could your work benefit from what they have done?
- As you look at the work others have been doing, what is one question you want to ask? Jot it down and be ready to share.
- Three-way sharing. Students meet in threes. Each student takes it in turn to be the (a) presenter, (b) interviewer and (c) feedback provider.

11: STRATEGIES FOR PEDAGOGICAL DOCUMENTATION

Purpose
Documentation can allow us to get a clearer picture of learning and it provides for continuous sharing and feedback between teachers and between students.

Procedure
There is no single way to go about documenting the learning in an inquiry classroom. Most teachers now use a combination of traditional and digital tools, anecdotal notes, photos, video snippets and audio recordings.

The idea is to find moments to 'stand back' from your students as they are engaged in learning and to capture that learning in some way. This learning memento can then be reviewed with students and with other teachers to help deepen understanding about the learning.

- Conversations and dialogue can be written up and displayed for students and parents to read and re-read.
- Photos can be included in blogs, journals or classroom wall displays with captions or quotes from the learning episode.
- Documented moments can be shared with other team members to help analyze and moderate our assessments of student learning.
- Bring an 'inquiring stance' to the episodes you have documented and be prepared to notice new things as you review a child's conversation or a video of them engaged in a task.

- Some questions to bring to documented learning moments:
  - What do we see when we look closely at this moment?
  - What is the student doing? Saying?
  - What does this reveal to us about their thinking?
  - What does this reveal about the student's misconceptions? Interests? Ideas?
  - What might we do next?
  - What questions does this raise for us?

Visible documentation of inquiry learning
Documentation holds a special place in the inquiry teacher's repertoire. Careful documentation not only contributes to assessment, it becomes part of the pedagogy.

Journals
The use of journals to document and reflect on journeys of inquiry has long been a significant part of the inquiry teacher's repertoire. Journals are vehicles through which students can record and self-assess, and they can provide both teachers and parents with insight into the children's evolving understanding. There are several ways to use journals and several types of journals that suit an inquiry classroom. Some teachers choose to use journals as the main place to house evidence of student learning as an inquiry progresses.

Whole class journal: the inquiry diary
Using a large sketch book or scrap book, write regular entries describing the progress of the inquiry. These entries can be co-written with students, used as a modeled writing session or written by individuals and small groups. Illustrate the journal with work samples and photos as the inquiry unfolds. Display the journal to share with parents and visitors. Once completed, the inquiry diary can go home with a different student each night and be commented on by parents. These diaries form a wonderful collection by the end of the year and can be used to inspire subsequent classes. They are also a great way to store some of the work samples and items that have been on the walls when the inquiry is complete.

Split-entry journals
This technique can be used for individual or whole-class journals. By dividing the entries up into these columns, we can helps students distinguish between recounting, analyzing and reflecting on their learning. Some sample column headings:

What did we do?	Why did we do it?	What did we learn?	What next?

Researcher's notebook/wonder journal

Giving each child their own personal researcher's notebook can be an engaging way to encourage students to document their own learning journey in a form that suits them. The researcher's notebook might be as simple as a place to keep thoughts, observations, jottings and questions, or something more involved that includes work samples and reflections. Some teachers issue a researcher's notebook at the beginning of the year and students keep this as a record of their inquiries throughout the year.

Digital alternatives

We are spoiled for choice when it comes to digital tools for documenting learning journeys. You can use virtually any app or program designed to record and document, whether it is a shared creation or each child's personal account of the journey. Class, group and individual blogs have brought a powerful dimension to the world of inquiry. Some schools are using individual blogs as children's own digital portfolios. Students who may be reluctant to record their thoughts and reflections through handwriting may become much more motivated to when they have the opportunity to blog about their experiences. Blogging meets all the purposes of the handwritten journal *and* allows for easier inclusion of photos, videos and, of course feedback and dialogue within and beyond the school. A class blog can act as a highly effective and authentic record of the inquiry journey and also provide parents with an ongoing, formative account of their child's learning. All this *and* an authentic purpose for writing!

Apps are designed specifically as 'journaling' tools. These include:

- Day One
- Memento
- My Wonderful Days
- My Daily Journal

12: STRATEGIES FOR MORE EFFECTIVE RESEARCH

A: PREDICT, PAUSE, REVIEW

Purpose

To help students develop the habit of thinking before they encounter new information and to help them become more thoughtful about what they are reading or viewing. When students spend a lot of time browsing for information, it can come at the expense of deeper thinking.

Procedure

Before students read, listen to or view a text, ask them to identify three things they think the text *might* say or three questions they bring to the text.

As they encounter the text, have them 'pause' at regular intervals in order to review the information against their predictions. This helps students read/view for meaning and encourages a slower and more methodical engagement with the material.

Adaptations and suggestions

If using this technique with a group, have students compare their predictions *and* their reviews. This will enhance their personal interpretation of the text.

B: POSSIBLE SENTENCES

Purpose

To help students engage with new material in a more discerning and deliberate way.

Procedure

- Provide students with a set of key words that appear in the text they are soon to encounter (through reading / listening / viewing).
- Ask them to consider what sentence that word *may* appear in, given what they know about the text.
- Have them record their 'possible sentences' for each word.
- As they engage with the text, they compare their possible sentence with the actual sentence as it appears in the text. Ask 'Does this mean the same thing despite being a different sentence? Is the meaning different? How? How do you now understand that word differently?'

REFERENCES AND FURTHER READING

- Richhart, R., Church, M. and Morrison, K. (2011) *Making Thinking Visible: How to Promote Engagement, Understanding and Independence for All Learners.* Jossey-Bass, San Francisco, CA.
- Williams, D (2011) *Embedded Formative Assessment: Pratical Strategies and Tools for K-12 Teachers.* Solution Tree Press, Bloomington, IN.

Adaptations and suggestions

Groups take a word each and develop possible sentences as a collaborative task. This is effective when the whole group is engaging with a shared text.

C: CAN WE TRUST THIS?

Purpose

To develop students' understanding of the need to use critical thinking when they encounter information and their ability to interrogate the worth of any text.

Procedure

- Ask students how they know if a secondary information source (book, website, clip) is trustworthy. What do they need to ask themselves?
- Provide the group with a question – for example, 'How does the government system work in Australia?' – and have them search for information in response to that question. They need to find one site/resource they regard as the most trustworthy and one they think is the least trustworthy. You may choose to deliberately provide each group with a selection to choose from and deliberately include some weak and some strong sites.
- Return to the class ready to share. Each group then explains the criteria they used to determine trustworthy/untrustworthy sites. Ask the class to decide which site they would regard as the *most* trustworthy and why.
- Now have students work in teams to list questions/criteria that they need to apply when searching for information. This becomes an anchor chart that can be used and added to throughout the year. (See the example on page 191.)

D: MODELLING THE PROCESS – RESEARCHING OUT LOUD

Purpose

To show students explicitly the process of 'critical searching' and have them identify the moves involved in deciding on what is worth engaging with.

Procedure

Inquiry teachers need to *show* students what it looks, sounds and feels like to go through a methodical process of locating, engaging with, recording and sharing information. This can be done simply yet powerfully through teachers modeling their *own* research into something they need to find out about. As you do this, make your thinking process audible and tell students why you are doing so, for example:

'I am interested in finding out how to best grow vegetables in my small front yard. I want to search for information on the internet and I am going to do this in front of you, to show you the process I go through. As I do this, I want you to notice what I am doing and the decisions I am making along the way. I

would like you to write your observations down and after I have done this, we will share what you noticed and see what connections you can make to your own experiences of being a researcher.'

As you model, try to consciously show:

- the questions you have and why they are important to you
- what you already think you know about this
- why you choose the search engine that you begin with
- how you scan the results and why you click on the ones you do
- why you choose *not* to click on some sites
- how you scan the site to check for relevance, trustworthiness and accessibility
- that you do 'one more search' and that you never stop at one site
- how you record the information you need – and the source itself
- how you then check that information against at least two other sites.

When students get to hear our 'thinking aloud', they gain a better insight into the questions and 'moves' that will help *them* as researchers. Once you have modeled and students have shared what they noticed, have them consider which parts of the process they already do well and which things they tend not to do. Give them an opportunity to practice their skills.

Modifications and suggestions:

Have a student take the 'hot seat' and demonstrate the process he/she uses to explore a question, and have other students observe and provide feedback.

Many teachers may not have the skills needed for critical, digital research themselves! The process I have just outlined above may need to be explored as a staff.

13: STRATEGIES FOR UNDERSTANDING AND MAKING MEANING

Inquiry teachers know about reading comprehension. They know that in order to help students understand the information they gather, they need to know how to make meaning. In the broad model for inquiry I have outlined in chapter 5, the 'sorting out' element is most closely aligned to the task of making meaning from information gathered. When students are working with secondary data sources such as books, articles and web pages, their ability to comprehend the material they encounter is critical to moving beyond simply 'fact finding' and achieving deeper understanding. Teachers can help students do this by explicitly focusing on the kind of thinking work that good readers do as they seek to understand a text. The following page offers some sample techniques.

STRATEGIES FOR UNDERSTANDING AND MAKING MEANING

THINKING FOR UNDERSTANDING	SAMPLE TECHNIQUE
A: Making connections between the information you are gathering and • your prior knowledge/ experience about this • information found in other texts about this • other topics/contexts.	1. Have students 'code' the text as they read/view: • TS (text to self) • TT (text to text) • TW (text to world). Model this process aloud for younger children. 2. Have students write down or share 3–6 things the text 'reminds them' of.
B: Making predictions	1. Have students write or discuss what they *think* the text is likely to say and how it may assist in answering their questions. Charts can be devised using the following headings: • What do we think it will say? • What it did say? • What surprised us? • What are we now wondering? 2. Use a 'concentric circles' organizer. As students work through a text, they add more information to the next circle on the organizer.
C: Asking questions	As they read through a text or watch a clip, have students stop and record questions they would ask the author or the filmmaker. Have students write questions in the margin or on sticky notes.
D: Monitoring	**1.** As they read the text, students use three highlighter pens: Red: don't understand at all. Yellow: have some uncertainty about. Green: understand. **2.** Stop and retell: Have students walk away from the text/video/computer and, in two minutes, orally paraphrase what they have just read. **3.** Note-taking and note-making. Model and have students practice: • dot points and word/phrases when note-taking • colored highlighters to emphasize key words • sticky notes to indicate important moments in the text • graphic organizers such as lotus diagrams, fishbone diagrams and other techniques for recording and summarizing as they read/view • using a margin to record thoughts as they read It is never too early to show children how to monitor their thinking and understanding as they read, view and listen.
E: Visualizing	As students engage with a text they sketch out information using diagrams, pictures, symbols and colours (many digital apps can be used for this purpose). Have students find a visual image to match each section of a text they have read.
F: Summarizing	Provide students with a grid of six, nine or 12 squares. As they gather their information they must summarize key points in each square using dot points, single words or phrases. Many graphic organizers are also very useful for summarizing.

CAN I TRUST THIS?

Questions to ask ourselves when we are searching for information

Who wrote this? Who is sponsoring the site? Who created this? Can I easily locate the name of person who has shared this information?

Is this person an expert on this subject? How do I know?

How up-to-date is this information? Is there a publication/upload date?

Are there advertisements on the site? (This might mean that the site is more about selling something than providing accurate information.)

Is this a forum/blog/chat-site? If so, I am probably reading *opinions* and I need to treat the information as such.

Does this information agree with information I have gathered from other sources?

Check the URL. Does it end with .gov, .org or .edu? If it does, it is more likely to be trustworthy.

Does the author acknowledge any other sources? If there are quotes or references to other work, does he/she indicate where I can find the original information?

And *if* the resource is trustworthy...will it be useful to *me?*

Do I understand what I am reading/viewing or hearing? (Scan the first section – does it make sense? Can I say this in my own words? If not, it may not be a useful site for me.)

Is this information relevant to my questions?

Do I need to seek permission to use the information?

Additional resources

DIGITAL RESOURCES

Rather than attempt to provide a list of who to follow, what to subscribe to, which online journals to read or which blogs to include in your feed, I am, instead encouraging you to… inquire! This will ensure that your digital resourcers are more current. Well-respected blogs such as "Inquirewithin" (www.inquiryblog.wordpress.com) receive contributions from teachers all over the world. These teachers often have their own blogs which can provide further insights and connections for the reader. My own blog (www.justwondering.com) and twitterfeed (@kjinquiry) will continue to explore the ideas raised in this book and will link to other useful and current resources.

Creating your own professional learning network using social media sites such as Twitter is an excellent way to connect with fellow inquiry teachers, current research, updates and resources. Hashtags such as the simple #inquiry or #inquiryed will yield a plethora of results. The most important thing to do in this process is, of course, to bring a critical stance to your search and to check the authors' credentials.

BOOK RESOURCES

I have referenced a number of texts throughout this book and urge you to follow these up for further reading. The list below is a small selection of additional recommendations:

- Barell, J.(2013) *Did You Ever Wonder?: Fostering Curiosity Here, There and Everywhere.* International Baccalaureate Publishing.
- Behrenbruch, B. (2012) *Dancing in the Light, Essential Elements for an Inquiry Classroom.* Sense Publishing, Melbourne.
- Bennet, B. and Rolhesier, C. (2001) *Beyond Monet.* Bookation Inc., Toronto.
- Blythe, T. and associates (1998) *The Teaching for Understanding Guide.* Jossey Bass, San Fransisco, CA.
- Brooks, J. and Brooks, M. (1999) *In Search of Understanding: The Case for Constructivist Classrooms.* ASCD, Alexandria, VA.
- Cam, P. (1995) *Thinking Together: Philosophical Inquiry for the Classroom.* PETA and Hale & Irenmonger, Sydney, NSW.
- Claxton, G. (2011) *The Learning Powered School: Pioneering 21st Century Education.* TLO Ltd, Bristol, UK.
- Claxton, G. *Educating Ruby: What Our Children Really Need to Learn.* Crown House Publishing, Carmathen, UK.

- Costa, A. and Kallick, B. (2009) *Learning and Leading with the Habits of Mind: 16 Characteristics for Success.* ASCD, Alexandria, VA.
- Daniels, H. and Harvey, S. (2009) *Comprehension and Collaboration: Inquiry Circles in Action.* Heinneman, Portsmouth, NH.
- Darling-Hammond, L. (et al) (2008) *Powerful Learning: What We Know about Teaching for Understanding.* Jossey Bass, San Francisco, CA.
- Dweck,C. (2007) *Mindset: The New Psychology of Success.* Random House Publishing Group, Ballantine, NY.
- Egan, K. (2010) *Learning In-depth: A Simple Innovation That Can Transform Schooling.* University of Chicago Press, Chicago.
- Elder, Z. (2012) *Full on Learning : Involve Me and I'll Understand.* Crown House Publishing, UK.
- Erickson, L. (2002) *Concept Based Curriculum and Instruction: Teaching Beyond The Facts.* Corwin Press.
- Erickson, L. and Lanning, L. (2014) *Transitioning to Concept-Based Curriculum and Instruction.* Sage, Thousand Oaks.
- Gallas, K. (1995) *Talking Their Way Into Science.* Teachers College Press, NY.
- Gardner, H. (1983) *Frames of Mind: The Theory of Multiple Intelligences.* Basic Books, NY.
- Halbert, J. and Kaser, L. (2013) *Spirals of Inquiry for Equity and Quality.* BC Principals' and Vice Principals' Association, Canada.
- Hattie, J. (2009) *Visible Learning: A Synthesis of Over 800 Meta-Analyses Relating to Achievement.* Routledge, London.
- Jackson, R. (2009) *Never Work Harder Than Your Students and Other Principles of Great Teaching.* ASCD, Alexandria, USA.
- Johnston, P. (2004) *Choice Words: How Our Language Affects Children's Learning.* Stenhouse. Portland, ME.
- Johnston, P. (2012) *Opening Minds: Using Language to Change Lives.* Stenhouse, Portland, ME.
- Juliani, Aj. (2014) *Inquiry and Innovation in the Classroom: using 20% Time, Genius Hour and PBL to Drive Student Success.* Routledge, London.
- Katz, L. *Engaging Children's Minds: the project approach.* Ablex Publishing Association.
- Kuhlthau, C., et al. (2007) *Guided Inquiry: Learning in the 21C.* Libraries Unlimited, Santa Barbara, CA.

- Littkey, D. and Grabelle (2004) *The Big Picture: Education Is Everyone's Business.* ASCD, Alexandria, VA.
- Loane, G. (2011) *I've Got Something to Say: Leading Young Writers to Authorship.* Airies Publishing LTD, NZ.
- Martin, B. and Hay, G. (2008) *Discovery Time: Developing Key Competencies Through Activity-Based, Child-Directed Learning.* Page Break, NZ.
- Marzano, R. (2003) *The Art and Science of Teaching: A Comprehensive Framework for Effective Instruction.* ASCD, Alexandria, VA.
- McTighe, G. and Wiggins, G. (2013) *Essential Questions: Opening Doors to Student Understanding.* ASCD, Alexandria, VA.
- Palmer, P. (1998) *The Courage to Teach: Exploring the Inner Landscape of the Teachers' Life.* Jossey Bass, San Fransisco, CA.
- Perkins, D. (2014) *Future Wise: Educating our Children for a Changing World.* Jossey-Bass San Francisco, CA.
- Powell, W. and Kusuma-Powell, O. (2011) *How to Teach Now: Five Keys to Personalized Learning in the Global Classroom.* ASCD, Alexandria, VA.
- Miller, D.(2008) *Teaching with Intention: Defining Beliefs, Aligning Practice, Taking Action.* Stenhouse, Portland, ME.
- Ricchart, Ron.(2015) *Cultures of Thinking: The 8 Forces We Must Master to Truly Transform Our Schools.* Jossey-Bass, San Francisco, CA.
- Ricchart, R. (2011) *Making Thinking Visible: How To Promote Engagement, Understanding, And Independence for All Learners.* Jossey- Bass, San Francisco, CA.
- Robinson, K. (2015) *Creative Schools: Revolutionizing Education from the Ground Up.* Allen Lane, London.
- Rothstein, D. and Santana, L. (2011) *Make Just One Change: Teach Students to Ask Their Own Questions.* Harvard Education Publishing Group, Cambridge, MA.
- Tomlinson, C. and McTighe, J. (2006) *Integrating Differentiated Instruction and Understanding by Design.* ASCD, Alexandria, VA.
- Wells, G. (2001). *Action, Talk & Text: Learning & Teaching Through Inquiry.* Teachers College Press, NY.
- Wiggins, G. and McTighe, J. (1998) *Understanding by Design.* ASCD, Alexandria, VA.
- Wilhelm, J. (2008) *Engaging Readers and Writers with Inquiry.* Teaching Resources, NY.
- Wilson (2013) *Activate Inquiry.* Education Services Australia, Melbourne, Vic.

OTHER BOOKS BY KATH MURDOCH

- Wilson, J. and Murdoch, K. (2008) *Learning for Themselves: Pathways to Independence in the Classroom.* Curriculum Corporation, Melbourne.
- Murdoch, K. (2006) *Take a Moment: Forty Frameworks for Reflection.* Seastar Education, Melbourne.
- Wilson, J. and Murdoch, K. (2006) *How to Succeed with Thinking.* Education Services Australia, Melbourne.
- Murdoch, K. and Wilson, J. (2005) *How to Succeed with Creating a Learning Community.* Education Services Australia, Melbourne.
- Murdoch, K. and Wilson, J. (2004) *How to Succeed with Cooperative Learning.* Education Services Australia, Melbourne.
- Wilson, J. and Murdoch,K. (2004) *How to Succeed with Learner Centred Assessment.* Education Services Australia, Melbourne.
- Hamston, J. and Murdoch, K (2004) *Australia Kaleidoscope.* Asialink and Curriculum Corporation, Melbourne.
- Murdoch, K. and Wilson,J. (2004) *Learning Links: Strategic Teaching In The Learner Centred Classroom.* Curriculum Corporation, Melbourne.
- Murdoch, K. and Hamston, J (1999) *Knowing Me, Knowing You: Units of Work about Identity and Difference.* Dellasta/ Eleanor Curtain, Melbourne.
- Murdoch, K. (1988) *Classroom Connections: Strategies for Integrated Learning.* Eleanor Curtain, Melbourne.
- Murdoch, K. and Hornsby, D. (1997) *Planning Curriculum Connections: whole school planning for integrated curriculum.* Eleanor Curtain Publishing, Melbourne.
- Hamston, J. and Murdoch, K. (1996) *Integrating Socially: Units of Work for Social Education.* Eleanor Curtain, Melbourne.
- Murdoch,K. (1992) *Integrating Naturally: Units of Work for Environmental Education.* Dellasta, Melbourne.

Literature to teach questions and stimulate curiosity

Sharing literature can be a powerful way to model and stimulate the dispositions of curiosity and wonderment, prompt questions and teach students about question forms. The list below is a small selection of titles that can enrich an inquiry classroom.

- Barnard, E. and Cho, T. (2005) *The Really, Really Big Beliefs Project*. Curriculum Corporation, Melbourne.
This book explores various belief systems but does so through a journey of inquiry taken by two students. Their discoveries are recorded in diary form – so this is both informative about the issue of beliefs AND a model of the inquiry process

- Brown. K. and Stewart, L. (2010) *Can I Cuddle the Moon*? Scholastic.
For young readers. A poetic and simple text that asks questions – allowing the reader to respond and think creatively. 'Can I cuddle a shining star?'

- Brown, P. (2009) *The Curious Garden*. Hachette Book Group.
This picture book raises the question: So what would happen if we just left nature to itself? What would the world really be like?

- Frost, H. and Lieder, R. *Step Gently Out*. Candlewick Press
An 'up close' look at nature. The amazing art work invites children to ponder the natural world in more detail – and offers the perfect springboard for questions.

- Gay, Marie-Louise. (2014) *Any Questions?* Groundwood Books.
A truly delightful book that explores not only the nature of questions but also the art of writing.

- Gay, Marie-Louse (1999) *Stella Star of the Sea, Stella Queen of the Snow, Stella Princess of the Sky, Stella Fairy of the Forest* and other titles in the series. Allen and Unwin.
The beautiful 'Stella' books are all about inquiry. Sam, Stella's little brother, asks many wonderful questions to which his big sister replies with her imaginative theories.

- Harris, A. (2013) *I Wonder*. Four Elephants Press.
A beautifully illustrated book about a young girl's walk with her mother. As she walks, she encounters a range of mysteries in the natural world – they wonder and wander together.

- Hornsey, C. and Perkins, G. (2010) *Why Do I Have To Eat Off The Floor?* Little Hare books.
The questions a dog would ask – if it could.

- Jenkins, S. *Hottest, Coldest, Highest, Deepest*. Haughton Mifflin.
Steve Jenkins' Books are wonderful for stimulating inquiry into the natural world. They appeal to students' thirst to find out fascinating facts about the world as well as using the power of comparison to stimulate curiosity and awe.

- Joyce, W.E. *The Fantastic Flying Books of Morris Lessmore*, Simon and Schuster.
An extraordinary book – and one that opens up a multitude of questions, inferences, ideas, possibilities. A book to respond to with wonderment and awe.

- King, Stephen M. (2008) *Leaf*. Scholastic.
A gorgeous, wordless text that invites imagination, creative thinking and wonderment.

- Minhós Martins, I. (2013) *Where Do We Go When We Disappear?* Tate Publishing.
This book explores a challenging, philosophical question in a beautiful, whimsical way.

- Ortas, R. (2014) *The Messy Monster Book*. Tate Publishing. In among this narrative are several philosophical questions to get little minds thinking.

- Papp, Lila. (2005) *Why?* Kane Miller books. Using the world of animals as her context, Lila Papp presents a series of questions about animals. For example, 'Why do kangaroos have pouches?', 'Why do rhinos have horns on their noses?'

- Perry, S. (1995) *If.* Getty/Children's Library Press. A book of 'surreal possibilities' that never fails to have children thoroughly curious and engaged.

- Pfister, M (2011) *Questions, Questions.* North South Books. A beautifully illustrated collection of questions to spark conversation and imagination.

- Reynolds, P. (2003) *The Dot.* Candlewick Press. This is a book about self expression and discovery told through the story of a child who thinks she can't draw.

- Russell, H. (2011) *Sixty Impossible Things Before Lunch.* www.harrietrussell.co.uk A collection of 60 questions or curiosities to which there are no clear answers – the author has a delightful 'play' with each.

- Most books by Shaun Tan (www.shauntan.net) stimulate questions, creative and divergent thinking. Both the text and illustrations in Tan's books leave the way open for interpretation and wonderment. Hachette Australia publishes most of Tan's titles, including *Arrival, The Red Tree* and *The Lost Thing. Tales from Outersuburbia* is published by Allen & Unwin.

- Silverstien, S. (1964) *The Giving Tree.* Harper and Row. This classic, beautiful story opens leads the way to questions about childhood, generosity, change, loss, growth and responsibility.

- Smith, K. (2008) *How To Be An Explorer of The World: Portable Life museum.* Perigree. A collection of ideas for exploring the world from the perspective of an artist. It encourages the user to document moments, patterns and every day occurrences and is definitely written in the spirit of inquiry!

- Strauss, S. (1999) *How Big Is Big?* Kay Porter Books. A great book for mathematical inquiry. Questions are posed throughout the text (How high is high? How stretchy is stretchy?) and some fascinating facts accompany each one. This book can trigger some wonderful scientific and mathematical investigations.

- Taylor, G. *Why Is The Sky Blue?* and *Do Dogs Dream?* Ladybird UK. Each of these pop-up books explores a range of questions about animals and the natural world. By hiding the answers under flaps and pop-ups, the books give scope for students to explore and share their own theories.

- Thompson, C. and Lissiat, A. (2005*) The Short and Incredibly Happy Life of Riley.* Lothian. This book explores the nature of happiness, of needs and wants. Big questions for young and old alike.

- Van Allsburg, C. (1984) *The Mysteries of Harris Burdick.* Haughton Mifflin. A series of powerful illustrations accompanied by a small thread of text. It begs to the reader to ask for more. What happened? What happened next? What could this mean?

- White, T. (2006) *Could You, Would You? A Book to Tickle Your Imagination*. Allen and Unwin. Trudy's whimsical questions and drawings not only inspire discussion and creative thinking, they often prompt students to ask their own questions. The random and non-linear nature of the text makes it delightfully fun to read and play with.

I am a teacher at heart, and there are moments in the classroom when I can hardly hold the joy. When my students and I discover unchartered territory to explore, when the pathway out of a thicket opens up before us, when the experience is illuminated by the lightning-life of the mind — then teaching is the finest work I know.

Parker J. Palmer

Palmer, P. (2007) *The Courage to Teach: Exploring the Inner Landscape of a Teacher's Life*, Jose-Bass, San Francisco.